ACCOUNTING

&

AUDITING RESEARCH

TOOLS AND STRATEGIES

7e

THOMAS R. WEIRICH
Central Michigan University

THOMAS C. PEARSON
University of Hawaii

NATALIE T. CHURYK
Northern Illinois University

WILEY

John Wiley & Sons, Inc.

VP AND PUBLISHER:	George Hoffman
SENIOR ACQUISITIONS EDITOR:	Jeff Howard
EDITORIAL ASSISTANT:	Kara Taylor
PROJECT EDITOR:	Ed Brislin
MEDIA EDITOR:	Greg Chaput
EXECUTIVE MEDIA EDITOR:	Allison Morris
SENIOR MARKETING MANAGER:	Julia Flohr
MARKETING ASSISTANT:	Laura Finley
DESIGNER:	RDC Publishing Group Sdn Bhd
PRODUCTION MANAGER:	Janis Soo
SENIOR PRODUCTION EDITOR:	Joyce Poh

Cover image by Colin Walton/Getty Images, Inc.

Permission Statements:

ACL Education Version software available at the text's Web site and screenshots are used with permission from ACL Services Ltd.

Images from AICPA services by the American Institute of CPAs are reprinted with permission.

Images from the FASB Accounting Standards Codification™ and the Governmental Accounting Research System are reproduced with permission from the Financial Accounting Foundation

I2 images remain the sole copyright of i2 Inc. and are used with permission.

LexisNexis screenshots are reproduced with the permission of LexisNexis, a division of Reed Elsevier Inc.

IASB screenshots are reproduced with permission from the International Accounting Standards Board.

RIA Checkpoint, published online at http://checkpoint.riag.com by Thomson Reuters/IRA © 2009 reprinted with permission. All rights reserved. This information or any portion thereof may not be copied or disseminated in any form or by any means or stored in an electronic database or retrieval system without the express written consent of Thomson Reuter/RIA.

Accounting Research Manager screenshots—© 2008 CCH INCORPORATED. All rights reserved. Reprinted with permission from Accounting Research Manager.

This book was set in 10/12 Times Roman by Thomson Digital and printed and bound by R.R. Donnelley. The cover was printed by R. R. Donnelley.

This book is printed on acid free paper.

To order books or for customer service please, call 1-800-CALL WILEY (225-5945).

Library of Congress Cataloging-in-Publication Data

Weirich, Thomas R.
   Accounting & auditing research : tools & strategies / Thomas R. Weirich, Thomas C. Pearson, Natalie T. Churyk. – 7th ed.
    p. cm.
   Includes index.
   ISBN 978-0-470-50697-4 (pbk.)

1. Accounting–Research. 2. Auditing–Research. I. Pearson, Thomas R. II. Churyk, Natalie T. III. Title. IV. Title: Accounting and auditing research.
   HF5630.W39 2010
   657.072–dc22

         2009026517

Printed in the United States of America

10 9 8 7 6 5 4 3 2 1

BRIEF CONTENTS

CONTENTS

CHAPTER 3 | THE ENVIRONMENT OF ACCOUNTING RESEARCH — 39

PREFACE

Dramatic changes are occurring in the accounting and auditing environment: U.S. GAAP is condensed in the FASB Accounting Standards Codification™, other accounting standards are changing faster than ever, mastery of international financial reporting standards is widely acknowledged, new technologies impact many financial statement filings with the government, other authorities that accountants must research generally continues to expand, auditing standards continues to evolve in new directions, a "clarity project" attempts to reform many auditing standards with enhanced writing and organization, and the need for specialized online database research skills continues to expand. Even changes in the CPA examination exist that include an identified skill set that incorporates research and analysis.

In response to the changes, understanding how to perform accounting, auditing, tax, and business research is becoming more important. Students and professional staff need practice to apply knowledge of research to problems in order to develop effective skills in research and analysis, without fear of the potential penalties that increasingly apply in the real world. Success in the profession depends on one's ability to effectively and efficiently research, analyze, communicate, and master other key business skills.

Accounting & Auditing Research: Tools & Strategies, Seventh Edition is an invaluable, step-by-step guide to practical professional research, both in understanding the authorities which govern as well as applying an effective methodology for research. This text focuses on today's professional research using online databases, supplemented with other tools in conducting the research and analysis. The text is more user-friendly, interactive, and powerful than earlier editions. The subtitle, *Tools and Strategies*, hints at the text's awesome integration of teaching and learning capabilities. Thus, *Accounting & Auditing Research: Tools & Strategies* enables users to find justifiable authoritative solutions to accounting, auditing, fraud investigations, tax, and business problems.

Various skills are developed in *Accounting & Auditing Research: Tools & Strategies, Seventh Edition* through reading and applying the knowledge presented. For example, the text enhances the reader's critical thinking and effective writing skills. Research and analysis skills are developed by completing exercises presented at the end of each chapter. The skills developed in this text helps prepare students who will conduct research in future practice and for the CPA Examination in simulation questions.

NEW, REVISED, AND EXPANDED FEATURES OF THE SEVENTH EDITION

This Seventh Edition of *Accounting & Auditing Research* presents new chapters on international accounting, the financial accounting environment including the FASB Codification System, and various online databases. While the emphasis of *Accounting & Auditing Research: Tools & Strategies* remains focused on providing useful guidance and information in conducting practical professional research, enhancements and updates in the Seventh Edition reflect significant changes in accounting research sources and technological advancements.

Revised for greater effectiveness and readability, the Seventh Edition presents the most extensive revision in the text's 25 year history. The text has enhanced the research tips, quick facts, and problems for assisting the learning process. Research Tips presented in sidebar boxes throughout the text provide help in conducting common research tasks effectively and efficiently. Quick Facts sidebar boxes summarize and expand on chapter concepts to provide new and useful research information. Various exercises are presented at the end of each chapter to reinforce the material and further develop one's expertise in professional research.

RESEARCH DATABASES EMPHASIZED

The Seventh Edition has also expanded its discussion of accounting, financial, and business databases. Many colleges and universities subscribe to these databases. Check with your university to determine the availability. If your college or university does not have access to some of the databases, the authors have provided screen shots at to the functionality of the various databases. The following research tools are emphasized throughout the text:

FASB Codification—The Financial Accounting Standards Board's Codification Research System discussed in Chapter 4 is the main research database for conducting financial accounting research for the private sector. This database is available to educators and students through the American Accounting Association. A demo of the database is available at the FASB's website www.fasb.org.

LexisNexis® Academic—This versatile research database is a subset of the widely recognized commercial LexisNexis® database. Both of these databases are presented in Chapter 6. In addition to various topical areas of law, the database has a business library which provides extensive information on public companies.

RIA Checkpoint®—This professional tax database is covered extensively in Chapter 7. The database contains a comprehensive research library for primary sources and secondary sources in federal taxation, as well as various specialized libraries.

AICPA reSOURCE—This invaluable database as presented in Chapter 8, includes a comprehensive collection of the AICPA literature consisting of Professional Standards, Accounting Trends and Techniques, Technical Practice Aids, Auditing and Accounting Guides, and Audit Alerts.

i2—Analyst's Notebook—This tool created by i2 Inc. is discussed in Chapter 10. This database is a visual investigative analysis software product that assists investigators by uncovering, interpreting, and displaying complex information in easily understood charts. More than 1,400 organizations in over 80 countries rely on i2 for investigations and intelligence analysis.

ACL™ (Educational Version)—This audit and fraud investigation software package is one of the most widely used audit software packages in the world. It is used by both auditors and fraud examiners, as well as most accounting firms and internal audit departments. Access through the text's website is provided by a downloadable executable file of the full educational version. A demo is provided (**ACL in Practice**) for those interested in fraud investigations.

ACCOUNTING CURRICULUM DEVELOPMENT OF RESEARCH AND ANALYTICAL SKILLS

Adopted over the years by many universities, *Accounting & Auditing Research: Tools & Strategies* has also assisted many public accounting firms and corporations in their staff training programs. The text guides the reader, step-by-step, through the research process. Faculty recognizing the essential need to incorporate research and analytical skills in the accounting curriculum will want their students to use this text for a comprehensive and systematic approach for students to learn research skills and analysis needed in the profession.

This text has versatile usage in most areas of the accounting curriculum. Many faculty assign the text to supplement traditional accounting courses, such as intermediate accounting, advanced accounting, governmental accounting, auditing, theory, tax or other courses. Alternatively, *Accounting & Auditing Research: Tools & Strategies, Seventh Edition* provides the information, insights, and research opportunities for a separate accounting and auditing research course. The text's website, *http://weirich.wiley.com*, provides additional problems and assistance in using the text for various classes.

ACKNOWLEDGMENTS

The authors greatly appreciate all the faculty members and former students who have used previous editions of this text and provided valuable suggestions for this new edition. The numerous accounting firms who have incorporated this text into their staff training programs are also appreciated.

Mahalo is extended to all those entities granting either database use or copyright permission to use screen images so as to enhance the readers' ability to understand. These entities include the ACL Services Ltd., American Institute of Certified Public Accountants, CCH, Financial Accounting Foundation, i2 Inc., LexisNexis, and RIA.

Special thanks go to our supportive spouses and other family members, who provided encouragement during the writing of this edition. Finally, we appreciate the work of the professional staff at Wiley who have also enhanced this text.

Thomas R. Weirich
Central Michigan University

Thomas C. Pearson
University of Hawaii

Natalie T. Churyk
Northern Illinois University

ABOUT THE AUTHORS

THOMAS R. WEIRICH

Thomas R. Weirich, Ph.D., CPA, is currently the Jerry & Felicia Campbell Endowed Professor at Central Michigan University and was also a former chair of its School of Accounting. He earned a Doctorate in Accountancy from the University of Missouri-Columbia, as well as an M.B.A. and B.S. degrees from Northern Illinois University. He has served on special assignment as the Academic Accounting Fellow to the Office of Chief Accountant at the U.S. Securities and Exchange Commission in Washington, D.C. He has completed a Faculty in Residence position with Arthur Andersen, LLP in their Business Fraud & Investigative Services Division whereby he participated in various fraud and background investigations. He also served as a consultant to the Public Oversight Board's Panel on Audit Effectiveness, and as an expert witness for the SEC and other organizations. Dr. Weirich was recently appointed by the Governor of the State of Michigan to serve on the Michigan State Board of Accountancy. Dr. Weirich has public accounting experience with an international firm as well as with a local firm.

Professor Weirich has written numerous articles in professional journals and assisted others, such as by serving on the Editorial Advisory Board to the *Journal of Accountancy*. He has extensive national, state, and local committee experience including a member of the American Accounting Association's Education Committee and the SEC Liaison Committee. He has completed assignments on the AICPA's SEC Regulation's Committee and on the AICPA's Technical Standards Subcommittee-Ethics, the Board of Examiners' Auditing Subcommittee and Content Committee that aid in the development of the CPA Examination. He also served on the AICPA's Pre-Certification Executive Education Committee, the Michigan's Association of CPAs' CPE Committee, Fraud Task Force, and the Environmental Issues Committee. He is currently serving on the National Association of State Boards of Accountancy—CPA Licensing Examinations Committee. Dr. Weirich has also served eleven years on the Mt. Pleasant, Michigan, City Commission and as mayor of the city. Professor Weirich has been the recipient of the School of Accounting/Beta Alpha Psi's Outstanding Teacher Award, Ameritech/SBC Teaching Award, the College of Business Dean's Teaching Award, the Michigan Association of Governing Boards' Distinguished Faculty Award and the Michigan Association of CPAs' Distinguished Achievement in Accounting Education Award.

THOMAS C. PEARSON

Thomas C. Pearson, LL.M., J.D., CPA is a Professor of Accounting at the University of Hawaii at Manoa and former Director of its School of Accountancy. He has earned two Masters of Letters of Law in taxation, the first from the University of Denver and the second from New York University. He has a Doctorate of Jurisprudence and M.B.A. from Vanderbilt University, and an A.B. from Dartmouth College. Professor Pearson has previously taught at the University of Wyoming and National Taiwan University. Professor Pearson has previously worked at Hospital Corporation of America.

Professor Pearson has published numerous articles, mostly in professional publications such as *Taxes* and the *Tax Advisor*. He has also published in leading academic publications such as *Accounting Horizons, Journal of Accounting Education,* and *Journal of the American Taxation Association.* as well as in prestigious law reviews such as the *Stanford Journal of Law, Business and Finance.* Professor Pearson has received numerous teaching awards including the University of Hawaii's Board of Regents Teaching Excellence Award and the Outstanding Achievement in Education Award by the Hawaii Society of CPAs. He has served as President of the Shidler College of Business Faculty Senate and on numerous university committees. He has also served on Hawaii's Tax Review Commission and is involved in several professional organizations.

NATALIE TATIANA CHURYK

Natalie Tatiana Churyk, Ph.D., CPA, is the Caterpillar Professor of Accountancy at Northern Illinois University. She earned her Doctorate in Accounting with a Finance Cognate from the University of South Carolina. She received her B. S. in Accounting and her M.B.A. with a specialization in Finance from California State University, Long Beach. Dr. Churyk has public accounting experience with a local California firm. She teaches in the undergraduate and M.A.S. programs. In addition to teaching accountancy for NIU, Professor Churyk develops and delivers continuing professional education in Northern Illinois University's CPA and CIA Review programs. Active with student groups, she is the faculty advisor for the Association of Latino Professionals in Finance and Accounting, the National Association of Black Accountants, and the campus mentor for KPMG's Future Diversity Leader Program.

Professor Churyk has published in professional journals such as the *Journal of Accountancy, Strategic Finance,* and *The CPA Journal.* She has various academic publications in journals such as *Journal of Business Research* and *Advances in Accounting Behavioral Research.* Professor Churyk has received several teaching awards, including the University-wide Educational Foundation Outstanding Teaching Award for Graduate Assistants. She serves on several state and national committees relating to education, student, and women initiatives, including the American Accounting Association's Teaching Learning and Curriculum Section and Midwest Steering Committee. She has received research grants from PricewaterhouseCoopers, the Institute of Management Accountants, and her university.

Introduction to Professional Research

LEARNING OBJECTIVES

After completing this chapter, you should understand:

- The importance of research in the daily activities of the professional accountant.
- The definition and nature of professional accounting research.
- The navigation steps to narrow one's research.
- The U.S. Securities and Exchange Commission's view on the importance of research.
- The role of research within a public accounting firm or within an accounting department of a business or governmental entity.
- The basic steps of the research process.
- The importance of critical thinking and effective communication skills.
- The importance of research on the U.S. CPA exam.

The accounting profession, like other professions, is witnessing major changes due to changes in the law, new services, technologies, and an ever-increasing number of professional standards. In addition to accounting, auditing, and tax compliance services, accountants are involved in such services as attestation reviews, forensic accounting, fraud examinations, and tax planning. Today's professional accountant must possess the knowledge to remain current and the skills to critically analyze various problems. Listening effectively and understanding opposing points of view are also critical skills for accountants. Often, one must present and defend his or her own views through formal and informal communications. Professional research and communication skills are essential in this environment.

Varying views and interpretations exist as to the meaning of the term **research**. In the accounting profession, research points to what the accounting practitioner does as a normal, everyday part of his or her job. In today's environment, to become proficient in accounting, auditing, and tax research, one must also possess the skills to use various professional databases, which are increasingly available on the Web. Using professional databases for research is even required on the computerized CPA exam.

The professional accountant, whether in public accounting, industry, or government, frequently becomes involved with the investigation and analysis of an accounting, auditing, or tax issue. Resolving these issues requires formulating a clear definition of the problem, using professional databases to search for the relevant authorities, reviewing the authoritative literature, evaluating alternatives, drawing conclusions, and communicating the results. This research process often requires an analysis of very complex and detailed issues. Therefore, researching such issues will challenge the **critical thinking** abilities of the professional. That is, the professional must possess the expertise to understand the relevant facts and render a professional judgment, even in some situations where no single definitive answer or solution exists. In such cases, the

QUICK FACTS

Accounting research is a combination of using accounting theory and existing authoritative accounting literature.

researcher would apply professional judgment in the development of an answer to the issue or problem at hand.

WHAT IS RESEARCH?

The objective of conducting any type of research, including professional accounting, auditing, and tax research, is a systematic investigation of an issue or problem utilizing the researcher's professional judgment.

Below are two examples of generalized research problems that can provide insight as to the types of research questions confronting the accounting practitioner:

1. A client is engaged in land sales, primarily commercial and agricultural. The company recently acquired a retail land sales project under an agreement stating that, if the company did not desire to pursue the project further, the property could be returned with no liability to the company.

   After the company invests a considerable amount of money into the project, the state of the economy concerning retail land sales declines, and the company decides to return the land. As a result, the client turns to you, the CPA, and requests the proper accounting treatment of the returned project. At issue is whether the abandonment represents a disposal of a segment of the business, an unusual and nonrecurring extraordinary loss, or an ordinary loss. The client may also want to understand the tax consequences.

2. A controller for a construction contracting company faces the following problem. The company pays for rights allowing it to extract a specified volume of landfill from a project for a specified period of time. How should the company classify the payments for such landfill rights in its financial statements?[1]

Research is often classified as either *theoretical research* or *applied research*. **Theoretical research** investigates questions that appear interesting to the researcher, generally an academician, but may have little or no practical application at the present time. In conducting theoretical research, one attempts to create new knowledge in a particular subject. Theoretical research sometimes uses empirical data based upon experimentation or observation. For example, a theoretical researcher may conduct a controlled experiment to determine the effects of informational complexity on analysts' forecasts.[2] Thus, theoretical research adds to the body of knowledge in a particular field and may ultimately contribute directly or indirectly to practical problem solutions. Theoretical research using empirical research studies based on experimentation or observation are frequently reviewed and evaluated by standard-setting bodies in drafting authoritative accounting and auditing pronouncements.

Applied research, the focus of this text, investigates an issue of immediate practical importance. One type of applied research is known as *a priori* (before the fact) research. This research is conducted before the client actually enters into the transaction. For example, assume that a public accounting firm needs to evaluate a client's proposed new accounting treatment for environmental costs. The client expects an answer within two days as to the acceptability of the new method and its impact on the financial statements. In such a case, a member of the accounting firm's professional staff would investigate to

---

[1] *AICPA Technical Practice Aids*, vol. 1 (Chicago: Commerce Clearing House, Inc.).

[2] Leslie Holder et al., "The Effects of Financial Statement and Informational Complexity on Analysts' Cash Flow Forecasts," *The Accounting Review* 83, no. 4 (July 2008): 915–956.

determine if the authoritative literature addresses the issue. If no authoritative pronouncement exists, the accountant would develop a theoretical justification for or against the new method.

Applied research relating to a completed event is known as *a posteriori* (after the fact) research. For example, a client may request assistance preparing his or her tax return for a transaction that was previously executed. Frequently, many advantages accrue to conducting *a priori* rather than *a posteriori* research. For example, if research reveals that a proposed transaction will have an unfavorable impact on financial statements, the client can abandon the transaction or possibly restructure it to avoid undesirable consequences. These options are not available, however, after a transaction is completed.

Society needs both theoretical and applied research. Both types of research require sound research design to effectively and efficiently resolve the issue under investigation. No matter how knowledgeable a professional becomes in any aspect of accounting, auditing, or tax, he or she will always have research challenges. However, using a systematic research approach will greatly help in resolving the problem.

RESEARCH QUESTIONS

Individual companies and CPA firms conduct research to resolve specific accounting, auditing, and tax issues relating to a company or client. The results of this research may lead to new firm policies or procedures in the application of existing authorities. In this research process, the practitioner (researcher) must answer the following basic questions:

1. Do I have complete knowledge to answer the question, or must I conduct research to consult authoritative references?
2. What is the law (tax law) or authoritative literature?
3. Does the law or authoritative literature address the issue under review?
4. Where can I find the law or authoritative literature and effectively and efficiently develop a conclusion?
5. Where can I find international accounting and auditing standards?
6. If there is no law or authoritative literature directly addressing the topic at issue, what approach do I follow in reaching a conclusion?
7. What professional databases or other sources on the Internet should I access for the research process?
8. If more than one alternative solution exists, what alternative do I select?
9. How do I document my findings or conclusions?

RESEARCH TIPS

Successful research requires answering various questions to find and apply relevant authorities.

The purpose of this text is to provide an understanding of the research process and the research skills needed to answer these questions. The whats, whys, and hows of practical professional accounting, auditing, and tax research are discussed with emphasis on the following topics:

• How do I research effectively?
• How do I apply a practical research methodology in a timely manner?
• What are the generally accepted accounting principles, auditing standards, and tax authorities?

- What constitutes substantial authoritative support?
- What are the available sources of authority for accounting, auditing, and tax?
- What databases are available for finding relevant authorities or assisting in researching a particular problem?
- What role does the Internet (the information superhighway) have in the modern research process?

In conducting research for an issue or question at hand, one of the primary tools utilized in financial accounting research is the Financial Accounting Standards Board (FASB) Codification System^{TM}, which is discussed in detail in Chapter 4. Similar to understanding the Codification's structure, navigating through the authoritative literature is necessary to analyze a variety of questions or issues. A useful instrument to help focus or narrow your research would be a navigation guide, such as the one depicted in Figure 1-1.

In navigating through the literature or Codification, the researcher should first focus on the functional area(s) that will help guide one to the appropriate professional literature and/or database as well as the authoritative body that issued the related literature. For instance, is the problem or issue under review a financial accounting question, managerial accounting issue, or technical SEC problem? Once the functional area is determined, the next step in the navigation is to determine the broad categorization of the topic, such as an asset, revenue, or expense issue. Then focus on the subtopic that allows for further segregation and navigation of the issue. For example, if the topical area is an expense issue, the subtopic might relate to cost of sales, compensation, or research and development.

The final phase in the navigation process is to focus on the section or nature of the content, which is often a recognition, measurement, or disclosure issue. For instance, if the functional area is financial accounting, the topic is assets, and the subtopic is financial instruments, the section or nature might address the proper measurement of the financial instrument either at cost or fair value. This navigation guide is explained in detail later in the text.

FIGURE 1-1 | RESEARCH NAVIGATION GUIDE

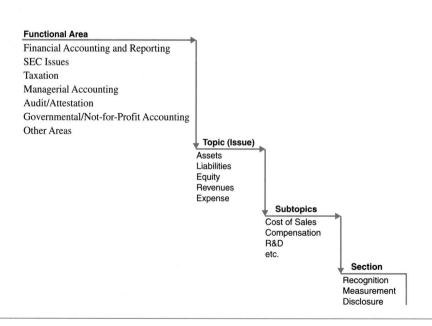

Functional Area
Financial Accounting and Reporting
SEC Issues
Taxation
Managerial Accounting
Audit/Attestation
Governmental/Not-for-Profit Accounting
Other Areas

Topic (Issue)
Assets
Liabilities
Equity
Revenues
Expense

Subtopics
Cost of Sales
Compensation
R&D
etc.

Section
Recognition
Measurement
Disclosure

A practical research approach, along with discussions of various research tools, is also presented in the text, as are demonstrations of this research approach using a number of end-of-chapter questions and exercises. The text also addresses the importance of critical thinking and effective writing skills that the researcher should possess and utilize in executing the research process. Specific tips on developing these skills are presented in subsequent chapters.

NATURE OF PROFESSIONAL RESEARCH

This text focuses on applied research, known as *professional accounting research*. Today's practitioner must conduct research effectively and efficiently to arrive at appropriate and timely conclusions regarding the issues at hand. Effectiveness is critical in order to confirm:

- The proper recording, classification, and disclosure of economic events.
- Compliance with authoritative pronouncements.
- The absence of preferable alternative procedures.

  Efficiency is needed to meet deadlines and manage research costs.
  Additional examples of issues frequently encountered by the practitioner include such questions as:

- What are the accounting, auditing, or tax implications of a new transaction?
- Does the accounting treatment of the transaction conform with generally accepted accounting principles (GAAP)? Does the tax treatment conform with the law?
- What are the disclosure requirements for the financial statements or tax returns?
- What is the auditor's responsibility when confronted with supplemental information presented in annual reports but not as part of the basic financial statements?
- What responsibilities and potential penalties exist for tax accountants?
- How does an accountant proceed in a fraud investigation?

Responding to these often-complex questions has generally become more difficult and time-consuming as the financial accounting and reporting requirements, auditing standards, and tax authorities increase in number and complexity. The research process is often complicated further when the accountant or auditor researches a practical issue or question for which no applicable authoritative literature exists.

As a researcher, the accountant should possess certain desired characteristics that aid in the research process. These characteristics include inquisitiveness, open-minded-ness, thoroughness, patience, and perseverance.[3] Inquisitiveness is needed while gathering the relevant facts to obtain a clear picture of the research problem. Proper problem definition or issue identification is the most critical component in research. An improperly stated issue usually leads to the wrong conclusion, no matter how carefully the research process is executed. Likewise, the researcher should avoid drawing conclusions before the research process is completed. A preconceived solution can result in biased research in which the researcher merely seeks evidence to support that position rather than search for the most appropriate solution. The researcher must carefully examine the facts, obtain and review authoritative literature, evaluate alternatives, and then draw conclusions based upon research evidence. The execution of an

QUICK FACTS

The **accounting researcher** is an investigator with strong analytical and communication skills.

RESEARCH TIPS

Conducting research requires the use of various electronic databases often available on the Web.

---

[3] Wanda Wallace, "A Profile of a Researcher," *Auditor's Report*, *American Accounting Association* (Fall 1984): 1–3.

efficient research project requires thoroughness and patience. This is emphasized in both the planning stage, where all relevant facts are identified, and the research stage, where all extraneous information is controlled. Finally, the researcher must work persistently in order to finish the research on a timely basis.

Perhaps the most important characteristic of the research process is its ability to add value to the services provided. A professional auditor not only renders an opinion on a client's financial statements, but also identifies available reporting alternatives that may benefit the client. A professional tax accountant not only prepares the returns, but suggests tax planning for future transactions. The ability of a researcher to provide relevant information becomes more important as the competition among accounting firms for clients becomes more intense and the potential significance and enforcement of penalties become more common. Researchers who identify reporting alternatives that provide benefits or avoid pitfalls will provide a strong competitive edge for their employers. Providing these tangible benefits to clients through careful and thorough research is essential in today's accounting environment.

CRITICAL THINKING AND EFFECTIVE COMMUNICATION

The researcher needs to know how to think. That is, he or she must identify the problem or issue, gather the relevant facts, analyze the issue(s), synthesize and evaluate alternatives, develop an appropriate solution, and effectively communicate the desired information. Such skills are essential for the professional accountant in providing services in today's complex, dynamic, and changing profession. In this environment, the professional accountant must possess not only the ability to think critically, which includes the ability to understand a variety of contexts and circumstances, but also apply and adapt various accounting, auditing, tax, and business concepts and principles to these circumstances to develop the best solutions. The development and nurturing of **critical thinking** skills will also contribute to the process of life-long learning that is needed for today's professional.

RESEARCH TIPS

Successful research requires critical thinking and effective communication.

Certain research efforts may culminate in memos or work papers, letters to clients, journal articles, or firm reports. The dissemination of your research, in whatever form, will require **effective communication skills** for both oral presentations and written documents. One's research output must demonstrate coherence, conciseness, appropriate use of Standard English, and achievement of the purpose for the intended reader. Critical thinking and effective writing skills are the focus of Chapter 2.

ECONOMIC CONSEQUENCES OF STANDARDS SETTING

Various accounting standards have far-reaching economic consequences. This was demonstrated by the Financial Accounting Standards Board (FASB) in addressing such issues as restructuring costs, financial instruments and fair value accounting, stock options, and post-employment benefits. Various difficulties sometimes arise in the proper accounting for the economic substance of a transaction within the current accounting framework.

Because financial statements must conform to GAAP, the standard-setting bodies, such as the FASB or Governmental Accounting Standards Board (GASB), will conduct research on the economic impact of a proposed standard. For example, the handling of off–balance sheet transactions has sometimes encouraged the selection of one business decision over another, producing results that may be less oriented to the users of financial statements.

In today's complex business and legal environment, the researcher conducting accounting and auditing research should understand the economic and social impact that various accepted accounting alternatives may have on society in general and individual entities in particular. Such economic and social concerns are becoming a greater factor in the evaluation and issuance of new accounting standards, as discussed more thoroughly in Chapter 4.

ROLE OF RESEARCH IN THE ACCOUNTING FIRM

Although research is often conducted by accountants in education, industry, and government, accounting, auditing, and tax research is particularly important in a public accounting firm. As a reflection of today's society, significant changes have occurred in the accounting environment. The practitioner today requires greater knowledge because of greater complexity in many business transactions, the proliferation of new authoritative pronouncements, and advances in technology. As a result, practitioners should possess the ability to conduct efficient research. An accountant's responsibility to conduct accounting/auditing research is analogous to an attorney's responsibility to conduct legal research. For example,

> A lawyer should provide competent representation to a client. Competent representation requires the legal knowledge, skill, thoroughness, and preparation reasonably necessary for the representation.[4]

A California court interpreted the research requirement to mean that each lawyer must have the ability to research the law completely, know the applicable legal principles, and find "the rules which, although not commonly known" are discovered through standard research techniques.[5] Thus, in the California case, the plaintiff recovered a judgment of $100,000 in a malpractice suit that was based upon the malpractice of the defendant in researching the applicable law.

The U.S. Securities and Exchange Commission (SEC) has also stressed the importance of effective accounting research through an enforcement action brought against an accountant. In Accounting and Auditing Enforcement Release No. 420, the SEC instituted a public administrative proceeding against a CPA. The SEC charged that the CPA failed to exercise due care in the conduct of an audit. The enforcement release specifically stated the following:

> In determining whether the [company] valued the lease properly, the [CPA] failed to consult pertinent provisions of GAAP or any other accounting authorities. This failure to conduct any research on the appropriate method of valuation constitutes a failure to act with due professional care.

Thus, it is vital that the professional accountant possess the ability to use relevant sources to locate applicable authoritative pronouncements or law and ascertain their current status. Due to the expanding complex environment and proliferation of pronouncements, many accounting firms have created a research specialization within the firm. Common approaches used in practice include the following:

1. The staff at the local office conducts day-to-day research with industry-specific questions referred to industry specialists within the firm.

> **QUICK FACTS**
> The accounting practitioner may be held liable for inappropriate or incomplete accounting or tax research.

---

[4] Model Rules of Professional Conduct of the American Bar Association, Rule One.
[5] Smith and Lewis, 13 Cal. 3d 349, 530 P.2d 589, 118 Cal Rptr. 621 (1975).

2. Selected individuals in the local or regional office are designated as research specialists, and all research questions within the office or region are brought to their attention for research.

3. The accounting firm establishes at the executive office of the firm a centralized research function that handles questions for the firm as a whole on technical issues.

4. Computerized files of previous research maintained by the firm provide consolidated expertise on how the firm has handled various issues in the past.

The task of accurate and comprehensive research is often complex and challenging. However, one can meet the challenge by becoming familiar with the suggested research process to solve the accounting, auditing, or tax issues.

A more in-depth look at a typical organizational structure for policy decision-making and research on accounting and auditing matters within a multi-office firm that maintains a research department is depicted in Figure 1-2. The responsibilities of a firmwide accounting and auditing policy decision function include:

- Maintaining a high level of professional competence in accounting and auditing matters.
- Developing and rendering high-level policies and procedures on accounting and auditing issues for the firm.
- Disseminating the firm's policies and procedures to appropriate personnel within the firm on a timely basis.
- Supervising the quality control of the firm's practice.

Research plays an important role in this decision-making process. A CPA firm's policy committee and executive subcommittee, as shown in Figure 1-2, generally consist of highly competent partners with many years of practical experience. The policy committee's primary function is to evaluate significant accounting and auditing issues and establish firmwide policies on these issues. The executive subcommittee's function is to handle the daily ongoing policy decisions (lower-level decisions) for the firm as a

> **RESEARCH TIPS**
>
> At times, conducting research will require consulting with research specialists.

FIGURE 1-2 | ORGANIZATIONAL FRAMEWORK FOR POLICY DECISION-MAKING AND RESEARCH WITHIN A TYPICAL MULTIOFFICE ACCOUNTING FIRM

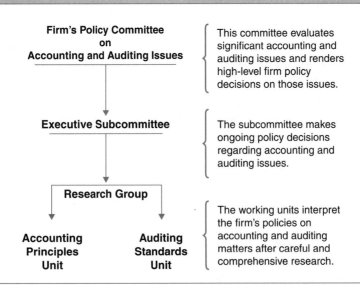

Firm's Policy Committee on Accounting and Auditing Issues — This committee evaluates significant accounting and auditing issues and renders high-level firm policy decisions on those issues.

Executive Subcommittee — The subcommittee makes ongoing policy decisions regarding accounting and auditing issues.

Research Group

Accounting Principles Unit   **Auditing Standards Unit** — The working units interpret the firm's policies on accounting and auditing matters after careful and comprehensive research.

whole. The responsibility of the accounting and auditing research personnel is to interpret firm policies in the context of specific client situations. Frequently, technical accounting and auditing issues that arise during the course of a client engagement are resolved through research conducted by personnel assigned to the engagement. When a local office cannot resolve a research matter satisfactorily, assistance is requested from the firm's specialized research units. These units conduct careful and comprehensive research in arriving at the firm's response to technical inquiries. This response is then disseminated to the various geographic offices of the firm for future reference in handling similar technical issues.

Practical accounting and auditing research is not confined to public accounting firms. All accountants should possess the ability to conduct effective research and develop logical and well-supported conclusions on a timely basis. The basic research process is similar whether the researcher is engaged in public accounting, management accounting, governmental accounting, auditing, or even taxation.

RESEARCH AND THE CPA EXAM

In licensing a new CPA, state laws or regulations typically require a combination of education, examination, and experience. State legislatures, state boards of accountancy, the Public Company Accounting Oversight Board (PCAOB), and the American Institute of Certified Public Accountants (AICPA) have strived to assure the professional competencies of CPAs. The important role that a CPA plays in society is so significant that the AICPA Board of Examiners have identified certain skills that are necessary for the beginning CPA to possess in order to protect the public interest. These skills and their definition are as follows:

- **Understanding:** The ability to recognize and comprehend the meaning and application of a particular matter.
- **Analysis:** The ability to organize, process, and interpret data to develop options for making decisions.
- **Judgment:** The ability to evaluate options for making decisions and provide an appropriate conclusion.
- **Communication:** The ability to effectively elicit and/or express information through written or oral means.
- **Research:** The ability to locate and extract relevant information from available resource materials.
- **Synthesis (deductive reasoning):** The ability to develop a solution based upon the data gathered from the research process (putting the pieces together).

For the CPA exam, not only are CPA candidates required to demonstrate their research ability in simulated problems, but they must also demonstrate understanding, analysis, and judgment through questions that will require the candidate to:

- Interpret and apply the relevant professional literature to specific fact patterns in various cases.
- Identify relevant information and draw appropriate conclusions from searching the professional literature.
- Recognize business-related issues as one evaluates an entity's financial condition.
- Identify, evaluate, analyze, and process an entity's accounting and reporting information.

On the computer-based CPA examination, candidates must demonstrate their research abilities by accessing various professional databases and searching through the legal or professional literature in order to identify the relevant authorities and draw conclusions related to the issues at hand. A candidate's research skills are tested by completing various simulations or case studies as part of the exam. The appendix to this chapter provides an overview of the basic format of the CPA exam's simulations. Examples of simulations are presented throughout subsequent chapters. This text will help you develop the necessary skills to utilize these databases for the computerized CPA exam and help you develop and refine the necessary skill sets and competencies necessary for your professional career. The following chapters will further focus on these skills, with particular emphasis on research skills.

OVERVIEW OF THE RESEARCH PROCESS

The research process in general is often defined as a scientific method of inquiry, a systematic study of a particular field of knowledge in order to discover scientific facts or principles. An operational definition of research encompasses the following process:[6]

RESEARCH TIPS

Carefully conduct each step in the research process.

1. Investigate and analyze a clearly defined issue or problem.
2. Use an appropriate scientific approach.
3. Gather and document adequate and representative evidence.
4. Employ logical reasoning in drawing conclusions.
5. Support the validity or reasonableness of the conclusions.

With this general understanding of the research process, practical accounting, auditing, and tax research is defined as follows:

> **Accounting, auditing, or tax research:** A systematic and logical approach employing critical thinking skills to obtain and document evidence (authorities) underlying a conclusion relating to an accounting, auditing, or tax issue or problem.

The basic steps in the research process are illustrated in Figure 1-3, with an overview presented in the following sections. As indicated in the illustration, carefully document each step of the research process. When executing each step, the researcher may also find it necessary to refine the work done in previous steps. The refinement of the research process is discussed more fully in Chapter 9.

Step One: Identify the Relevant Facts and Issues

QUICK FACTS

The research process is appropriate to any type of accounting or tax issue confronted.

The researcher's first task is to gather the facts surrounding the particular problem. However, problem-solving research cannot begin until the researcher clearly and concisely defines the problem. One needs to analyze and understand the "why" and "what" about the issue in order to begin the research process. Unless the researcher knows why the issue was brought to his or her attention, he or she might have difficulty knowing what to research. The novice researcher may find it difficult to distinguish between relevant and irrelevant information. When this happens, it is advisable to err on

---

[6] David J. Luck, Hugh C. Wales, and Donald A. Taylor, *Marketing Research* (Englewood Cliffs, N.J.: Prentice Hall, Inc., 1961), 5.

FIGURE 1-3 | THE RESEARCH PROCESS

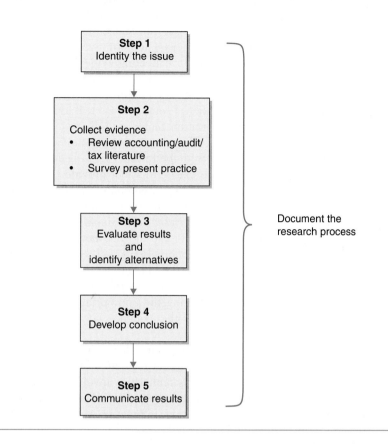

the side of gathering too many facts rather than too few. As the researcher becomes more knowledgeable, he or she will become more skilled at quickly isolating the relevant facts.

In most cases, the basic issue is identified before the research process begins, for example, when a client requests advice as to the proper handling of a specific transaction. However, further refinement of the exact issue is often required. This process of refining the issue at hand is referred to as **problem distillation**, where a general issue is restated in sufficiently specific terms. If the statement of the issue is too broad or general, the researcher is apt to waste valuable time consulting sources irrelevant to the specific issue.

Factors to consider in the identification and statement of the issue include the exact source of the issue, justification for the issue, and determination of the scope of the issue. To successfully design and execute an investigation, state the critical issue clearly and precisely. As explained in Chapters 4 and 6, many research tools, especially computerized databases, are indexed by a set of descriptive words. Because keywords aid in reference identification, failure to use the appropriate keywords or understand the facts in sufficient detail can cause a researcher to overlook important authorities. Undoubtedly, writing a clear, concise statement of the problem is the most important task in research. Failure to frame all the facts can, and often will, lead to an erroneous conclusion.

Step Two: Collect the Evidence

RESEARCH TIPS

Use electronic databases and the Internet to help collect the evidence.

As previously stated, problem-solving research cannot begin until the researcher defines the problem. Once the issues are adequately defined, the researcher is ready to proceed with step two of the research process, the collection of evidence. This step usually encompasses a detailed review of relevant authoritative accounting or auditing literature and a survey of present practice. In collecting evidence, the researcher should have familiarity with the various sources available, know which sources to use, and know the order in which to examine the sources and applicable authorities.

QUICK FACTS

The Internet opens a vast world of information for the professional accountant/researcher.

This early identification of the relevant sources will aid in the efficient conduct of the research. A number of research tools, including electronic databases and the Internet, that will aid in the collection of evidence are available and discussed in detail in Chapters 4 through 8. With the Internet growing at an exponential rate as new Web sites are added on a daily basis, this tool provides an increasingly significant impact on the way people, including accountants, auditors, and tax professionals, conduct business. The Internet permits an accounting professional to use various discussion groups or webinars whereby professionals discuss topics on accounting, auditing, or tax issues. Accountants use the Internet to search for federal and state legislation that may have an impact on clients and retrieve financial statements from SEC filings. Figure 1-4 provides an example of how a small CPA firm might utilize the Internet. Many accountants also use the Internet to interact quickly and effectively with the client to assist in collecting the appropriate evidence, such as requesting additional facts that may influence the evidence needed or results from the relevant authorities.

RESEARCH TIPS

Different search engines on the Internet can give you different hits. Therefore, use more than one search engine when conducting research.

In cases where authoritative literature does not exist on a specific issue, the practitioner should develop a theoretical resolution of the issue based upon a logical analysis of the factors or analogous authorities involved. In addition, the researcher needs to evaluate the economic consequences of the various alternatives in the development of a conclusion. Note that, in practice, a solution is sometimes not readily apparent. Professional judgment and theoretical analysis are key elements in the research process.

FIGURE 1-4 AN EXAMPLE OF A SMALL CPA FIRM UTILIZING THE INTERNET

Mark Jensen, CPA, states that the Internet has become the "greatest equalizer" because it provides his small practice with many of the research tools utilized by the big international accounting firms. "It lets me offer resources and services to my clients and future clients that the big firms have to offer," says Jensen.

Mark was asked by a would-be entrepreneur to help write a business plan to open a computer software store in southern New York. Both Jensen and the client were computer literate, but neither of them knew much about the software business. So Mark accessed the Internet and, within an hour, was deluged with information about software stores.

A word search for "software" yielded more than one hundred articles about computer stores, including one from the *Washington Post* about a software store start-up. Jensen also gleaned information about software stores from the small business forums on the Internet. Mark and his client used the information to prepare a business plan that helped secure financing for the business.

Being online via the Internet allows Jensen to search through news sources throughout the world. Publications and news services such as the *New York Times*, Associated Press, United Press International, Reuters, *Financial Times of London*, and Dow Jones News Service are just a few of the sources available on the Internet.

Mark also retrieves news items for clients as an effective way to maintain relationships and attract new clients. One of his clients is involved in the machine tools industry, and Mark frequently notifies the client when a major industry event takes place.

Besides tracking news, Jensen uses the Internet to exchange e-mail with clients and associates. He also can access the SEC's Web site and obtain recent SEC filings of major public companies, such as their 10-K, 10-Q, or other filings.

Step Three: Analyze the Results and Identify the Alternatives

Once a practitioner has completed a thorough investigation of the facts and collection of evidence, the next step is to evaluate the results and identify alternatives for one or more tentative conclusions to the issue. Fully support each alternative by authoritative literature or a theoretical justification with complete and concise documentation. One cannot expect to draw sound conclusions from faulty information. Soundly documented conclusions are possible only when the information has been properly collected, organized, and interpreted.

Further analysis and research are sometimes needed as to the appropriateness of the various alternatives identified. This reevaluation may require further discussions with the client or consultations with colleagues. In discussing an issue with a client, the researcher should use professional skepticism and recognize that management is not always objective in evaluating alternatives. For example, the issue may involve the acceptability of an accounting method that is currently being used by the client. In such cases, the research is directed toward the support or rejection of an alternative already decided on by management. The possibility of bias should cause the researcher to retain a degree of professional skepticism in discussions with the client regarding a conclusion.

Step Four: Develop a Conclusion

After a detailed analysis of the alternatives, including economic consequences, the researcher develops a conclusion and thoroughly documents the final conclusion selected from the alternatives identified. The conclusions should be well supported by the evidence gathered. The conclusion and details of the proposed solution are then presented to the client.

Step Five: Communicate the Results

The most important point in the communication is the conclusion reached. The communication often takes the form of a research memorandum, requiring an objective and unbiased analysis and report. The memorandum should contain a statement of facts, a clear and precise statement of the issue, a brief and straightforward conclusion, and discussion of the authoritative literature and explanation as to how it applies to the set of facts. The written communication should communicate clearly and follow the conventional rules of grammar, spelling, and punctuation. Particularly, because a client often cannot evaluate the quality of research, nothing diminishes a professional's credibility with the client faster than misspellings, incorrect grammar, or misuse of words. Sloppy communications may suggest sloppy research and analysis.

> **RESEARCH TIPS**
>
> After analyzing the results, develop a conclusion and communicate the results.

In drafting the appropriate written communication, avoid making common errors such as:

1. Excessive discussion of the issue and facts in a memo, which indicates the memo was not drafted with sufficient precision.
2. Excessive citations to authoritative sources (cite only the relevant authorities for the conclusion reached).
3. Appearing to avoid a conclusion by pleading the need for additional facts.

Novice researchers too often include irrelevant information. This distracts from the fact that the proposed solution to the problem is appropriate.

A serious weakness in any part of the research and communication process undermines the entire effort. Therefore, address each segment of the process with equal seriousness as to its impact on the entire research project.

SUMMARY

The research work of a practicing professional accountant is very important. Few practitioners ever experience a workweek that does not include the investigation and analysis of an accounting, auditing, or tax issue. Thus, every professional accountant should possess the ability to conduct practical research in a systematic way. The goal of this text is to aid current and future practitioners in developing a basic framework or methodology to assist in the research process.

The emphasis of the following chapters is on practical applied research that deals with solutions to immediate issues rather than theoretical research that has little or no present-day application. **Chapter 2** presents an overview of the importance of critical thinking and effective writing skills that every researcher (accountant/auditor/tax professional) must possess to be effective. **Chapters 3** and **8** provide an overview of the environment of accounting and auditing/attestation research, with an emphasis on the standard-setting process. The FASB's Codification Research System™ is presented in **Chapter 4**. The sources of authoritative literature in dealing with international accounting issues is discussed in **Chapter 5**. **Chapter 6** presents other available research tools that may aid in the effective and efficient conduct of practical research, with an emphasis on computerized research via various databases that exist. **Chapter 7** provides the basic steps of tax research and valuable databases and Web sites. The chapter highlights the RIA tax database, part of which is also utilized on the CPA exam. **Chapter 9** concludes with a refinement of the research process by presenting specific annotated procedures for conducting and documenting the research process via a comprehensive problem.

Chapter 10 provides an overview of fraud and insights into the basic techniques of fraud investigation, an area that is particularly pertinent as more practitioners are entering the specialized field of forensic accounting. The basic steps of a fraud investigation are quite similar to accounting research.

DISCUSSION QUESTIONS

1. Define the term *research*.

2. Explain what accounting, auditing, and tax research are.

3. Why are accounting, auditing, and tax research necessary?

4. What is the objective of accounting, auditing, and tax research?

5. What role does professional research play within an accounting firm or department? Who primarily conducts the research?

6. What are the functions or responsibilities of the policy committee and executive subcommittee within a multi-office firm?

7. Identify and explain some basic questions the researcher must address in performing accounting, auditing, or tax research.

8. Differentiate between *theoretical* and *applied* research.

9. Identify the characteristics that an accounting practitioner should possess.

10. Provide an example of utilizing the research navigation guide.

11. Distinguish between *a priori* and *a posteriori* research. Which research is used more for planning work?

12. Explain the analogy of the California court decision dealing with legal research as it relates to the accounting practitioner.

13. Explain how the research process adds value to the services offered by an accounting firm.

14. What consequences are considered in the standard-setting process?

15. Explain the importance of identifying keywords when identifying relevant facts and issues.

16. Explain the five basic steps involved in the research process.

17. Discuss how research can support or refute a biased alternative.

18. Explain what is meant by *problem distillation* and its importance in the research process.

19. What skills are important and tested on the CPA exam?

20. Your conclusion to the research is often presented to your boss or client in the form of a research memorandum. Identify the basic points to include in this memo. Also, identify at least two common errors to avoid in the drafting of the memo.

21. Explain the necessity of critical thinking in the research process.

22. Why did the SEC bring an enforcement action against a CPA concerning research?

23. If authoritative literature does not exist, what steps might the researcher take?

APPENDIX

Research Focus on the CPA Exam

Skills in practice identified for the CPA are classified in three categories: knowledge and understanding; application skills, which include research and analysis; and communication skills. Knowledge is acquired through education or experience, and familiarity with information. Understanding is the process of using concepts to address the facts or situation. Knowledge and understanding skills represent almost half of the skills tested on the CPA exam.

Application skills of judgment, research, analysis, and synthesis are required to transform knowledge. Judgment includes devising a plan of action for any problem, identifying potential problems, and applying professional skepticism. Research skills include recognizing keywords, searching through large volumes of electronic data, and organizing data from multiple sources. Analysis includes verifying compliance with standards, noticing trends and variances, and performing appropriate calculations. Synthesis includes solving unstructured problems, examining alternative solutions, developing logical conclusions, and integrating information to make decisions. Application skills require technological competencies in using spreadsheets, databases, and computer software programs. Application skills represent one-third to almost one-half of the skills tested on the CPA exam.

Communication skills include oral, written, graphical, and supervisory skills. Oral skills include attentively listening, presenting information, asking questions, and exchanging technical ideas within the firm. Written skills include organization, clarity, conciseness, proper English, and documentation skills. Graphical skills include organizing and processing symbols, graphs, and pictures. Supervisory skills include providing clear directions, mentoring staff, persuading others, negotiating solutions, and working well with others. Communication skills represent 10 to 20 percent of the skills tested on the CPA exam. Using the five-step research process demonstrated in this chapter substantially helps to develop the necessary skills for the CPA exam. For any research problem, learn the facts, and understand the problem or issues. Acquire knowledge about the client's needs and desires in order to understand the alternative and best solutions to the problem. Knowledge and understanding of accounting should also include the various standard setters and their authoritative sources and the nonauthoritative sources available in various databases, Web sites, hardbound books, newsletters, and other secondary sources.

Use application skills, such as identifying keywords for research. Develop the skills of locating and reviewing the relevant authorities. Analyze how the authorities apply to the particular facts in the research problem. Synthesize information with the help of insightful, nonauthoritative sources. Use professional judgment as you refine the issues with greater specificity and develop well-reasoned conclusions. Develop strong communication skills not only for the CPA exam and research memos, but in handling the day-to-day tasks and interactions that typify the work of accountants and business professionals. Communicate the results of the research, as appropriate.

Many of the previously mentioned skills are tested on the CPA exam in what are called simulations. The AICPA defines a simulation as "an assessment of knowledge and skills in context approximating that found on the job through the use of realistic scenarios and tasks and access to normally available and familiar resources." In other words, simulations are condensed case studies that utilize real-life, work-related examples. These case studies require the use of tools (computerized databases) and skills that accountants use in the real world. These primary computerized databases are similar in functionality to the AICPA Professional Standards (Auditing and Attestation literature), FASB Codification Research System, and Thomson Reuters/RIA Checkpoint® tax database.

To successfully complete a simulation, the CPA candidate is expected to possess basic computer skills that include the use of spreadsheets and word processing functions. As to the research component of the simulation, the candidate will be required to search various authoritative literature databases in order to answer accounting, auditing, and tax questions to support his or her judgments and prepare formal communications.

Figure A1-1 presents the opening screen shot of the Auditing and Attestation simulation. Notice the Professional Standards entry on the left. This database is explained in Chapter 8, which provides access to the auditing literature to carry out the simulation. Figure A1-2 provides the opening screen shot for the FARS simulation, whereby one accesses the FASB literature to obtain a solution. Finally, Figure A1-3 provides the opening screen shot for Regulations, where the candidate conducts research in the tax code. Notice the Internal Revenue Code selection on the left, which opens up the IRS Code for research. Chapter 7 provides further details of tax research. Each of these databases is explained in detail, with examples, in Chapters 4, 7, and 8. Note on each screen the simulation question being tested under Step One: Research Question.

RESEARCH TOOLS
- ACL
- AICPA reSOURCE
- Codification
- eIFERS
- Internet
- i2
- LexisNexis
- RIA Checkpoint

OPENING SCREEN SHOT OF THE AUDITING AND ATTESTATION SIMULATION

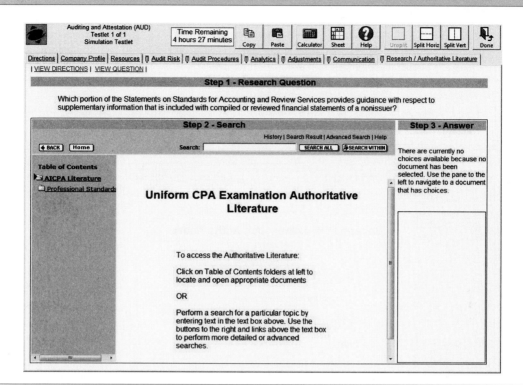

OPENING SCREEN SHOT OF FARS SIMULATION

FIGURE A1-3   OPENING SCREEN SHOT OF REGULATIONS SIMULATION

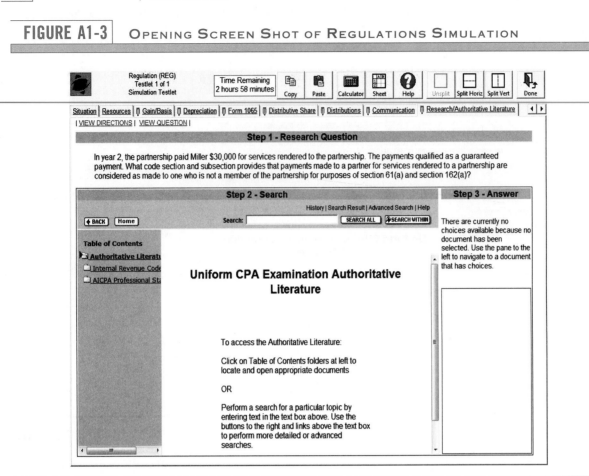

Critical Thinking and Effective Writing Skills for the Professional Accountant

LEARNING OBJECTIVES

After completing this chapter, you should understand:

- Critical thinking skills.
- Levels of thinking.
- How critical thinking skills can help professional accountants "add value" to their services.
- How competent writing forms a key element of critical thinking skills.
- How to strengthen and improve writing skills.
- The proper use of punctuation.
- The U.S. Securities and Exchange Commission's "Plain English" initiative.
- How to write effective client letters and e-mails.
- How to write memos to a file.

Change is accelerating in today's environment and the pressure to respond is intensifying. As new technology, accounting standards, laws, business methods, and global economic realities work their way through the accounting profession, these changes and realities are becoming increasingly complex. Critical thinking is necessary for effectively addressing these dynamic changes and is considered an important component of accounting education. All professionals must also know how to write effectively.

Clients now expect professional accountants to "add value" to what they observe, read, and write. Accountants must evaluate complex systems and information, as well as detect, predict, advise, and recommend appropriate courses of action. Critical thinking is needed throughout the process. Effective writing communicates the results to others.

CRITICAL THINKING SKILLS

Today's professional accountants must respond to the progressive diversity and complexity of accounting, auditing, and tax practice and develop life-long learning skills that focus on their ability to think critically. Critical thinking skills are essential to understanding, applying, and adapting concepts and principles in a variety of contexts and circumstances. The accountant's professional skepticism, that of questioning management's responses, involves critical thinking that entails an attitude of examining and recognizing emotion-laden and explicit or hidden assumptions behind each question. Accountants must master critical thinking skills particularly because business organizations continue to evolve in response to new information technology and greater worldwide competition.

Descriptions of critical thinking are summarized as follows:

1. Critical thinking is difficult because it is often complex.
2. Critical thinking applies multiple criteria.
3. Critical thinking requires an ability to tolerate ambiguity and uncertainty.
4. Critical thinking involves self-regulation of the thinking process.
5. Critical thinking may impose meaning and find structure in apparent disorder.
6. Critical thinking requires effort. It entails intense elaboration and careful judgment.
7. Critical thinking often yields multiple solutions and requires cost and benefit analysis.
8. Critical thinking involves making interpretations.[1]

RESEARCH TIPS

Use critical thinking to assess issues, problems, data, and other concerns.

Nothing is more important and practical to the accounting practitioner than developing critical thinking skills. Poor thinking will inevitably cause new problems, waste time, and ensure frustration. As you become more proficient in critical thinking, you also become more proficient in assessing issues and objectives, problems and solutions, information and data, assumptions and interpretations, different points of view, and frames of reference.

Critical thinking has many definitions. The *American Heritage Dictionary* defines **critical** as "characterized by careful and exact evaluation and judgment." Critical thinking points to a positive ability in those who possess it. Critical thinking focuses on problem definition and problem solving; it is a rational response to questions that may lack definite answers or may be missing some relevant information. Its purpose is to explore situations to arrive at justifiable conclusions and optimal solutions. Critical thinking rests on a willingness to take nothing for granted and to approach each experience as if it were unique. Although the purpose of critical thinking is to understand, its practice usually leads to evaluation and, therefore, to judgment. Simply stated, critical thinking is the art of using your best thinking given your knowledge and skills.

Critical thinking is purposeful, goal-oriented, and creative. Critical thinking is an active process involving rethinking the problem, and refusing to consider merely the most obvious or easiest solutions. The qualities that lie behind rethinking are these:

- A willingness to say, "I don't know"
- An openness to alternatives in ways of seeing and doing—alternatives that are based on understanding how things work
- An interest in the ideas of others that is shown by paying attention—even when the ideas conflict with your own
- Thoughtfulness that is shown by genuine, not just idle, curiosity
- A desire to discover what other people have done and thought
- An insistence on getting the best evidence before choosing between alternatives
- An openness to your own intuition[2]

---

[1] Lauren B. Resnick, *Education and Learning to Think* (Washington, D.C.: National Academy Press, 1987).

[2] Robert Boostrom, *Developing Creative and Critical Thinking: An Integrated Approach* (Chicago: National Textbook Co., 1992), 24–25.

Critical thinking is a process of understanding how thinking and learning work, using *higher-order* skills for comprehending issues and for analyzing, synthesizing, and assessing ideas logically. The higher-order reasoning skills include:

1. **Analysis** of a problem, or breaking ideas into their component parts to consider each of them separately.

2. **Synthesis,** or connecting different components or ideas in order to derive relationships that tie the parts of an answer together.

3. **Critical assessment** of the conclusions reached, examining them for sound logical reasoning. Accountants must master critical thinking skills in order to engage effectively in the process of research and problem solving.

The ability to reason critically is an essential, fundamental skill that enables one to acquire more knowledge more easily. To summarize, critical thinking includes:

1. Recognizing any explanatory relationship among statements.

2. Recognizing the structure of arguments (the premises, implicit assumptions, and conclusions).

3. Assessing consistency or inconsistency, equivalence among statements, and logical implications.

4. Formulating and identifying deductively and inductively justified conclusions based on the available evidence.

LEVELS OF THINKING

The difficulty in discussing critical thinking concisely arises from two characteristics of critical thinking itself.

> First, clear thinking results less from practicing skills than from adopting such attitudes as persistence, open-mindedness, thoroughness, and flexibility. Second, thinking is not a single process that can be divided into a series of steps. Instead, it is a family of processes that enlighten and support each other.[3]

The noted nineteenth-century writer Oliver Wendell Holmes characterized people as to their thinking skills. The lowest-level thinkers were fact collectors with no aims beyond the facts; thinkers on the next level were able to compare, reason, and generalize using the results of the fact collectors' work; and the highest-level thinkers demonstrated the ability to idealize, imagine, and predict.

One current classification of thought, generated by the Illinois Renewal Institute, distinguishes recall, process, and application. The lowest level of thought is **recall**, in which one defines, describes, lists, recites, and selects. The second level of thought is **process**, in which one compares, contrasts, classifies, sorts, distinguishes, explains, infers, sequences, analyzes, synthesizes, and analogizes. The highest level of thought is **application**, in which one evaluates, generalizes, imagines, judges, predicts, speculates, hypothesizes, and forecasts.

Bloom's taxonomy is probably the most famous classification of thought. Bloom's six-level taxonomy proceeds from knowledge, comprehension, application, analysis, and synthesis to evaluation, as presented in Figure 2-1. Bloom hypothesized that higher-order knowledge occurs with the use of higher-level skills (i.e., critical thinking skills).

---

[3] *Ibid.*, Teacher's Manual, 1.

Practitioners can use higher-level application skills to complement lower-level recall skills by both focusing on what successful accountants do to "add value" to their organizations and by always questioning assumptions.

Bloom's taxonomy implies that the levels of thinking are incremental: The ability to perform at level 4, for example, is necessary before moving up to level 5. (The ideal reader, writer, accountant, or auditor moves up the levels until he or she can perform at the top level.) To exercise the highest-level, level 6, skills, one must already possess the skills at the other levels. To *infer* properly, for example, one must first define and describe accurately the objects or situations from which one will infer. The skills increase in complexity as the level rises. To analyze a situation, for example, is a far more complicated process than simply to recall a situation, and to evaluate a situation (using definite criteria for a given purpose) is more complicated than either of the others. The

FIGURE 2-1 | EXAMPLES OF APPLYING AND UNDERSTANDING BLOOM'S TAXONOMY

Level No.	Major Categories in Bloom's Taxonomy	Illustrative General Instructional Objectives	Illustrative Behavioral Terms for Stating Specific Learned Outcomes
1.	**Knowledge** represents recalling previously learned materials.	Knows common terms, specific facts, basic concepts, and principles.	Defines, describes, labels, lists, reproduces, selects, and states.
2.	**Comprehension** involves "grasping" the material, including translating words into numbers, summarizing or interpreting the materials, and estimating future trends.	Understands facts and principles; translates verbal materials into mathematical formulas; estimates future consequences implied in the data; and justifies methods and procedures.	Converts, defends, distinguishes, estimates, extends, explains, predicts, rewrites, and summarizes.
3.	**Application** of the use of previously learned materials into new situations.	(Correctly) applies laws and theories into new and practical situations.	Changes, computes, demonstrates, discovers, manipulates, modifies, shows, solves, and uses.
4.	**Analysis** breaks down the material into its component parts to better understand its organizational structure.	Recognizes unstated assumptions and logical gaps in reasoning; distinguishes between facts and inferences; and evaluates the relevancy of data.	Breaks down, diagrams, differentiates, discriminates, distinguishes, infers, outlines, relates, selects, separates, and subdivides.
5.	**Synthesis** puts parts together to form a new whole, usually involving creative behaviors and new patterns or structures (e.g., developing a new schema for classifying information).	Writes a well-organized research paper; gives a well-organized speech; integrates learning from different areas into a new plan to solve a problem; and formulates a new schema to classify objects or events.	Assigns, categorizes, combines, compiles, composes, creates, devises, explains, generates, plans, recognizes, reorganizes, revises, rewrites, tells, or writes.
6.	**Evaluation** judges the value of the statement (based upon definite criteria) for a given purpose. The criteria can be internal (organization) or external (relevant to the given purpose).	Judges the logical consistency of the presented material, how well the data "support" the "conclusions" and how well the end product adheres to the internal and external criteria.	Appraises, compares, concludes, contrasts, criticizes, explains, interprets, justifies, relates, summarizes, and supports.

basic differences between the levels are largely a matter of attitude, not procedure. That is, the ability to progress up through the levels partly depends on one's ability to internalize the qualities previously noted.

Bloom's framework of thought has had a practical impact on accountants. It has influenced many professional accounting examinations to modify their exam questions and format in order to test higher-level critical thinking skills of candidates (levels 4, 5, and 6). For example, the Uniform CPA Exam, now completely computerized, emphasizes heavily the critical thinking and research skills that accountants need in the workplace.

Critical thinking also depends on the ability to make specific decisions, such as:

1. Deciding on the meaning (and intent) of a statement.
2. Deciding whether a definition is adequate.
3. Deciding whether an observation statement is reliable.
4. Deciding whether a statement is an assumption.
5. Deciding whether a statement made by an alleged authority is acceptable.
6. Deciding whether a conclusion follows necessarily from the underlying data.
7. Deciding whether an inductive conclusion is warranted.

In critical thinking "you decide first what the words mean, then whether they make sense, and finally whether you believe them."[4] A simplified example that helps to reinforce the critical thinking process is presented in Figure 2-2.

UNIVERSAL ELEMENTS OF REASONING

It is helpful for the professional accountant/researcher to concentrate on the universal elements of reasoning when using critical thinking to arrive at a solution to a problem. The eight elements of purpose, issue, information, concepts, assumptions, interpretation, implications, and conclusions provide a central focus in critical thinking.[5] Whenever we think, we should use these eight elements of analysis, as depicted in Figure 2-3.

RESEARCH TIPS

As you analyze a problem, you need to proceed through the eight elements of reasoning.

AN EXAMPLE OF USING CRITICAL THINKING SKILLS

The use of critical thinking skills in a business organization is illustrated in Goldratt and Cox's[6] best-selling business book, *The Goal*. This book describes a company that has "floundered" because it conducted its business under certain time-honored assumptions, such as:

1. Keep all employees busy all of the time.
2. Order materials in the largest quantities possible to receive the lowest price.
3. Keep the manufacturing robots working all the time (minimize downtime).
4. Measure the "cost" of an idle machine as its depreciation expense.
5. Allow management to change the priority of jobs in process to meet customer needs.

---

[4] Boostrom, *op. cit.*, 198.
[5] Richard Paul, *Critical Thinking: Basic Theory &Instructional Structures* (Foundation for Critical Thinking, 1998).
[6] E.M. Goldratt and J. Cox, *The Goal* (New Haven, Conn.: North River Press, 1992).

FIGURE 2-2 | CRITICAL THINKING ACCOUNTING EXAMPLE

Purpose: To prepare a report based upon your research to answer the following client request.

Issue/Question: A major client, who maintains homes in both New York and Florida and uses both frequently throughout the year, asks you, from an economic standpoint, which state would be the best for her to establish residency in.

Answering this question quickly, intelligently, and accurately requires critical thinking to identify all the relevant factors regarding this decision and to develop proper conclusions, including focusing on such issues as (a) income tax rates of both states, (b) state sales tax rules and rates (e.g., buying and using such "discretionary" assets as a new car), (c) property taxes (e.g., buying or selling a home), unemployment/welfare taxes, municipal taxes, inheritance taxes (e.g., considering the client's age), and (d) costs of other essentials (e.g., food, clothing, and shelter).

After identifying the relevant factors, you should focus this analysis by asking specific questions to narrow the scope of this decision to such relevant issues as:

1. Does the client anticipate selling one of the homes? If so, which one?
2. Where will the client purchase and use her assets (e.g., the new car)?

The answers to these and other, similar questions will affect how you proceed with this analysis while fully considering all of the relevant factors. Considering relevant issues and eliminating irrelevant ones forms the crux of critical thinking.

This example can also help you better understand such critical thinking skills. For example, the researcher must analyze, synthesize, and critically assess the relevant factors. This process requires using the available evidence effectively. Specifically, the accountant should ascertain that the evidence is:

1. **Sufficient.** Does the accountant have adequate evidence to reach a proper conclusion or should he or she ask further questions (e.g., are state inheritance tax rates under review by the respective state legislatures)?
2. **Representative.** Is the evidence provided objective (e.g., will the client actually spend the requisite days in Florida to be considered a legal resident of that state)?
3. **Relevant.** Does the evidence relate directly to the provided assertion (e.g., will the client's plans to spend much time visiting her grandchildren in California impact her legal residence status)?
4. **Accurate.** Does the evidence come from reliable primary or secondary sources (e.g., can CPA firm employees observe the times spent in Florida or New York)?

Thus, the ability to reason critically is essential to the acquisition of knowledge in any discipline and may, therefore, be appropriately regarded as a fundamental skill, one that new accountants should acquire as soon as possible. Critical thinking includes:

1. Formulating and identifying deductively and inductively warranted conclusions from available evidence.
2. Recognizing the structure of arguments (premises, conclusions, and implicit assumptions).
3. Assessing the consistency, inconsistency, logical implications, and equivalence among statements.
4. Recognizing explanatory relations among statements.

Goldratt and Cox demonstrate that the company could operate much more profitably by challenging these assumptions (i.e., by using higher-order critical thinking skills) and thereby yielding dramatically improved results. They showed that adhering to these "old" policies made the company less efficient. Some "new" results included the following policies:

FIGURE 2-3 | EIGHT ELEMENTS OF REASONING

1. **Purpose.** You reason things out in order to meet some specific end, goal, or objective. If the purpose or goal is unclear or unrealistic, various problems can occur as you proceed. As an accountant/researcher, your primary goal or purpose is to complete accounting/auditing research in order to develop an answer to a particular practical issue/problem. You should select clear and realistic purposes and evaluate your reasoning periodically to make sure you still are on target with your stated purpose.

2. **Issue.** The second element is to reason out a question or issue. This requires the formulation of the issue in a clear and relevant way. Because accounting/auditing authoritative literature is organized around keywords or concepts, clearly identifying the issue will greatly aid you in researching it.

3. **Information.** Data or information exists concerning the issue about which you are reasoning. Any defect in the data or information is a possible source of problems in conducting research. As an accounting practitioner, you will use client-provided data and both authoritative and nonauthoritative sources in reasoning out a solution. Therefore, you need to be mindful that the data or information may contain defects or contradictions, especially in the client data or nonauthoritative sources.

4. **Concepts.** Reasoning uses concepts that include theories, principles, or rules. A basic understanding of the concepts is important as you reason out an accounting/auditing issue.

5. **Assumptions.** All reasoning begins somewhere. Incorrect assumptions in your reasoning can be a source of problems and can bias your research. You must determine that your assumptions are justifiable and how they will shape your point of view in conducting research.

6. **Interpretation.** The sixth element of reasoning requires that what you infer from your research is based upon the evidence gathered. All reasoning requires some type of interpretation of the data in order to draw conclusions from the research process.

7. **Implications.** As you conclude the research process and begin to develop conclusions, you need to consider the various implications or consequences that arise from your reasoning. Consider both negative and positive implications as you develop your conclusions.

8. **Conclusion.** The final element of reasoning is the conclusion to the research question or issue. As you develop the conclusion, be careful to have the proper point of view—one that is not too narrow or broad, or based on misleading information or contradictions.

---

1. Because busy employees produce unneeded inventory, wasting large amounts of resources, have certain production employees perform quality control and preventive maintenance, rather than produce nonessential parts.

2. Because ordering large amounts of materials increases unnecessary inventory, order smaller quantities of parts inventory.

3. Because robots, like employees, only increase unneeded inventory, consider the cost of the inventory they produce in deciding whether to allow the robots to work.

4. Because "bottlenecks" often prevent a factory from working to its full potential, focus on reducing operating bottleneck constraints.

5. Because rush orders generally impair the optimal timing of the production process, rarely alter the normal work flow for "special" jobs.

> **RESEARCH TIPS**
>
> Use careful analytical reasoning (critical thinking skills) for effective research.

Similarly, professional accountants should develop and use critical thinking skills to add value to their services, an important goal for all professionals—including newly hired employees. A summary of some necessary basic critical thinking skills appears in Figure 2-4.

FIGURE 2-4 | BASIC CRITICAL THINKING SKILLS

Skill	Description
Value-added services	Advise, predict, detect, recommend, and evaluate.
Wariness	Take nothing for granted. Approach each experience as a "unique" event.
Rethinking	Do not perform tasks in an obvious and routine manner. Use innovative, alternative ways to perform the necessary jobs. Insist on obtaining the "best" available evidence, considering the related costs.
Evaluation and judgment	Use definitive criteria to obtain the goal of the assignment, and then apply reasonable judgment after this evaluation.
Incremental levels of thinking	Apply lower levels of thinking before progressing to higher ones.

EFFECTIVE WRITING SKILLS

The ability to communicate effectively, in both oral and written form, is essential for today's practitioner. In the workplace, an accountant may write to a supervisor, a shareholder, a company's management, government agency, or others. Strong communication skills are emphasized in the following personal statements shared by two leading business professionals:

QUICK FACTS

Written communication skills are considered one of the researcher's most important skills.

In accounting and all other professions, we must have the appropriate technical skills. But, if we cannot communicate what we know, the value of technical skills is lessened. For example, knowing how to compute corporate income taxes is a valuable skill. Being able to tell others how to do it magnifies the value of that technical skill. Others can capitalize on your knowledge only if you can communicate it.

Dennis R. Beresford, Former Chair of the Financial Accounting Standards Board

Learning to communicate well should be a top priority for anyone aspiring to lead or advance in a career. Strong technical skills are needed, but technical ability alone will not result in career advancement. Those who develop only technical skills always will work for people who have both technical and leadership abilities, and communication is the key ingredient in leadership.[7]

Hugh B. Jacks, Former President, BellSouth Services

Accounting practitioners have ranked written communication as the most important of 22 skills to develop in students, according to research conducted by Albrecht and Sack.[8] Similarly, writing skills are among the most important attributes considered in the hiring process, according to a survey of Fortune 500 senior tax executives.[9] Thinking and writing are somewhat related: Thinking determines what one wants to say, and writing records

---

[7] From William C. Himstreet, Wayne M. Baty, and Carol M. Lehman, *Business Communications: Principles and Methods*, 10th edition. © 1993.

[8] W.S. Albrecht, and R.J. Sack, *Accounting Education: Charting the Course Through a Perilous Future*. Accounting Education Series, vol. 16 (Sarasota, Fla: American Accounting Association, 2000).

[9] Paice, G., and M. Lyons, "Addressing the People Puzzle," *Financial Executive*, September 2001. Available online: *http://www.fei.org/magazine/articles/9-2001_corptaxes.cfm.*

these ideas for future communication. However, effective writing is more than making a draft, jotting down isolated ideas, writing reminders to oneself, making outlines, or charting different sides of an issue. Writing is a process that enables one to make his or her more precise and effective, rather than merely relying on reading or discussion.

Since thinking and writing are related, it follows that critical thinking and effective writing are also connected. Effective writing is a matter not just of form but of quality content arising from critical thought. One must think critically in order to write effectively.

Writing as a Process

Writing is a way to make meaning of our experiences and knowledge. Writers perform many functions at the same time, such as:

RESEARCH TIPS

Review writing requirements any time you write a professional report, or when you study for the CPA exam.

- Remembering past experiences or readings while determining what they intend to write.

- Trying to convey major concepts while at the same time supplying supporting evidence and details.

- Considering personal knowledge while considering what the audience needs to know for its unique purposes.

- Continually editing and revising as needed while trying to retain the central idea and purpose.

Envisioning the intended final product helps to bring logical order to the writing. The AICPA defines effective writing in essay answers for the CPA examination as requiring the following six characteristics:

1. **Coherent organization:** Organize responses so that the ideas are arranged logically and the flow of thought is easy to follow. Generally, knowledge is best expressed by using short paragraphs composed of short sentences. Moreover, short paragraphs, each limited to the development of one principal idea, can better emphasize the main points in the answer. Place each principal idea in the first sentence of the paragraph, followed by supporting concepts and examples.

2. **Conciseness:** Conciseness requires that candidates present complete thoughts in as few words as possible, while ensuring that important points are covered adequately. Short sentences and simple wording also contribute to concise writing.

3. **Clarity:** A clearly written response prevents uncertainty concerning the candidate's meaning or reasoning. Clarity involves using words with specific and precise meanings, including proper technical terms. Well-constructed sentences also contribute to clarity.

4. **Use of Standard English:** Standard English is characterized by exacting standards of punctuation and capitalization, by accurate spelling, by exact diction, by an expressive vocabulary, and by knowledgeable usage choices.

5. **Responsiveness to the requirements of the question:** Answers should directly address the requirements of the question and demonstrate the candidate's awareness of the purpose of the writing task. Avoid making broad expositions on the general subject matter.

RESEARCH TIPS

Write concisely and clearly, using Standard English and coherent organization.

6. **Appropriateness for the reader:** Writing that is appropriate for the reader takes into account the reader's background, knowledge of the subject, interests, and concerns. The requirements of some essay questions may ask candidates to prepare a written document for a certain reader, such as an engagement memorandum for a CPA's client. When the intended reader is not specified, the candidate should assume the intended reader is a knowledgeable CPA.[10]

---

[10] Examination Division, AICPA, *Report of the Testing of Writing Skills Subtask Force of the CPA Examination Change Implementation Task Force*, September 18, 1990.

FIGURE 2-5 | WORD SELECTION AND SENTENCE STRUCTURE GUIDELINES

1. Visualize your reader and select words familiar to him or her.
2. Use the active voice in your writing.
3. Choose short words.
4. Use technical words and acronyms with caution.
5. Select your words for precise meanings.
6. Limit your sentence content. Use short sentences.
7. Use proper punctuation in sentence development.
8. Arrange your sentences for clarity and unity.

Any professional accountant should apply these same six criteria of coherent organization, conciseness, clarity, use of Standard English, responsiveness to the requirements of the question, and appropriateness for the reader to his or her writing. Let us further examine these six criteria by classifying them as composing or editing skills.

Composing skills are primarily used for a focused first draft. Three of the criteria are essential **composing** skills:

- **Organization:** Is the writing organized in a logical manner? Apply this concept not only to the document as a whole, but within each section and paragraph.
- **Responsiveness:** Does the writing respond to what is asked for and needed?
- **Appropriateness:** Is the writing appropriate for the reader, considering his or her capacity and level of experience?

Editing skills are primarily used in revising a draft. Editing is what one does to the draft; it is largely a matter of rewriting to produce a more concise presentation, yet one with greater clarity of expression. Thus, editing skills include:

- **Conciseness:** The writing contains no extraneous matter and does not repeat itself.
- **Clarity:** The right word choices and the most effective sentence patterns are used.
- **Use of Standard English:** The writing reflects Standard English both in usage and mechanical exactness

The first draft should focus on the substantive ideas to convey in an organized fashion that is appropriate and responsive to the reader's needs. One does not worry about conciseness, clarity, and Standard English until revising the draft. Often several revisions are necessary and some composing skills are also used. Some basic suggestions for revising word selection and sentence structure for effective writing are presented in Figure 2-5.

Success in critical thinking and effective writing comes from life-long learning. The skills develop from education, practice, and experience. If effective writing is not developed, the accountant may lose business or the potential for career advancement. Clients who are unable to judge the quality of work may form impressions of a professional's quality based on the quality of the accountant's writing. Bad writing may indicate poor thinking.

QUICK FACTS

Effective writing is a process that includes proper grammar as well as proper punctuation.

PUNCTUATION PRIMER

Successful writing requires proper grammar and punctuation. Figure 2-6 provides a basic primer on the main punctuation issues with examples. Remember that proper punctuation is very important not only for business writing, but also on the CPA exam. Proper punctuation on the CPA exam essays improves one's grade.

FIGURE 2-6 | PUNCTUATION PRIMER

PERIODS

Rule 1. Use a period after a declarative sentence (one that states a fact) or an imperative sentence (one that states a command).

Examples: Our accountant resigned yesterday. Get me the reconciliation report immediately.

Rule 2. Use a period with abbreviations and initials. If the last word in the sentence ends in a period, do not follow it with another period.

Examples: Robert received his M.B.A. from Harvard. The meeting will begin at 2:00 p.m.

COMMAS

Rule 1. Use commas when a sentence contains words in a series.

Examples: Her previous employers were the SEC, AICPA, and FBI.
The auditor requested support for the accounts payable balance, the accounts receivable balance, and the vacation accrual balance.

Rule 2. Use a comma when two or more adjectives describe the same noun.

Examples: That was a long, tiring meeting. Susan is a loyal, dedicated employee.
Note: If the word "and" can be inserted between the two adjectives, a comma is needed.

Rule 3. Use a comma to separate two independent clauses that are joined by a conjunction. An independent clause is a group of words that can stand alone as a sentence.

Examples: The audit has been concluded, but an opinion has not been issued. We are pleased to have you join our firm, and we hope this will be a rewarding experience for you.

SEMICOLONS

Rule 1. Use a semicolon to separate two independent clauses when no conjunction is used.

Examples: The president declined the raise; he was already making $2 million a year. Fifty people attended the conference; most of them were accountants.

Rule 2. Use a semicolon to avoid confusion where commas are already present.

Examples: The auditors traveled to Los Angeles, California; Chicago, Illinois; and Little Rock, Arkansas, to conduct the fraud investigation.
Will, partner of the firm, interviewed three potential staff members; but not one of them was hired.

COLONS

Rule 1. Use a colon after a complete sentence to show that something is to follow.

Examples: Please get me the following items: payroll register, list of vendors, and list of accounts payable.
Please get the payroll register, a list of vendors, and a list of accounts payable. (No colon after *get* because *Please get* is not a complete sentence.)

Rule 2. Use a colon after the salutation of a business letter.

Example: Dear Mr. Williams:

QUESTION MARKS

Rule 1. Use a question mark after a direct question.

Examples: Are you sure the tax forms were filed before the deadline?
I asked John if he was sure the tax forms were filed before the deadline. (No question mark because it is not a direct question.)

Rule 2. When quotation marks are used, place the question mark inside the final quotation mark only if the quoted part of the sentence is a question.

Examples: The partner asked, "Will you be at the audit committee meeting tomorrow?" Did Thomas say, "Can we push the deadline back until Friday"? (The question mark is placed outside the quotation mark because the entire sentence is a question.)

(*continued*)

FIGURE 2-6 | PUNCTUATION PRIMER (CONTINUED)

EXCLAMATION POINTS

Rule 1. Use an exclamation point to show emphasis or surprise.

Example: Help me!

Rule 2. Do not use an exclamation point in formal business letters.

QUOTATION MARKS

Rule 1. Periods and commas always go inside quotation marks.

Examples: Jill said, "I will not have time to reconcile the bank statement tomorrow." The professor said, "Remember the accounting equation for tomorrow's test."

Rule 2. Use single quotation marks for quotes within quotes. Remember that the period goes inside all quote marks.

Examples: He said, "The boss said, 'Make sure to disclose the inventory method used in our notes to financial statements.'" Bob said, "The professor said, 'The quiz tomorrow only covers the journal entries regarding cash and accounts receivable.'"

APOSTROPHES

Rule 1. Use an apostrophe to show singular possession by placing the apostrophe before the *s*.

Examples: Today's assignment will involve performing some tax research on the Internet. Bill's presentation was excellent.

Rule 2. Do not use an apostrophe with possessive pronouns—his, her, our, their, etc.

Examples: His accounting professor was one of the best. Our company should have caught the error—not theirs.

Rule 3. Use an apostrophe with contrac-omitted letters with the apostrophe.

Examples: Sue doesn't care if you use LIFO or FIFO. Don't assume that the financial statements are free of error.

HYPHENS

Rule 1. Use a hyphen in a compound expression when a noun follows the expression.

Examples: The vendor has a past-due account. The vendor's account is past due. (No hyphen because a noun does not follow *past due*.)

Rule 2. Use a hyphen in compound numbers and fractions.

Examples: Sixty-three employees signed the code of ethics. Please sell me the 10-year-old bonds.

CAPITALIZATION

Rule 1. Capitalize the first word in a sentence.

Examples: The balance sheet presents information for a certain date. The income statement presents information over a period of time.

Rule 2. Capitalize the first word of a direct quote.

Examples: The manager said, "Please have the statement of cash flows ready by tomorrow." Peter asked, "Should we expense this item or capitalize it?"

Rule 3. Capitalize proper nouns.

Examples: During our business trip we saw the Golden Gate Bridge. The SEC office is close to the Washington Monument.

IMPROVED WRITING SKILLS REQUIRED

Improved writing skills are required by many key accounting organizations, including the AICPA, and the managing partners of the country's largest public accounting firms. Improved writing skills will enhance an organization's productivity and lower training costs. Thus, the Uniform CPA Examination now requires CPA candidates to possess more effective research and writing skills.

The Securities and Exchange Commission (SEC) has criticized dense writing styles, technical jargon, and repetitive disclosures in various prospectuses. A prospectus is a document provided to the public when a company is issuing new stock. The prospectus outlines the business and principal purposes for the company's proposed use of the capital funds raised from the stock offering. The SEC Release 33-7380, "Plain English Disclosures," requires public company registrants to use "plain english" in a prospectus's cover page, summary, and risk factor sections. The SEC also issued *A Plain English Handbook: How to Create Clear SEC Disclosure,* which specifies six principles for clear writing: active voice, short sentences, everyday language, tabular presentation of complex material, limited legal jargon, and no multiple negatives.

The SEC plain writing concepts apply to any writing. However, let's first discuss the concepts in the context that most concerns the SEC.

RESEARCH TIPS

Use plain English with short sentences, everyday language, active voice, tabular presentation of complex material, limited legal jargon, and no multiple negatives.

Active Voice

The active voice uses strong, direct verbs. Thus, the active voice creates more confidence. The active voice follows the way we think and process information. Technically, the subject of the sentence performs the action described by the verb. The active voice is often easier to understand than the passive voice.

The passive voice is easy to spot because it uses the word "be" or "been" as part of the verb. In the passive voice, the action is done to somebody or something by another agent that might not be identified in the sentence. Did you notice that the previous sentence included an example of the passive voice, "be identified"? The passive voice is less effective because it often forces the reader to reread information, particularly if it is part of a long, complex sentence. Therefore, when revising work, modify sentences that contain the passive voice to use the active voice.

The SEC provides the following example of how to change from the passive voice to the active voice to achieve effective writing. The "before" material is from an actual corporate filing with the SEC.

Before: No person has been authorized to give any information or make any representation other than those contained or incorporated by reference in this joint proxy statement/prospectus, and, if given or made, such information or representation must not be relied upon as having been authorized.

The SEC's proposed revision not only changes the voice, but reinforces its clarity, conciseness, and use of Standard English:

After: You should rely only on the information contained in this document or incorporated by reference. We have not authorized anyone to provide you with information that is different.

QUICK FACTS

The active voice helps to keep the reader's attention.

Short Sentences

Short sentences help to prevent such problems as run-on sentences and sentence fragments, which are constructions that represent just part of a sentence. Typically, in a sentence fragment, either the subject or verb is left out. Run-on sentences have two independent

RESEARCH TIPS

Divide long sentences into short sentences to convey your research results.

clauses joined without any punctuation. Having more than one idea in a sentence often makes the sentence difficult to read. The SEC suggests that a registrant strive to use shorter sentences, of 25 to 30 words, as in the following "before and after" example.

Before: Machine Industries and Great Tools, Inc., are each subject to the information requirements of the Securities Exchange Act of 1934, as amended (the "Exchange Act"), and in accordance therewith file reports, proxy statements, and other information with the Securities and Exchange Commission (the "Commission").

After: We must comply with the Securities Exchange Act of 1934. Accordingly, we file annual, quarterly and current reports, proxy statements, and other information with the Securities and Exchange Commission.

Definite, Concrete, Everyday Language

Clearer communication results when writers and readers use definite and concrete words. Similarly, providing examples using one investor helps make complex information more understandable. The SEC provided the following "before and after" example to help registrants communicate in clearer, less vague language. The SEC uses greater specificity in the "after" example.

Before: *History of Net Losses.* The Company has recorded a net loss under generally accepted accounting principles for each fiscal year since its inception, as well as for the interim nine months of this year. However, these results include the effect of certain significant, non-cash accounting transactions.

After: *History of Net Losses.* We have recorded a net loss under general accounting principles for each year since we started business, and for the interim nine months of this year. Our losses were caused, in part, by the annual write-off of a portion of the goodwill resulting from the ten acquisitions we made during this period.

Tabular Presentation

Tabular presentations often help to organize complex information. SEC registrants using "if-then" tables, for example, can make the presentation of such information more accessible. For example, the following tabular headings define two columns to enhance the identification of information that might not stand out in a paragraph:

The Event of Default (if) | **Remedy** (then)

Limited Jargon and Technical Terms

Use legal and other jargon sparingly in registration statements. Jargon often forces readers to learn a new vocabulary that inhibits their understanding of the information. In certain circumstances, jargon is unavoidable; technical terms are sometimes needed to communicate technical information as efficiently as possible. However, the writer should define or explain any technical terms used. The SEC suggests the use of clear and common terms for better understanding, as demonstrated in the following example.

Before: The following description encompasses all the material terms and provisions of the Notes offered hereby and supplements, and to the extent inconsistent therewith replaces, the description of the general terms and provisions of the Debt Securities (as defined in the accompanying Prospectus) set forth under the heading "Description of Debt Securities" in the Prospectus, to which description reference is hereby made.

After: We disclose information about our notes in two separate documents that progressively provide more detail on the notes' specific terms: the prospectus, and this pricing supplement. Since the specific terms of notes are made at the time of pricing, rely on information in the pricing supplement over different information in the prospectus.

No Multiple Negatives

The SEC suggests that registrants' filings avoid multiple negatives. Comprehending documents is more difficult when readers must "decipher" the meaning of the combination of negatives. Avoidance of negatives clarifies the writing, as demonstrated in the following example.

Before: Except when an applicant has submitted a request for withdrawal without the appropriate tax identification number, the request will be honored within one business day.

After: We will send your money within one business day if you include your tax identification number in your withdrawal request.

Elements of Plain English

The SEC has also stated that using plain English is part of writing well. Plain English uses common language; however, it is not overly simplified English. Plain English is the opposite of obscure language, for it seeks to have the message understood on the first reading. Successful plain English depends on whether the writing is clear, straightforward language for that audience.

The SEC has identified the following four basic requirements for plain English.

1. **Know your audience:** Successful communicators first identify the investor groups for whom they write. Effective writing includes analyzing the readers' needs and expectations. Writers should tailor their tone and style to their intended audience, select words that contribute to an effective writing style, and choose language based on current and future investors' educational and financial knowledge.

   Other pertinent factors in audience targeting include investor demographics (e.g., job experience, age, and income) and how the investors will read and use the document. Authors should remember that the least sophisticated investors often have the greatest need for an "understandable" disclosure document.

2. **Know what material information needs to be disclosed:** After identifying the readers' needs and expectations, the author should gather the necessary information to communicate. The SEC has stated that too many disclosure documents combine material and immaterial information into long, dense sentences; they do not prioritize the information or organize it logically for the reader. The SEC notes that prospectus cover pages typically include very dense printing with sentences running 60 to 100 words in length and include superfluous information. In this respect they do not "invite" the investor to read the remainder of the prospectus for key information concerning the offering.

   In coherent writing, main points stand out. Registrants should emphasize main points by placing them where they will attract the reader's attention. Therefore, the cover page should provide a clear, concise, and coherent "snapshot" of the offering. Subsequent sections of the prospectus then present the details in a logical fashion.

3. **Use techniques of clear writing:** Two overriding themes in clear and effective writing are **conciseness** and **clarity**. In writing documents, one should eliminate digressions and irrelevant detail. Precise diction is another important element of clear writing.

FIGURE 2-7	KEY POINTS OF EFFECTIVE WRITING

Content	Add relevant, "value-added" content, a process enhanced with the use of critical thinking skills.
Chain of processes	Convey "large" concepts while supplying evidence supporting these ideas, to add meaning from your experiences.
Coherent organization	Organize ideas logically, making the flow of thought easy to follow.
Conciseness	Use as few words as are necessary to convey "complete thoughts."
Clarity	Select "effective" words to state ideas with "certainty."
Use of Standard English	Use appropriate punctuation and grammar, perhaps with the help of a computer-based spelling/ grammar checker.
Responsiveness	Ensure that the answers directly address the research question.
Appropriateness for the reader	Consider the intended reader's background and experience.

4. **Design and structure the document for ease of readability:** Readers demand properly designed documents, and the dense printing typical of most prospectuses discourages reading. Good use of white space and margins increases the readability of documents. Headings, bullet points, and graphic illustrations make a long document more pleasing to the eye.

Plain English in writing does not omit complex information. Instead, plain English presents information in an orderly and clear fashion so that the reader can better understand and absorb the ideas.

A summary table of some elements of effective writing is presented in Figure 2-7.

WRITING EFFECTIVE E-MAILS AND LETTERS

Written communication is used if the information is complex and warrants repeating, or if a copy will help for later reference. Oral communication, such as telephone calls or in-person meetings, is used if an immediate response is needed, if one needs to hear a voice to read between the lines, or if greater concern about privacy applies.

Written communication by today's accountants includes both e-mails and letters. The increased use of e-mail has reinforced the need to develop strong writing skills, as well as technological skills to ensure the security of the transmissions, as well as the sophistication of the presentation. Apply the writing and thinking concepts previously discussed in the context of typical written communications with clients. Also, strive to maintain a cordial and respectful tone, which connects with the client. While one might use a conversational style in a client letter, it should be limited for most letters. Write directly and clearly.

Four basic types of business letters that are often delivered via e-mail are transmittal letters, status update letters, "action requested" letters, and opinion letters. Before studying each type, review the basic letter contents: date, address, greeting, message, polite closing, signature, and special notations, such as for attachments.

A transmittal letter merely transmits information; it does not seek an action An effective transmittal letter must quickly summarize any information the accountant will be delivering in more detail. The letter often closes with an offer to provide additional assistance. A firm newsletter is a common transmittal letter example. Since the

QUICK FACTS

Business letters include transmittal, status update, "action requested," and opinion letters.

accountant's real goal is to impress clients and potential clients with the firm's knowledge and potential services, it's essential to ensure that the newsletter and its transmission meet the firm's quality standards. If the transmittal occurs via e-mail, it is particularly important that the subject line state the contents accurately, so as not to produce any surprise.

A status update letter typically reminds the client about a situation by providing an update. In writing such a letter, assume that not everyone reading the letter will remember everything about the past events. Thus, reference previous correspondence on a subject or summarize major actions already taken. Then summarize new developments or activities. You might close the status update letter with a suggestion that the reader call if there are any questions.

A letter requesting action needs to make the request clearly and up front. List precisely what is needed from the client in order to minimize his or her burden. Briefly mention why the information is needed, to help motivate the desired response. Close the letter by politely mentioning an approaching deadline or likely follow-up.

An opinion letter summarizes the situation very briefly, but should restate the critical facts that are the basis for the advice provided. While the client is primarily interested in the conclusions and planning implications, provide some level of detail depending upon the sophistication of the client. Include language to limit potential misunderstanding, such as "based on the facts provided" or "based on a due diligence review" as of a given date.

RESEARCH TIPS

Use an update letter to remind the client about a matter.

WRITING MEMOS TO THE FILE

Writing a memo to the file is often an important part of documentation that is required in accounting, auditing, and taxation. Memos should provide important information up front. For example, the top of the memo will list the date, whom the memo is written to, whom the memo is from, and the subject matter. Similarly, the content of the memo states important conclusions early. A memo rarely waits until the end to provide a conclusion. Busy business people do not always read the entire memo.

In tax practice, the typical memo will have the following headings: *Facts, Issues, Conclusion,* and *Reasoning*. Sometimes the reasoning is divided by issue. The reasoning must discuss the law or authorities, as well as apply the law or authorities to the client's set of facts. Writing the memo so that each sentence integrates some aspect of the specific facts with some aspect of the law is difficult, but is a necessary skill to develop. Some firms will wish to separate discussion of the law and authority from the analysis. In such cases, every law and authority explained in the discussion should be referenced in the memo. Don't just provide conclusions; state how each element of the legal test or authority applies in that particular case.

A memo should not amount to an academic lecture about a topic. Instead, you should carefully write the memo to present only the potentially relevant facts, laws, and authorities. However, it is generally better to err on the side of providing too many facts than too few. Potentially relevant authority is sometimes referred to as "colorable authority." Colorable authority is usually discussed but distinguished from authority having real relevance to the problem.

Discuss the facts, as well as the law and authorities, logically. Thus, the facts are often best provided in chronological order. A tax memo may need to discuss both the client's position and the government's position. Generally, the strongest authority is discussed first, before citations of other authority that may interpret the strongest authority. Most firms will want the writer to discuss objectively all relevant authorities. Do not omit discussion of law or authorities on the ground that it may prevent the client from achieving the desired results.

RESEARCH TIPS

Write a memo to the file to document the reason for your conclusion.

A strong memo provides great insight when identifying the issues. Thus, the issue statement is refined to include the most critical facts, along with pinpointing where in the law the real issue arises. For example, even if an accountant is told that the issue is whether the client gets a home office deduction, the accountant must refine that issue toward more precision using the facts and law. In this case, detailed knowledge of the law on home offices will help determine which facts are critical. Then pinpointing precisely what part of or what phrase in the law is at issue enables the reader to assess the situation much more quickly and accurately.

A memo is a formal document. Use the third person in the memo (the person's name, "he," "she," "it," "they") to keep the constant focus on the subject. Avoid using the first person ("I," "we," "our") and the second person ("you," "yours"), which creates a less objective appearance. The length of the memo may vary, but edit it for conciseness. A chitchatty writing style does not go over well in a memo.

SUMMARY

Accounting professionals—whether in auditing, management accounting, not-for-profit accounting, taxation, or business—provide value-added services to others in a dynamic, complex, expanding, and constantly changing profession. Therefore, accountants must learn to *rethink*, to develop life-long learning skills to think critically—to grasp the meaning of complex concepts and principles—and to judge and apply these concepts and principles to specific issues.

Additionally, quality writing requires continual practice. Just as SEC registrants must recognize the importance of developing strong writing skills, accountants must follow many of the above suggestions to meet their goals.

Critical thinking and effective writing are essential tools for accounting, auditing, and tax research. The concepts outlined in this chapter are used throughout the remainder of this text.

DISCUSSION QUESTIONS

1. Define critical thinking.

2. Discuss the highest level of thinking according to Bloom's taxonomy.

3. Discuss what *grasping the meaning of a statement* or *comprehension* implies.

4. Discuss how critical thinking relates to the term *professional skepticism.*

5. What are the qualities that lie behind rethinking?

6. Discuss the three levels of thought as defined by the Illinois Renewal Institute.

7. Discuss the AICPA list of effective writing characteristics. Which are editing skills and which are composing skills?

8. What six principles of clear writing does SEC Release 33-7380 identify?

9. Explain why plain English writing does not mean deleting complex information.

10. What are the elements of plain English?

11. What is the difference between the active voice and the passive voice? Give an example.

12. What are special concerns with e-mails?

13. What types of client letters exist?

14. How does writing a client letter differ from writing a memo to the file?

15. How is a tax memo usually organized?

EXERCISES

1. There are five houses in a row, each of a different color, that are inhabited by five people of different nationalities, with different pets, favorite drinks, and favorite sports. Use the clues below to determine who owns the monkey and who drinks water. Utilize the chart to develop your answer.

   a. The Englishman lives in the red house.

   b. The Spaniard owns the dog.

   c. Coffee is drunk in the green house.

   d. The Russian drinks tea.

   e. The green house is immediately to the right of the white house.

   f. The hockey player owns hamsters.

   g. The football player lives in the yellow house.

   h. Milk is drunk in the middle house.

   i. The American lives in the first house on the left.

   j. The table tennis player lives in the house next to the man with the fox.

   k. The football player lives next to the house where the horse is kept.

   l. The basketball player drinks orange juice.

   m. The Japanese resident likes baseball.

   n. The American lives next to the blue house.

	HOUSE 1	HOUSE 2	HOUSE 3	HOUSE 4	HOUSE 5
Color					
Country					
Sport					
Drink					
Pet					

2. Develop a chart similar to Figure 2-3 for the following assignment: Johnson Electronics has requested your advice as to when assets need to be classified as current assets.

3. Develop a chart similar to Figure 2-3 for the following assignment: Your client, Baxter Controls, has requested your advice as to when a contingent liability should be booked (recorded) as a liability.

4. Insert the correct punctuation in the following sentences.

   a. A general ledger contains all the assets liabilities and owners equity accounts

   b. The purpose of a trial balance is to prove that debits equal credits but does not prove that all transactions have been recorded

   c. The current assets section of the balance sheet contains items such as cash accounts receivable and prepaid expenses and the current liabilities section contains items such as accounts payable notes payable and short term debt

   d. The auditing exam was to begin at 200 pm but the professors car broke down so we didn't begin until 230 pm

   e. Did William ask How can we finish the audit tonight because Linda said We have twenty hours of work left to do

5. Rewrite the following sentences into shorter, more concise sentences while maintaining the main points of the sentence.

   a. For good reasons, the secretary may grant extensions of time in 30-day increments for filing of the lease and all required bonds, provided that additional extensions requests are submitted and approved before the expiration of the original 30 days or the previously granted extension.

   b. If the State agency finds that an individual has received a payment to which the individual was not entitled, whether or not the payment was due to the individual's fault or misrepresentation, the individual shall be liable to repay to the State the total sum of the payment to which the individual was not entitled.

   c. Universities differ greatly in style, with some being located on out of town campuses in parkland, others having buildings scattered about parts of city centers and others being at various points between these two extremes.

6. Rewrite the following double-negative sentence to eliminate the double negative.

   No termination will be approved unless the administrator reviews the application and finds that it is not lacking any requisite materials.

7. Rewrite the following sentences using active voice.

   a. The fraud was reported by the employee.

   b. The book was enjoyed by me because the seven fraud investigation techniques were described so well by the author.

8. Utilizing your critical thinking skills, solve the following problem.

   Three auditors checked into a hotel under one reservation. After paying $100 each to the hotel manager, they went to their individual rooms. The manager, noting that the total rate for the three rooms is $250, gives $50 to the bellboy to return to the three auditors. On the way to the rooms, the bellboy reasons that $50 would be difficult to share among three individuals, so he pockets $20 and gives each auditor $10. At this point, each person has paid $100 and gotten back $10. So they paid $90 each, for a total of $270. The bellboy kept $20, making the total $290 ($270 + $20). Where is the remaining $10?

9. Critically analyze why an asset is an asset.

10. Critically evaluate the pros and cons of the following statements:

    a. Financial statements are useless because they are incomplete. Not all assets or liabilities are included.

    b. Financial statements are useless because they present assets at their historical costs rather than their fair market values.

11. When should a liability first be reported? When should reporting of a liability cease?

12. What are the benefits of utilizing a contra "accumulated depreciation" account rather than crediting the asset account directly?

13. Insert the correct punctuation.

    a. The professor received his PhD from the University of Illinois and he continued teaching there after he was finished with the program

    b. The general ledger does not balance it must balance before we leave

    c. Did Robert say Can this item be classified as an asset

    d. Susans investigation didn't discover any fraud but theres new evidence that might keep the investigation going

    e. Dear Mr Smith

14. Indicate the needed capitalization in the following sentences.

    a. the auditor said, "we must have these work papers completed by tomorrow."

    b. when do we have to file our taxes?

    c. is the conference in dallas or austin, texas?

The Environment of Accounting Research

LEARNING OBJECTIVES

After completing this chapter, you should understand:
- The SEC's role and the complex environment for accounting.
- The FASB, which sets accounting standards for the private sector.
- The GASB, which sets accounting standards for state and local government accounting.
- Other organizations that influence the accounting standard-setting process.
- The types of authoritative pronouncements.
- The meaning and levels of GAAP.

THE ACCOUNTING ENVIRONMENT

Research on accounting issues is conducted in a dynamic environment. New professional standards are constantly issued, and existing standards are updated or deleted. In researching accounting issues, one needs to use the most recent authoritative pronouncements.

The development of accounting standards is influenced by a variety of factors, including:

1. The requirements of the federal government and other regulatory bodies.
2. The influence of various tax laws on the financial reporting process.
3. The practices of certain specialized industries, such as the motion picture and insurance industries.
4. Inconsistencies in practice.
5. Disagreements among accountants, business executives, and others as to the objectives of financial statements.
6. The influence of professional organizations.
7. International differences among countries in setting international accounting standards.
8. Increasing litigation concerns.
9. The public's confidence in financial reporting.

Accounting research has a complex environment, as illustrated in Figure 3-1. The acronyms shown for the various organizations influencing accounting are explained later in this and in subsequent chapters. Within this environment are numerous accounting standards, rules, and recommended practices. Yet, with so many directions in which to

> **RESEARCH TIPS**
>
> Acquire a comprehensive understanding of the dynamic accounting environment to add depth of understanding to your research.

FIGURE 3-1 | ACCOUNTING RESEARCH ENVIRONMENT

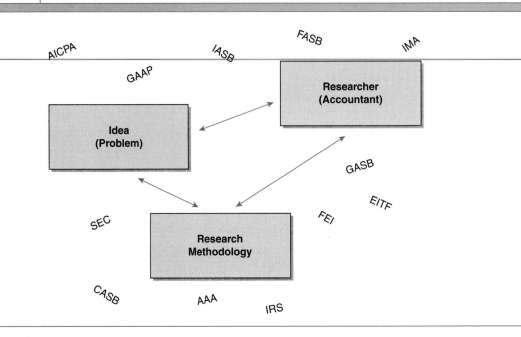

turn for guidance and with the need to solve the dilemma efficiently, the accountant must have a basic understanding of when an organization's standards apply.

This chapter concentrates on the standard-setting process in accounting, including the process conducted by the private sector (FASB) and its predecessors, the public sector for state and local government accounting (GASB), and selected other standard-setting bodies in the United States. International standards are discussed in Chapter 5. Besides the SEC, IRS, and the Cost Accounting Standards Board (CASB), many other professional organizations have also set or influenced certain accounting standards for entities in their domains.

THE SEC AND THE STANDARD-SETTING ENVIRONMENT

The SEC in the United States was established by the Securities and Exchange Act of 1934. The law charged the SEC with the duty of ensuring full and fair disclosures of all material facts relating to publicly traded securities. Public companies, those with more than $10 million in assets whose securities are held by more than five hundred owners, must comply with U.S. securities laws, such as filing annual and periodic reports with the SEC. Congress empowered the SEC to specify the documents that public companies must file with the SEC and prescribe the accounting principles used in generating the financial data.

The SEC has the statutory authority to issue rules and regulations to administer the securities statutes. Those rules and regulations are formal SEC policy, as approved by the five SEC commissioners. All other SEC employees are accountants, lawyers, economists, and securities analysts.

The SEC's Office of the Chief Accountant (OCA) works to establish the accounting policies followed by the SEC. Some believe the SEC's Chief Accountant is the most powerful accounting position in the world. The OCA is divided into three groups:

- Accounting to develop accounting and disclosure requirements for domestic private companies.
- Professional Practice to develop auditing policies and procedures.
- International Affairs to develop international auditing and regulatory policies.

The SEC divisions—Corporation Finance, Enforcement, Investment Management, and Trading and Markets—are consulted by the OCA groups. The first three each have a Chief Accountant's Office.

The Division of Corporation Finance reviews the financial statements of all public companies at least once every three years. Their review sometimes leads to financial restatements. The Enforcement Division investigates potential securities law violations, including those related to accounting, auditing, and financial issues discussed in Chapter 4. Some believe that audit firms often respond to the Division of Enforcement decisions by pressing the accounting standard setter to establish a rule on that issue to prevent further problems. Investment Management reviews financial reporting by investment companies. Trading and Markets examines stockbrokers and self-regulatory agencies, such as the stock exchanges.

The SEC term *rules and regulations* refers to all rules and regulations adopted by the SEC, including the forms and instructions that are used to file registration statements and periodic reports. Some rules provide definitions of terms in certain statutes or regulations and are called *general rules*. Other rules are found in regulations, a compilation of rules related to a specific subject (for example, Regulation 14A on solicitation of proxies). Still other rules relate to procedural matters, such as the steps to be followed in proceedings before the SEC, where to file documents, and what font size to use in materials filed with the SEC. Additional discussion of SEC issuances is provided in a subsequent chapter on accounting research.

The SEC has delegated the major responsibility for accounting standard setting to the FASB but has retained an oversight function. The SEC recognizes the use of these accounting principles as acceptable for use in filings with the SEC. In monitoring the FASB's activities, the SEC has occasionally overruled the FASB or its predecessor, the AICPA Accounting Principles Board (APB), as in the issues of accounting for the investment tax credit, accounting for inflation, and accounting for oil and gas exploration.

> **QUICK FACTS**
> The SEC retains an oversight function with respect to accounting standards for public companies.

Over time, accounting standards have emerged to meet the needs of financial statement users. The number of users of financial statements—primarily investors, lenders, and governmental entities—has increased enormously over the past eighty years, and the complexity of the business enterprise has increased with it. These changes have resulted in a greater demand by users for more uniformity in accounting standards to facilitate comparison of financial statements. Government agencies, legislative bodies, and professional organizations have gradually responded to this demand.

Prior to 2009, the FASB had the sole responsibility for setting accounting standards in the private sector. The International Accounting Standards Board (IASB) is now recognized by the SEC for foreign registrants. The GASB is the standard setter for the public sector for state and local governments. Before 1973, the AICPA set standards for both the private and public sectors. Following is a discussion of these accounting standard-setting bodies and their processes, except for the IASB, which is discussed in Chapter 5.

Rules-Based versus Principles-Based Accounting Standards

The SEC has studied the approach by which accounting standards are established in response to the Sarbanes-Oxley Act of 2002, which sought to improve the U.S. system of financial reporting. The study concluded that imperfections exist when standards are created either on a principles-only or rules-only basis. Rules-only standards provide detailed and structured technical guidance; however, the intention of the standard is often overlooked. Conversely, principles-only standards may state a goal or objective while providing little technical guidance or structure for complying with the standard.

The SEC recommends a more consistent and efficient system of principles-based or objective-oriented standards with guidance for operational sufficiency. Such standards would provide a more useful conceptual framework and more timely information to the practitioner or user of financial statements. These objective-oriented standards should have the following characteristics:

- Arise from an improved and consistently applied conceptual framework.
- State clearly the accounting objective of the standard.
- Provide sufficient detail and structure so the standard can be operationalized and applied on a consistent basis.
- Minimize exceptions from the standard.
- Avoid use of percentage tests ("bright lines") that allow financial engineers to achieve technical compliance with the standard while evading the intent of the standard.[1]

As accounting standard-setting moves forward, the SEC concluded that principles-based or objectives-based standards should characterize the FASB's standard-setting process.

FINANCIAL ACCOUNTING STANDARDS BOARD

The role of the FASB in today's capital markets is to develop high-quality financial reporting standards that result in credible and transparent financial information in order to service the investing public. The FASB's financial accounting standard-setting process actually involves several entities: the Financial Accounting Foundation (FAF), the FASB board itself, the FASB staff, and the Emerging Issues Task Force (EITF), as noted in Figure 3-2. The GASB, which is also under the umbrella of the FAF, is discussed later in this chapter.

The five-member FASB Board represents a broad spectrum of the financial community. It might include partners from large and small CPA firms, corporate executives, financial analysts, and an academic. The FASB pursues its investigative activities with a full-time research staff of approximately seventy professionals from various backgrounds. The FASB acquires advice from the Financial Accounting Standards Advisory Council (FASAC) on the priorities of its current and proposed projects, selecting and organizing task forces, and any other matters that the FASB requests. In addition to the regular FASB staff, the Board has several formal channels for gathering information in the standard-setting process, including various advisory councils and project resource groups. These information channels aid the Board when considering the appropriateness of current standards or conducting research for creating new accounting standards.

FASB Strives to Simplify Standards

In response to the growing number of increasingly complex accounting standards, the FASB has realized the need for simplification of its standards. The term *standards overload* is often used to describe the profession's concern as to the number and

---

[1] Study Pursuant to Section 108(d) of the Sarbanes-Oxley Act of 2002 on the Adoption by the United States Financial Reporting System of a Principles-Based Accounting System (The Study). SEC, 2003.

FIGURE 3-2 | ORGANIZATION OF FAF, FASB, AND GASB

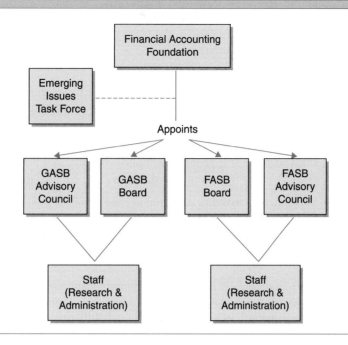

complexity of accounting rules and required disclosures and the difficulty of finding all the accounting rules on any given subject. This new framework emphasizes issuing standards that focus more on objectives (substance) than on detailed rules (form).

Another project aimed at simplifying the FASB standards focuses on improving the quality of the cost-benefit analysis performed on proposed standards. Through this project, the FASB strives to reduce the costs of issuing a new standard (for example, development time, learning time, or monetary expense) without decreasing its benefits to financial reporting. Overall, the FASB's goal is to make accounting standards or authorities that are easier to understand and apply, and financial statements that are more useful to and utilizable by ordinary investors.

Content of Authorities

The FASB Codification project of accounting standards, the topic of Chapter 4, has superseded most[2] accounting authorities. However, standards are still issued in a similar format with an additional section containing Codification update instructions. The standards themselves are no longer authoritative, but contain background information the practitioner may find of interest.

It is useful to understand the structure of authorities. For a period of time, many practitioners will probably still rely on what the prior authority dictated. Also, much of this authority is still incorporated in governmental accounting standards.

The FASB issues pronouncements labeled Statements of Financial Accounting Standards (SFASs) and Interpretations of Financial Accounting Standards, which

RESEARCH TIPS

Use the FASB's pre-codification Statements of Financial Accounting Standards (SFASs) for supplementary and background information.

---

[2] The FASB Accounting Standards Codification Notice to Constituents provides a list of the following grandfathered material: paragraph B217 of FAS 141; paragraphs 25 and 341 of FAS 140; paragraph 77 of FAS 87; paragraphs 97 and 102 of SOP 93-6; paragraph 24 of FAS 118; paragraph 83 of FAS 124(R); and paragraph 1.05 of the Investment Company Audit and Accounting Guide.

interpret the FASB's own statements as well as predecessor authorities from the AICPA, Accounting Research Bulletins (ARBs) and Accounting Principle Board Opinions (APBOs). New pronouncements are issued in the format of year-sequential update number (for example, 2009–10, the tenth pronouncement issued in 2009) and include typical content as follows:

1. A summary.
2. A table of contents.
3. Introduction and other narrative.
4. The actual standard.
5. A list of the FASB members actually voting.
6. The basis for a qualifying or dissenting vote of an FASB member.
7. Appendices containing background information, a glossary of terms, numerical and other examples of applying the standard, and other ancillary information.
8. Upon adoption of the Codification, SFASs will contain Codification Update Instructions, similar to current SFAS Amendment sections.

To help practitioners and their clients implement the provisions of FASB Standards, the FASB staff has periodically issued Technical Bulletins to provide timely guidance on implementation issues. These Technical Bulletins allowed conformity with FASB pronouncements without the need for the entire FASB Board to issue a new authoritative statement.

The EITF was established in 1984 to help answer questions by financial statement preparers and users about issues not clearly covered by an existing set of authoritative pronouncements. Chaired by the FASB Director of Research and Technical Activities, the EITF consists of highly knowledgeable individuals with the foresight to identify issues before they become prevalent and conflicting practices regarding them become well established. The EITF normally addresses industry-specific issues rather than those encompassing accounting and financial reporting as a whole. For example, pre-codification EITF No. 03-5, "Applicability of AICPA Statement of Position (985-605-15-3) Software Revenue Recognition to Non-Software Deliverables in an Arrangement Containing More-Than-Incidental Software," applied primarily to the software industry. Similarly, Pre-codification EITF No. 03-8 (720-20), "Accounting for Claims-Made Insurance and Retroactive Insurance Contracts by the Insured Entity," applied to the insurance industry.

If the EITF is unable to reach a consensus on an issue under consideration and decides that the problem merits further action, it will forward the file to the FASB Board for further deliberation. Conversely, if the EITF can reach a consensus on an issue, the FASB can usually infer that no Board action is necessary. Thus, EITF's consensus positions are still included in the levels of GAAP for financial and state and local government reporting, as detailed in a subsequent section of this chapter, and are now issued in sequential order along with other FASB authorities

The FASB staff often receives questions regarding the appropriate application of FASB literature. The FASB staff issues application guidance through FASB Staff Positions (FSP) in order to more quickly and consistently respond to practitioners' and users' needs. After receiving approval from FASB Board members, a thirty-day exposure period exists for interested parties to comment on a proposed FSP. The FSPs are posted on the FASB Web site (www.fasb.org) and remain there until they are incorporated into printed FASB literature. Prior to 2003, the FASB issued Staff Implementation Guides in response to such issues.

FIGURE 3-3 | FASB STANDARD-SETTING PROCESS

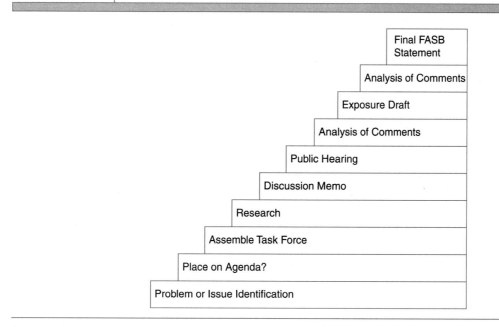

FASB Due Process

Given the importance of FASB standards, the Board uses an extensive due process so much so that it has spent over eleven years deliberating on certain standards. The standard-setting process followed by the Board appears in Figure 3-3. Briefly, the FASB is held to a fixed procedure. Before issuing a SFAS, it must take the following steps:

1. Identify the problem or issue and take into account legal or SEC pressures.
2. Decide whether to consider the issue. At this point, the board generally seeks opinion from the FASAC, advisory councils, project resource groups, and professional organizations such as the Financial Executives International (FEI), the Institute of Management Accountants (IMA), and the Risk Management Association.
3. Establish a task force (usually about fifteen people) to study the problem.
4. Have its research staff investigate the issues.
5. Issue a discussion memo to interested parties.
6. Hold public hearings and request written comments on the issue. Several hundred responses are usually received.
7. Analyze the results of the investigation, communicate responses, and conduct public hearings.
8. If action is appropriate, issue an exposure draft, a preliminary SFAS. The normal exposure period is at least sixty days.
9. Request additional comments on the exposure draft and hold further public hearings.
10. After analyzing the public response, issue a final SFAS.

Having gone through this due process procedure, the FASB's final pronouncement is placed in the "authoritative" level of the GAAP hierarchy. SFASs are issued in a standard format and located at the FASB Web site, reprinted in the Official Release section of the *Journal of Accountancy*, and available in the FASB Accounting Standards Codification database, discussed in Chapter 4.

FASB Conceptual Framework Project

In certain situations, an accounting issue may arise for which no precedent exists and no authoritative pronouncement has been issued. In such cases, the researcher must develop a theoretically justifiable conclusion. A number of organizations and individuals have directed their efforts toward the development of accounting theory in order to provide a framework for resolving issues in a theoretically consistent manner. For example, the American Accounting Association (AAA), an international professional organization primarily consisting of accounting professors, sponsors and conducts extensive research of a theoretical or conceptual nature. The AICPA also promotes research in accounting theory, has published a series of Accounting Research Monographs, and has issued four Concept Statements.

Despite these and other efforts, however, a widely accepted theoretical framework of accounting still does not exist. Recognizing the need for such a framework, the FASB has undertaken a comprehensive, long-range project called the conceptual framework project. This project encompasses a series of pronouncements entitled Statements of Financial Accounting Concepts (SFACs), which describe concepts and relationships that underlie financial accounting standards. These pronouncements have addressed (or will address) such issues as:

- Elements of financial statements and their recognition, measurement, and display.
- Capital maintenance.
- Unit of measure.
- Criteria for distinguishing information to be included in financial statements from that which should be provided by other means of financial reporting.
- Criteria for evaluating and selecting accounting information (qualitative characteristics).[3]

Statements of Financial Accounting Concepts Nos. 1–7

The conceptual framework project seeks to establish objectives and concepts for the development of accounting standards and in the preparation of financial statements, especially where no published standards exist. The project's focus is to produce a constitution for accounting, resulting in a coherent set of accounting standards. However, because the FASB did not use full due process in this project, the SFACs are not authoritative. CPAs need not justify departures from their guidance. However, the researcher normally utilizes these pronouncements when no authoritative pronouncement is directly on point to the issue under consideration. In such cases, the researcher needs to develop a theoretical foundation for the solution to the problem.

The first seven Concept Statements issued under the conceptual framework project are as follows:

---

[3] FASB, Statement of Financial Accounting Concept No. 1, "Objectives of Financial Reporting by Business Enterprises" (1978).

1. **Objectives of Financial Reporting of Business Enterprises:** SFAC No. 1 sets forth the objectives of general-purpose external financial reporting by business enterprises. For example, it states that financial reports should help society better allocate scarce economic resources.

2. **Qualitative Characteristics of Accounting Information:** SFAC No. 2 examines the characteristics of accounting information that make the information useful.

3. SFAC No. 3 was superseded by SFAC No. 6.

4. **Objectives of Financial Reporting of Nonbusiness Organizations:** SFAC No. 4 establishes the objectives of general-purpose external financial reporting by nonbusiness organizations.

5. **Recognition and Measurement in Financial Statements:** SFAC No. 5 establishes recognition criteria and guidance regarding what information should be incorporated into financial statements. It also describes and defines the concept of earnings and what should be included in a full set of an entity's financial statements.

6. **Elements of Financial Statements:** SFAC No. 6 redefines the ten interrelated elements of financial statements: assets, liabilities, equity, investment by owners, distributions to owners, comprehensive income, revenues, expenses, gains, and losses. It also defines three classes of net assets for nonprofit organizations as well as accrual accounting and other related concepts. Besides amending portions of SFAC No. 2, SFAC No. 6 also supersedes SFAC No. 3.

7. **Using Cash Flow Information and Present Value in Accounting Measurements:** SFAC No. 7 provides a framework for using future cash flows as the basis for accounting measurements and for the interest method of amortization. It also provides general principles that govern the use of present value.

AMERICAN INSTITUTE OF CERTIFIED PUBLIC ACCOUNTANTS (AICPA)

Before the establishment of the FASB in 1973, the AICPA was the recognized standard-setting body for the private sector. The AICPA Committee on Accounting Procedures published fifty-one ARBs from 1939 to 1959, dealing with a wide spectrum of accounting issues. Because of FASB approval and clearance, some of the ARBs from the AICPA still apply. However, FASB Statements have superseded some ARB pronouncements and modified the application of others.

In 1959, the APB began. The APB issued thirty-one APBOs, now binding on all CPAs. Since 1984, the AICPA has required disclosure of departures from APBOs either in the notes to financial statements or in the audit reports. CPAs could not give their approval to financial statements that deviated from APBOs unless they wanted to assume the considerable personal risk and the burden of proof of defending the "unauthorized practices." Because few business enterprises or auditors were anxious to assume the burden of defending financial statements that differed from APBOs, this action gave new strength and authority to the APBOs. The APB issued four non-authoritative Statements, which address broad concepts rather than specific accounting principles, and several unofficial Interpretations.

Following the formation of the FASB, the AICPA created an Accounting Standards Division to influence the development of accounting standards. The Accounting Standards Executive Committee (AcSEC) of the Accounting Standards Division became

QUICK FACTS
The AICPA was replaced by the FASB as the standard setter for accounting standards for the private sector.

the spokesperson for the AICPA on financial accounting matters. AcSEC responds to FASB and SEC accounting pronouncements by issuing comment letters and preparing issues papers to develop financial accounting and reporting issues that the FASB should consider. AcSEC also often publishes brief notes and news releases in the AICPA's monthly online publication, the *CPA Letter*, which reaches more than 340,000 members.

In the past, AcSEC also issued Statements of Position (SOPs) to propose revisions of AICPA-published Industry Audit and Accounting Guides. However, due to recent changes in the profession, authority for issuing SOPs will reside with the FASB. Prior SOPs do not establish enforceable accounting standards; however, members of the AICPA must justify departures from practices recommended in the SOPs.

Various committees of the AICPA also publish material applicable to special concerns, such as business valuation. These publications—*Accounting Research Monographs*, *Accounting Trends and Techniques*, and others—are discussed in Chapter 6. The annual *Accounting Trends and Techniques* publication summarizes current accounting practices of over six hundred publicly owned companies. It presents tabulations of the numbers of surveyed companies that use particular practices; it also presents excerpts of actual reports issued by the surveyed companies.

GOVERNMENTAL ACCOUNTING STANDARDS BOARD (GASB)

For many years, financial reports of local and state units of government have varied in quality and lacked uniformity due to an absence of clearly defined principles. A body of GAAP for local units of government has slowly evolved. However, given the high value of assets that governmental entities manage as well as infamous financial crises in municipal units such as New York, Cleveland, and Orange County in California, the financial community has paid increasing attention to governmental units' financial statements.

Public sector (governmental) accounting is only now reaching the plateau of responsibility and credibility inhabited by private sector (proprietary) accounting. The GASB has developed in a fashion similar to the FASB. The GASB received authoritative status for its standards under Rule 203 of the AICPA Rules of Conduct and legislation in the various states.

The GASB's role is to set financial accounting and reporting standards for the public sector (state and local governmental entities) as the FASB does for all private entities. The GASB was established in 1984 by the FAF. This led to the addition of two government organizations (the Government Finance Officers Association [GFOA] and the National Association of State Auditors, Comptrollers, and Treasurers) to the list of FAF sponsors. Both organizations continue to focus primarily on GASB standards for the public sector.

The GASB consists of seven members who are required to have knowledge of governmental accounting and finance and a concern for the public interest in matters of financial accounting and reporting. The GASB professional staff works with the Board and its task forces, partakes in public hearings, performs research, analyzes oral and written comments received from the public, and prepares drafts of documents for consideration by the Board.

The GASB uses the following due process for major projects:

- Research the subject to define the issues and determine the scope of the projects.
- Appoint a task force to advise the Board on the issues and aid in developing alternative solutions prior to the issuance of a discussion document.

QUICK FACTS

The GASB sets financial accounting standards for state and local government accounting.

- Issue a discussion memorandum or invitation to comment, which will set forth the definition of the problem, the scope of the project, and the issues involved; discuss relevant research; and include alternative solutions to the issues identified.

- Hold a public hearing at which concerned individuals will be encouraged to state their views on the issues contained in the discussion document.

- Issue an exposure draft of a proposed statement for public comment prior to adoption of a final statement.

- Issue a final statement. A majority vote of the board members is needed to issue a statement.

During these steps, the Board deliberates the issues in meetings open to the public. The Board may issue a statement in an expedited process following exposure for public comment if, in the judgment of its members, the Board can make an informed decision based on available information. GASB pronouncements serve as a beginning reference for the researcher in addressing an issue associated with state or local governmental accounting. Because GASB uses a due process procedure, its pronouncements occupy the highest level of governmental GAAP.

Similar to its FASB counterpart, the GASB has an advisory council. The Governmental Accounting Standards Advisory Council (GASAC) is responsible for consulting with the GASB as to major policy questions, technical issues on the Board's agenda, project priorities, matters likely to require the attention of the GASB, selection and organization of task forces, and such other matters as may be requested by the GASB or its chairperson. The GASAC also is responsible for helping develop the GASB's annual budget.

State and local government accounting first developed in 1968 with the publication of *Government Accounting, Auditing, and Financial Reporting* (GAAFR), or simply the "Blue Book." GAAFR brought together different governmental accounting practices and provided an authoritative source for such accounting. It became the basis for many state laws for uniform municipal accounting. In an attempt to eliminate the accounting differences and to update, clarify, amplify, and reorder the principles of GAAFR, the National Council on Governmental Accounting (NCGA) in 1979 issued Statement 1, Governmental Accounting and Financial Reporting Principles. Statement 1 contained significant modifications to the basic fund accounting and financial reporting philosophy of GAAFR.

Three major primary research publications exist in the governmental arena. First, the *GASB Codification of Government Accounting & Financial Reporting Studies* contains all GASB Statements, Interpretations, Technical Bulletins, and Concept Statements. It also codifies the National Council on Government Accounting's Statements and Interpretations as well as the AICPA Audit Guides of State and Local Governments and Statements of Position. The GASB Codification corresponds to the private sector's FASB Accounting Standards.

Second, the U.S. Comptroller General's "Yellow Book" contains a codification of audit standards for government organizations, programs, activities, and functions. This text operates much the same as the AICPA Professional Standards.

Finally, the U.S. Congress's Single Audit Act of 1984 requires all state and local government units receiving at least $300,000 of federal assistance per fiscal year to have an audit made in conformity with the standards of this act. These audits contain both financial and compliance components and are subject to oversight by federal agencies designated by the United States Office of Management and Budget.

RESEARCH TIPS

Use the "Blue Book" for state and local government accounting. The "Yellow Book" is for government auditing standards.

OTHER ORGANIZATIONS INFLUENCING STANDARD SETTING

The Cost Accounting Standards Board (CASB) is an independent board within the Office of Management and Budget's Office of Federal Procurement Policy. The CASB has increased the uniformity of cost allocations among companies holding large government contracts. It has exclusive authority to issue cost accounting standards that govern the measurement, assignment, and allocation of costs on federal government contracts over $500,000. The CASB was created by Congress in 1971, discontinued in 1980, and re-created in 1989, but is currently inactive and without staff. Yet the CASB continues to serve as an important source of authoritative guidance.

Income tax laws have significantly influenced the development and implementation of GAAP because of the willingness of the accounting profession to accept tax accounting requirements as GAAP. In order to save the expenses of maintaining two sets of books, many smaller businesses use tax-basis statements as their external financial statements. CPAs must recognize certain reporting problems when the two statements are not identical. The Internal Revenue Code (IRC), IRS Regulations, Revenue Rulings, and other tax accounting pronouncements also affect accounting practice. Researching a tax issue is discussed in Chapter 7.

Many other professional organizations influence directly or indirectly the setting of accounting standards:

- The Securities Industry Associates (SIA), which represents investment bankers and manages the portfolios of large institutional investors, and the Financial Analysts Federation are typical of the kind of organizations that influence the setting of standards and the shaping of GAAP. They help select members of the FAF, which, in turn, selects the members of the FASB and the GASB. These groups represent users of financial statements and usually favor standards providing for additional disclosures.

- The National Association of State Auditors, Controllers, and Treasurers (NASACT) is an information clearinghouse and research base for state financial officials. Although it publishes no journal, NASACT performs financial management projects for state fiscal officers and appoints members to the FAF.

- The FEI influences accounting standards development by having an active committee make recommendations on discussion memoranda issued by the FASB. It also conducts its own research on important issues through the Financial Executives Research Foundation (FERF).

- The IMA also has a committee providing formal input to the FASB.

- The AAA emphasizes the need for a theoretical foundation for accounting. The AAA influences standard setting through research and analysis of accounting concepts presented in committee reports and in its quarterly journal, *The Accounting Review*, and other publications.

Figure 3-4 summarizes the constituencies and the missions of organizations affecting standard-setting and the shaping of GAAP.

GENERALLY ACCEPTED ACCOUNTING PRINCIPLES (GAAP)

GAAP is "a technical accounting term which encompasses the conventions, rules, and procedures necessary to define accepted accounting practice at a particular time," according to APB Statement No. 4 (105-10-65-1). This definition implies two points:

| FIGURE 3-4 | THE ROLE OF PROFESSIONAL ACCOUNTING ORGANIZATIONS IN DEVELOPING GAAP |

Organization	Principal Professional Membership	Principal Mission	Journal
*1. American Accounting Association (AAA) www.aaahg.org	Accounting professors	Helps develop a logical, theoretical basis for accounting. Promotes research and education in accounting.	*Accounting Horizons*
*2. American Institute of Certified Public Accountants (AICPA) www.aicpa.org	Certified public accountants	Its various committees have issued authoritative pronouncements on accounting principles and auditing standards. Conducts programs of research and education, surveys practice, and communicates concerns of members.	*Journal of Accountancy*
*3. Association of Government Accountants (AGA) www.agacgfm.org	Federal, state, and local government accountants	Professional society of accountants, auditors, comptrollers, and budget officers employed by federal, state, and local governments in management and administrative positions. Monitors the activities of and often provides input to the Government Accounting Standards Board (GASB).	*Journal of Government Financial Management*
*4. Association for Investment Management and Research www.aimr.com	Financial analysts and chartered financial analysts	Promotes the development of improved standards of investment research and portfolio management. An organization of primary users of accounting information, it represents those who analyze information and provide professional advice on investment matters.	*Financial Analysts Journal*
*5. Financial Executives International (FEI) www.leadership.opm. gov/Locations/FEI/ index.aspx	Corporate financial executives	Professional organization of financial and management executives performing duties of a controller, treasurer, or VP finance, primarily from large corporations. Sponsors research activities through its affiliated Financial Executives Research Foundation (FERF).	*Financial Executive*
*6. Governmental Finance Officers Association (GFOA) www.gfoa.org	State and local public finance officials	Provides technical service center and technical inquiry service for public finance officials. Monitors the activities of and often provides input to the GASB.	*Governmental Finance Review*
*7. Institute of Internal Auditors (IIA) www.theiia.org	Internal auditors and certified internal auditors	Cultivates, promotes, and disseminates knowledge concerning internal auditors. Sponsors research on the internal auditor's role in promoting more reliable financial information.	*The Internal Auditor*
*8. Institute of Management Accountants (IMA) www.imanet.org	Corporate controllers and financial officers and certified management accountants	Conducts research primarily on management accounting methods and procedures. Has recently increased its role in the development of financial accounting standards.	*Strategic Finance*

(continued)

FIGURE 3-4	THE ROLE OF PROFESSIONAL ACCOUNTING ORGANIZATIONS IN DEVELOPING GAAP (CONTINUED)

Organization	Principal Professional Membership	Principal Mission	Journal
*9. National Association of State Auditors, Controllers, and Treasurers *www.nasact.org*	State financial officials	Serves as an information clearinghouse and research base for state financial officials.	
10. Risk Management Association *www.rmahq.org*	Bank officers	Promotes studies on comparative industry practices to provide bench marks against which to judge corporate performance.	*The RMA Journal*
11. Securities Industry Association (SIA) *www.sia.com*	Broker-dealers in securities	Monitors and provides input to stockbrokers regarding SEC, stock exchanges (such as NYSE and AMEX), and congressional actions.	*Securities Industry Trends*

*Also appoints members to the FAF

1. GAAP is not a static, well-defined set of accounting principles, but a fluid set of principles based on current accounting thought and practice. GAAP changes in response to changes in the business environment. Therefore, the researcher must review the most current authoritative support, recognizing that recent pronouncements sometimes supersede or modify older pronouncements.

2. GAAP is not composed of mutually exclusive accounting principles. Alternative principles for similar transactions sometimes may be considered equally acceptable. The researcher must not quit when one acceptable principle is found.

GAAP performs two major functions:

1. **Measurement:** GAAP requires recognizing or matching expenses of a given period with the revenues earned during that period (for example, depreciating fixed assets and recognizing stock options and bad debt allowances). Besides attempting to measure periodic income objectively, the measurement principle focuses on the valuation of financial statement accounts (for example, reporting inventories at the lower of cost or market valuations).

2. **Disclosure:** GAAP provides information necessary for the users' decision models (for example, methods to group accounts and descriptive terminology, as in reporting lease obligations in the footnotes). However, GAAP does not require disclosure of certain macroeconomic factors (for example, interest rates and unemployment rates) that may interest the entity, bankers, and other financial statement users.

CPAs may not express an opinion that the financial statements are presented in conformity with GAAP if the statements depart materially from an accounting principle promulgated by an authoritative body designated by the AICPA Council, such as the FASB and the AICPA APB. While opinions from these bodies previously provided the "substantial authoritative support" necessary to create GAAP, other sources of GAAP were available. Most notable were standard industry practices either when a practice addresses a principle that does not otherwise exist in GAAP or when a practice seems to conflict with GAAP. In either case, management must justify the practice, and the CPA must evaluate the case to ascertain whether the practice violates established GAAP. In addition, if unusual circumstances would make it misleading to follow the normal procedure, management must disclose departures from the authoritative guidelines and justify the alternative principle.

The FASB arrives at GAAP by considering three objectives of financial reporting set out in Statement of Financial Accounting Concepts No. 1. Financial reporting should provide information that:

1. Is useful to present and potential investors, creditors, and other users in making rational investment, credit, and similar decisions. The information should be comprehensible to those who have a reasonable understanding of business and economic activities and are willing to study the information with reasonable diligence.

2. Helps present and potential investors, creditors, and other users in assessing the amounts, timing, and uncertainty of prospective cash receipts from dividends or interest, as well as the proceeds from the sale, redemption, or maturity of securities or loans. Since investors' and creditors' cash flows are related to enterprise cash flows, financial reporting should provide information to help investors, creditors, and others assess the amounts, timing, and uncertainty of prospective net cash inflows to the related enterprise.

3. Provides information about the economic resources of an enterprise, the claims to those resources (obligations of the enterprise to transfer resources to other entities and owners' equity), and the effects of transactions, events, and circumstances that change its resources and claims to those resources.[4]

The Levels of GAAP[5] and FASB Accounting Standards Codification™

A five-level hierarchy existed for the components of U.S. GAAP prior to FASB Accounting Standards Codification™. To create a single authoritative source of GAAP, in the Codification the FASB flattened the hierarchy to two levels (authoritative and nonauthoritative) via the Codification.[6] The sources used to write the two new GAAP levels are provided in Figure 3-5. The Codification is discussed more in Chapter 4.

The basic five-level hierarchy for government GAAP is presented in Figure 3-6. Those in level one have the highest level of authority.

Authoritative guidance is founded on the basic assumption or concepts of financial or government accounting. These basic assumptions and principles underlying financial reporting include the going-concern assumption, substance over form, neutrality, the accrual basis, conservatism, materiality, objectivity, consistency, and full disclosure. As described below, the authoritative level was based on reference sources containing established accounting principles. Nonauthoritative GAAP is comprised of other accounting literature not necessarily based on accounting principles, such as notable industry practices, or other literature not adopted by the FASB, such as International Financial Reporting Standards.

The following additional information about the levels of the Codification should enhance understanding of the items within each level. FASB Interpretations have clarified, explained, or elaborated on prior FASB, APB, and ARB Statements.

---

[4] FASB, Statement of Financial Accounting Concept No. 1, "Objectives of Financial Reporting by Business Enterprises" (1978).
[5] FASB, Pre-codification Statement of Financial Accounting Standards No. 162, "The Hierarchy of Generally Accepted Accounting Principles" (2008).
[6] FASB, Pre-codification Proposed Statement of Financial Accounting Standard, "The Hierarchy of Generally Accepted Accounting Principles a replacement of FASB Statement No. 162" (2009).

QUICK FACTS
The two major functions of GAAP are measurement and disclosure.

RESEARCH TOOLS
AICPA reSOURCE
ACL
Codification
eIFRS
Internet
i2
LexisNexis Academic
RIA Checkpoint

RESEARCH TIPS
The Codification allows users to access all authoritative U.S. GAAP literature on a particular topic in one location.

QUICK FACTS
The FASB Codification contains only essential standards and implementation guidance.

| FIGURE 3-5 | BASIC PRINCIPLES AND ASSUMPTIONS UNDERLYING FINANCIAL REPORTING MAPPED INTO FASB ACCOUNTING STANDARDS CODIFICATION |

Prior to July 1, 2009

Level   Components

1   Pronouncements of an authoritative body designated by the AICPA Council in Rule 203 of the Code of Professional Conduct
a. FASB Statements and Interpretations
b. APB Opinions
c. AICPA Accounting Research Bulletins
d. Rules and Interpretative Releases of the SEC for SEC registrants

2   Pronouncements of bodies composed of expert accountants who follow a due process procedure
a. Cleared AICPA Industry Audit and Accounting Guides
b. Cleared AICPA Statements of Position (SOP)
c. FASB Technical Bulletins

3   Pronouncements of bodies organized by the FASB or AICPA but that do not necessarily go through due process procedures
a. AcSEC Practice Bulletins cleared by the FASB
b. Consensus Positions of the FASB EITF

4   Practices or pronouncements that are widely recognized as being generally accepted because they represent prevalent practice in a particular industry or the knowledgeable application to specific circumstances of pronouncements that are generally accepted
a. AICPA Accounting Interpretations
b. Implementation Guides by the FASB Staff, now referred to as FASB Staff Positions (FSPs)
c. Notable Industry Practices
d. Uncleared SOPs, and audit and accounting guides

5   Other Accounting Literature
a. APB Statements
b. AICPA Issues Papers
c. FASB Concepts Statements
d. International Accounting Standards Committee Statements
e. AICPA Technical Practice Aids
f. Textbooks
g. Journal articles and monographs

Subsequent to July 1, 2009

Item   Components

Authoritative
1   Financial Accounting Standards Board (FASB)
a. Statements (FAS)
b. Interpretations (FIN)
c. Technical Bulletins (FTB)
d. Staff Positions (FSP)
e. Staff Implementation Guides (Q&A)
f. Statement No. 138 Examples

2   Emerging Issues Task Force (EITF)
a. Abstracts
b. Topic D (other technical matters)

3   Derivative Implementation Group (DIG) Issues

4   Accounting Principles Board (APB) Opinions

5   Accounting Research Bulletins (ARB)

6   Accounting Interpretations (AIN)

Item	Components
7	American Institute of Certified Public Accountants (AICPA)
	a. Statements of Position (SOP)
	b. Audit and Accounting Guides (AAG)
	c. Practice Bulletins (PB)
	d. Technical Inquiry Services (TIS) (only for Software Revenue Recognition)
	Nonauthoritative
8	Notable Industry Practices
	a. APB Statements
	b. AICPA Issues Papers
	c. FASB Concepts Statements
	d. International Accounting Standards
	e. Committee Statements
	f. AICPA Technical Practice Aids
	g. Textbooks
	h. Journal articles and monographs

FIGURE 3-6	BASIC PRINCIPLES AND ASSUMPTIONS UNDERLYING STATE AND LOCAL GOVERNMENT REPORTING

NOTE: For federal governmental entities, the first four levels would also include pronouncements issued by the Federal Accounting Standards Advisory Board (FASAB).

Level	Components
1	Pronouncements of an authoritative body
	a. FASB Pronouncements acknowledged by the GASB
	b. NCGA Pronouncements acknowledged by the GASB
	c. GASB and AICPA Pronouncements
	Note: If the accounting treatment of a transaction or event is not specified by a pronouncement of 1a or 1b, then 1c is presumed to apply.
2	Pronouncements of bodies composed of expert accountants who follow a due process procedure
	a. GASB Technical Bulletins
	b. Cleared AICPA Industry Audit and Accounting Guides, such as:
	Audits of State and Local Governmental Units
	Audits of Certain Nonprofit Organizations
	Audits of Colleges and Universities
	c. Cleared AICPA SOP
3	Consensus positions of the GASB, EITF, and cleared AcSEC practice bulletins for state and local government
4	Practices or pronouncements that are widely recognized as being generally accepted because they represent prevalent practice in a particular industry or the knowledgeable application to specific circumstances of pronouncements that are generally accepted
	a. Uncleared SOPs and Audit and Accounting Guides
	b. Questions and answers issued by GASB staff
	c. Industry practice
5	Other accounting literature
	a. GASB Statements of Financial Accounting Concepts
	b. Elements of the Financial Statement Hierarchy
	c. Textbooks
	d. Journal articles

Authoritative Level: This level is based on literature issued by the following standard-setters:

1. FASB
   a. Statements (FAS): Original pronouncements
   b. Interpretations (FIN): Clarify, explain, or elaborate on prior FASB, APB, and ARB Statements
   c. Technical Bulletins (FTB): Provide guidance in applying pronouncements
   d. Staff Positions (FSP): Offer application guidance
   e. Staff Implementation Guides (Q&A)
   f. Statement No. 138 Examples: Accounting for Certain Derivative Instruments and Certain Hedging Activities
2. EITF: Research resulting from unclear original pronouncements
   a. Abstracts
   b. Topic D: Other technical matters and implications and implementation of Abstracts
3. Derivative Implementation Group (DIG) Issues: 189 originally issued
4. APB Opinions: Thirty-one opinions of the AICPA APB
5. ARB: Fifty-one ARBs, issued by the Committee on Accounting Procedures (CAP) of the AICPA
6. Accounting Interpretations (AIN)
7. AICPA
   a. SOP
   b. Audit and Accounting Guides (AAG): Only incremental accounting guidance, normally reviewed by the AICPA AcSEC and cleared by the FASB
   c. Practice Bulletins (PB): Include the Notices to Practitioners elevated to Practice Bulletin status by Practice Bulletin 1
   d. Technical Inquiry Services (TIS): Only for Software Revenue Recognition

Nonauthoritative Level: This level provides other accounting literature and industry practice that the researcher could reference in the absence of a higher-level authority. Examples include textbooks, journal articles, AICPA Issue Papers, and International Financial Reporting Standards.

While reference to an authoritative pronouncement usually provides adequate support for an accounting decision, accountants forced to rely on lower levels of support must often build a case involving multiple references. Figure 3-7 provides a division between primary, self-supporting references and secondary, non-self-supporting references.

In researching an issue, the question often arises, Where does the researcher start and when can he or she stop the research process? To begin, the researcher would focus on the primary authoritative support, which has the highest level of authority according to the hierarchy of GAAP. If no primary sources are cited, the researcher would then drop down and review the secondary support.

If the researcher determines that the answer to the question is located in a primary authoritative support, he or she can stop the research process because these sources are sufficient for a conclusion. However, if the researcher cited secondary support, additional research is needed because any secondary source individually is insufficient authority. The researcher must recognize that many research questions will not have

RESEARCH TIPS

If possible, start your research with primary support.

RESEARCH TIPS

When using lower levels of support, attempt to reference multiple authorities.

FIGURE 3-7 | ACCOUNTING AUTHORITATIVE SUPPORT

Primary Authoritative Support: Sources that provide sufficient authoritative support for including a particular accounting principle within GAAP

1. General application to the field of accounting
   a. FASB, FASAB, and GASB Statements of Financial and Governmental Accounting Standards
   b. FASB, FASAB, and GASB Interpretations
   c. Opinions of the AICPA Accounting Principles Board
   d. Accounting Research Bulletins of the Committee on Accounting Procedures
   e. Consensus Positions of EITF of the FASB

2. Special application to certain entities
   a. Regulations of the Securities and Exchange Commission
   b. AICPA Industry Accounting Guides
   c. AICPA SOPs
   d. Statements of the CASB
   e. Interpretations of the CASB

Secondary Authoritative Support: Sources that support inclusion of particular accounting principles within GAAP, but individually are not sufficient authoritative support

1. Official publications of authoritative bodies
   a. FASB Statements of Financial Accounting Concepts
   b. GASB Concept Statements
   c. FASB Technical Bulletins*
   d. APB Statements of the AICPA
   e. Interpretations of APB Opinions*

2. Other sources of information
   a. Pronouncements of industry regulatory authorities
   b. Substantive industry practices
   c. Published research studies of authoritative professional and industrial societies
   d. Publications of recognized industry associations
   e. Accounting Research Monographs of the AICPA
   f. SEC Staff Accounting Bulletins
   g. Pronouncements of the IFAC and other international accounting bodies
   h. Accounting textbooks and reference books authored by recognized authorities in the field

*After July 1, 2009, Secondary Support Items (c) and (e) become Primary Support.

clear-cut answers. Therefore, professional judgment is a key element in deciding when to stop the research process.

Using Authoritative Support

Accountants rely heavily on GAAP authorities in supporting their positions. CPAs may not attest to the validity of financial statements (that is, they may not express an opinion that the statements are presented in conformity with GAAP) if the statements depart materially from an accounting principle promulgated by an authoritative body (that is, a senior technical committee) designated by the AICPA Council, such as the FASB or the GASB. Sometimes an accountant attempts to discover a consensus among users of financial information to document industry practices.

A CPA may sometimes justify using an alternative principle to GAAP if unusual circumstances would make it misleading to follow the normal GAAP principles. That is, under Rule 203 of the AICPA Code of Professional Conduct, if the entity's management believes the circumstances do not warrant compliance with the accounting standard, an exception is permitted. Under these circumstances, however, the auditor's report must clearly disclose the nature of the exception and the reason for it in the financial statements.

READING AN AUTHORITATIVE PRONOUNCEMENT

In researching an issue, the researcher may desire to read a specific GASB Statement or superseded FASB Statement. In such a case, the researcher should know the basic format that is followed in these pronouncements. Depending upon the complexity of the pronouncement, the following elements usually appear:

RESEARCH TIPS

Full text of FASB standards can be found on the FASB Web site.

- An introduction to the accounting issues addressed by the pronouncement.
- The background of the business event and accounting issues.
- The basis of the Board's conclusions.
- The actual opinion or statement of accounting standard.
- The effective date to implement the standard.
- Illustrations of application.
- Disclosures required.

These basic elements are not necessarily presented as separate sections of the pronouncement. Those that are relatively short may combine the introduction and background information and eliminate the illustration of applications section if it is not a complicated principle. However, there is always a separate section designated as the Opinion or Standard of Accounting. Codified FASB Statements (discussed in detail in Chapter 4) include Codification Update Instructions. SFASs are archived and accessible through a navigation panel at the FASB Codification Web site (http://asc.fasb.org).

The introductory section of a pronouncement defines the accounting issue that necessitated the pronouncement. This section gives the scope of the pronouncement, that is, it defines the type of entity affected. It can also limit the application of the pronouncement to companies of specific size (for example, sales exceeding $250 million). The introduction also gives the effects of the new pronouncement on previously issued standards. It specifies which pronouncements or sections of prior pronouncements are superseded by the new standard. Generally, within the introduction, there is a summary of the standard so the researcher can see quickly if the standard applies to the specific situation under investigation.

The background information section describes in more detail the business events and related accounting treatments presented in the pronouncement. This section develops the various arguments supporting alternative approaches to resolving the issue. The underlying assumptions for these alternatives are defined, and the different interpretations of the economic impact of the business event are presented. The FASB generally places the background information in an appendix to the official pronouncement.

The basis for conclusion of the authoritative standard is described in the opinions and statements. This section explains the rationale for the accounting principles prescribed in the pronouncement, indicating which arguments were accepted and which were rejected. The FASB incorporates dissenting viewpoints at the end of its main section, Standards of Financial Accounting and Reporting, and positions the basis for conclusion in a separate appendix. The background information and basis for conclusion provide the researcher with a description of the business events and transactions covered by the pronouncement. These sections can help in determining if the pronouncement addresses the specific issue under investigation. If the researcher is in the early stages of investigation, these sections can help in defining the business transactions, determining their economic impact, and relating them to the proper reporting format.

The opinion or standard section prescribes the accounting principles for the business transactions described in the pronouncement. This standard section represents the heart of the official pronouncement. Accountants must follow it when concluding that the standard applies to the business transactions under investigation. The length of this section will depend upon the complexity of the business events involved. The standard length varies from short, as in the case of FASB pre-codification Statement No. 129, "Disclosure of Information about Capital Structure," to very long and complicated, as in FASB pre-codification Statement No. 142, "Goodwill and Other Intangible Assets."

The Effective Date section states when the new pronouncement goes into effect. It also identifies any transition period that a company might use to implement a new standard. For example, FASB pre-codification Statement No. 13, "Accounting for Leases," had a four-year transition period to permit companies to gather data for retrospective application of this complicated pronouncement on lease transactions. While some standards may take effect retrospectively, others take effect shortly after their issuance. If the Board prescribes the method of implementation, retrospective application, or prospective application, this section of the pronouncement will indicate the permissible method.

Accounting Choices Have Economic Consequences

Selecting an accounting alternative often affects economic decisions within a business. For example, debates as to the proper accounting for stock options and the use of market values for derivatives have resulted in major economic implications for many companies. When alternatives within GAAP exist, accountants should consider the probable economic impacts when selecting among various accounting principles.

The development of financial accounting standards can affect economic behavior and wealth distribution in three ways, according to Rappaport.[7] The standards can influence intended external users (competitors and stockholders, for example), unintended external users (such as competitors, labor unions, and special interest groups) and internal users (corporate management). For example, assume that the research suggests the future value of equipment is impaired so as to immediately expense it rather than continuing to capitalize it over several years. This reduction in income could adversely impact the company's earnings per share and stock price. It could reduce the union members' profit-sharing payouts or make their competitors' financial statements look relatively stronger, enabling them to attract new investors. It could reduce the bonuses available to corporate management, thereby causing them to relocate to their competitors' organizations.

The previous example demonstrates the "law of unintended consequences," which often generates many unexpected ramifications from the decisions. Nonetheless, accountants are ethically bound to follow GAAP to help report accurate financial information, regardless of future economic consequences. Legally, various civil and criminal penalties exist after Sarbanes-Oxley for defrauding shareholders of public

> **QUICK FACTS**
>
> Accounting standards sometimes affect economic behavior and wealth distribution.

---

[7] Alfred Rappaport, "Economic Impact of Accounting Standards: Implications for the FASB," *Journal of Accountancy* 2 (May 1977): 89–97.

companies, altering documents, improper certification of financial reports, and engaging in other improper conduct.

SUMMARY

This chapter has presented an overview of the bodies that set standards in accounting, the process of standard setting, the types of authoritative pronouncements, the meaning and levels of GAAP, and the Financial Accounting Standards Codification System. Because GAAP is a fluid set of principles based on current accounting thought and practice, and not a static, well-defined set of accounting principles, accountants must research updates to the Codification or changes in the pronouncements. Given that GAAP is not composed of mutually exclusive accounting principles, research in accounting does not consist of searching for a single acceptable principle. Often, it involves searching for alternative principles that one must carefully examine.

DISCUSSION QUESTIONS

1. Discuss the environmental factors that influence the standard-setting process.
2. What is an underlying reason for the establishment of accounting standards?
3. Describe the rule-making or due process procedures of the FASB in the establishment of a standard.
4. What is the FASB conceptual framework project? Explain the benefit of this project to the practitioner.
5. Discuss the authority of the Statements of Financial Accounting Concepts.
6. Identify the authoritative publications of the AICPA.
7. Give examples of authoritative and nonauthoritative GAAP.
8. What is the purpose of the GASB? Why should the public have an interest in governmental financial reporting?
9. What constitutes GAAP?
10. What are the implications of GAAP and authoritative support to the researcher?
11. To conduct efficient research, where should one start in reviewing the accounting literature in search of a solution to a problem?
12. How can the promulgation of an accounting standard impact economic behavior? Discuss a specific example.
13. Distinguish between primary authoritative support and secondary authoritative support.
14. What two governmental organizations were added to the list of sponsoring organizations of the FAF due to the establishment of the GASB's authoritative status?
15. Identify the advantages and disadvantages of rules-based versus principles-based accounting standards.
16. Explain the overload of accounting standards. How is the FASB attempting to overcome this issue?

EXERCISES

1. Utilizing Figure 2-3 (Eight Elements of Reasoning), develop the eight elements for the following issue: Daimler Auto Parts, Inc., headquartered in Munich, Germany, is attempting to register with the SEC in order to list its stock on the New York Stock Exchange. Daimler currently is capitalizing most of its research and development (R&D) costs. Management of Daimler has requested your advice in regards to the proper accounting for R&D as to conformity with U.S. GAAP and/or International Accounting Standards.
2. Access the FASB Web site (www.fasb.org), click the FASB Facts link, and name the current FASB Board members.

3. Access the FASB Web site (www.fasb.org) and identify the three most recent exposure drafts issued by the FASB.

4. Access the GASB Web site (www.gasb.org). List and summarize the GASB Concept Statements.

5. Access the GASB Web site (www.gasb.org). Identify the two most recent exposure drafts issued by the GASB.

6. Access the FASB Web site (www.fasb.org) and answer the following:

   a. List the titles of the two most recently issued FASB Statements.

   b. What is the primary function of the FASAC?

7. Access the SEC Web site (www.sec.gov) and answer the following:

   a. List the two most recently issued proposed rules.

   b. Locate and briefly describe the SEC's Internet Enforcement Program located under the Enforcement Division.

8. Access the FEI Web site (www.leadership.opm.gov/Locations/FEI/index.aspx). Locate and list the three most recently issued comment letters to the FASB.

9. Access the AICPA Web site (www.aicpa.org). Under Accounting Standards, locate and list the three most recently issued exposure drafts of the Accounting Standards Executive Committee.

10. Access the IIA web site (www.theiia.org). List three upcoming training events along with the respective venues.

Financial Accounting Research Tools

LEARNING OBJECTIVES

After completing this chapter, you should understand:

- Database research strategies: the five steps.
- The challenges that accounting research presents.
- The contents of the FASB Accounting Standards Codification Research System (the Codification).
- Using the Codification and other accounting databases to locate GAAP authorities.
- Examples of using the Codification effectively and efficiently.
- Cases that assist in practicing accounting research.
- SEC accounting for public companies.
- SEC regulations.

This chapter provides the researcher with a comprehensive five-step research process as introduced in Chapter 1 for financial accounting research. It focuses primarily on the FASB's Accounting Standards and the new online FASB Accounting Standards Codification™ Research System (the Codification). The chapter also includes discussion on SEC accounting pronouncements. Finally, two examples of simulations for the Financial Accounting and Reporting section of the CPA exam are included in the appendix.

Due to the recent increase in accounting and auditing pronouncements and the increase in financial reporting in general, more and more organizations use an electronic database to gain rapid access to key accounting authorities for decision-making. Research skills are increasingly needed on the part of the future accounting professional.

Professional accounting research is challenging because of the volume of accounting rules, their level of complexity, the extensive detail and length of accounting standards, and the difficulty in finding all relevant accounting rules on a particular topic. To address this issue for financial reporting, the FASB has consolidated authoritative, non-governmental U.S. GAAP into a single database, the Codification. The SEC involvement for accounting standard setting for public companies is also examined. The databases and their content as well as Web sources of information are discussed for each of these accounting standard-setting bodies in this chapter.

ACCOUNTING RESEARCH ONLINE

Database systems are designed to retrieve relevant documents from a vast library or collection of data. Compared to free Internet sources, commercial databases have several advantages. They generally provide a more comprehensive document retrieval system. Commercial databases usually have better search capabilities and make an effort to seek out reliable sources of information. They are used extensively in many professions and have become essential in the accounting profession. Such retrieval systems help the researcher search quickly through large amounts of data for words or phrases that are pertinent to the research inquiry and, in turn, refer to authoritative pronouncements or other topical sources of information.

By understanding the electronic research costs, you can avoid creating a negative impression of your research skills. Basic pricing structures can vary as to how your employer pays for its electronic databases. While universities generally provide unlimited access to student searches, some firms may pay on a search basis or document printing basis. It also helps to understand the billing system that the firm uses in order to appreciate the client's priority that electronic research is not only effective but efficient in its use of the client's money. If the client sees a separate charge for research, it's especially important to document your research activities and review them to ensure that the time spent and any database costs passed on to the client are properly chargeable.

DATABASE RESEARCH STRATEGIES

A research strategy suggested for using databases is as follows:

1. Define the specific information needed.
2. Determine the sources to search.
3. Use appropriate search methods.
4. View the results and manage the information.
5. Communicate the search results.

Although the five steps for database research are presented in order, the reality is that most research projects involve some type of iterative process of these steps.

Step One: Define the Information Needed

Take the time to identify the preliminary information needs of any research project before proceeding in the task. The more focused one is on the specific research needs for the project, the more quickly the desired results are achieved. Accountants use databases for many reasons, including finding the appropriate financial accounting research standards to apply to a problem.

Step Two: Determine the Sources to Search

To assess a database, consider the source of the data and reliability of the information presented and evaluate the information's current relevance. While the FASB codification database is very reliable for financial accounting, even when scrutinized by a court, consider whether one needs to examine the SEC part of the database. One may sometimes need to use a database providing international financial reporting standards, as discussed in the next chapter. For other databases presented in subsequent chapters, one must determine whether the source is a well-known author, part of an open government, a leading university, or a prestigious private vendor. Consider the reliability of the information for objectivity, accuracy, and insight. Ask about statistical calculations. Reconsider the source's reliability if any obvious errors, omissions, or inconsistent information is discovered. Materials that depend on foreign language translation may be unreliable.

Relevance depends on timeliness, resource updates, practical insights, and overall usefulness of the data.

Step Three: Use Appropriate Search Methods

Search methods in a database include keyword searches, a drill-down in a table of contents, citation retrieval, or index search. A keyword search looks for those documents that contain a specified pattern of words, phrases, or numbers. Keyword searches have become most popular. Drill down in a table of contents by progressing from the big topics to more detailed refinements. If the structure of the authority is clear, this drill-down approach may help. Use citation retrieval to pull up a document if the precise document location is known. An index system helps particularly when the index is comprehensive, the precise terminology varies, and the index is in a specialized service providing insights and leading to authoritative results.

RESEARCH TIPS

Searches may use keywords, an index, a citation, or the table of contents.

Step Four: View the Results and Manage the Information

Customized options for a database may enable the subscriber to view both external and internal documents integrated into the subscriber's view of the database. Many firms maintain their own research files on various accounting and auditing issues from the firm's own practice. The primary purpose of accessing internal files is to provide firm personnel with the firm's conclusions on a previously researched issue. If confronted with a research issue in a firm and the firm's documents are not integrated into a research database, one should check if a file index exists for previous firm research on that issue and where to locate that research. Always ask for help, especially if in doubt.

Develop the habit of documenting research activities and the time spent on the activity. Document research findings in a consistent manner. Follow firm procedures in managing the information, which is often kept confidential within the firm. Periodically, review client bills to review the charges for research time spent and database costs passed on to the client. Recognize that clients will want understandable answers and practical advice. Learn to pay attention to all details and the real needs of the client.

Step Five: Communicate the Search Results

Citing sources of data and information accurately is essential in communicating the database search results. Maintaining this record also enables an easy return to the source later if questions arise. Financial accounting research results are often communicated via a memo to the client file.

FASB ACCOUNTING STANDARDS CODIFICATION™ RESEARCH SYSTEM

RESEARCH TOOLS

ACL
AICPA reSOURCE
Codification
eIFRS
i2
Internet
LexisNexis Academic
RIA Checkpoint

The Financial Accounting Standards Board (FASB) Codification™ Research System (the Codification) enables comprehensive, but not complete, research on accounting issues for the private sector. A link to the demo of the Codification highlighting the functionality of the system is available by accessing the author's Web site (www.weirich.wiley.com). It is suggested that you access and review this demo before proceeding with this chapter. Currently, at the FASB Web site, the FASB has released many of its pronouncements in nonsearchable format.

RESEARCH TIPS

To read a former pronouncement, select Pre-codification standards from the left navigation panel in the Codification.

RESEARCH TIPS

The Codification consolidates a majority of nongovernmental GAAP authorities in one location.

RESEARCH TIPS

Limited SEC guidance is included in the Codification.

QUICK FACTS

The four major topic areas in the Codification include Presentation, Financial Statement Accounts, Broad Transactions, and Industries.

The Codification includes essential[1] content and implementation guidance of prior level A–D GAAP[2] (see Chapter 3, Figure 3-5) and organizes it into approximately ninety topical areas described later in this chapter. A master glossary is also contained in the Codification.

To provide users with a more comprehensive database, the Codification team included limited SEC content (Regulation S-X, Financial Reporting Releases, Accounting Series Releases, Interpretive Releases, Staff Accounting Bulletins, EITF Topic D, and SEC Staff Observer comments) in the Codification. The included SEC literature is for user convenience only.

Upon adoption, the Codification supersedes all preexisting nongovernmental accounting and reporting standards. The Codification replaced the prior five-level GAAP hierarchy with two levels: authoritative and nonauthoritative, as described in Chapter 3. Thus, the Codification supersedes standards and implementation guidance issued by the FASB and prior standard-setters. Included in the Codification are the following pre-codification standards:

1. The FASB category contains Statements (FAS); Interpretations (FIN) that clarify, explain, or elaborate on prior FASB, APB, and ARB statements; Technical Bulletins (FTB) that provide guidance in applying pronouncements; Staff Positions (FSP); Staff Implementation Guides (Q&A), and Statement No. 138 Examples, "Accounting for Certain Derivative Instruments and Certain Hedging Activities."

2. EITF includes Abstracts that are the result of research related to new and unusual financial transactions or controversial issues. The EITF reaches a consensus on how to account for the specific transaction and will then release an Abstract. Topic D includes other technical matters related to the implications and implementations of the Abstracts.

3. The Derivatives Implementation Group (DIG) was organized in 1998 and had its last meeting in 2001. Its primary purpose was to examine issues related to derivatives and hedges. Among the 189 issuances, some were previously superseded, some were integrated in SFAS 133, and some were revised to meet current market conditions.

4. Thirty-one opinions of the AICPA APB, along with Accounting Interpretations (AIN), were still in effect in 2009. (Many were previously superseded.)

5. Fifty-one ARBs were issued by the Committee on Accounting Procedures (CAP) of the AICPA.

6. The AICPA category contains Statements of Position (SOP); Audit and Accounting Guides (AAG) (only incremental accounting guidance that normally is reviewed by the AICPA AcSEC and cleared by the FASB); Practice Bulletins (PB) (including the Notices to Practitioners elevated to Practice Bulletin status by Practice Bulletin 1); and Technical Inquiry Services (TIS) for Software Revenue Recognition only.

The citation coding for the authoritative guidance in the Codification begins with the four main topical areas: Presentation, Financial Statement Accounts, Broad Transactions, and Industries, as illustrated in Figure 4-1.[3] Each topic is further refined into

---

[1] While developing the Codification Research System, the Codification team organized literature into essential and nonessential literature. Nonessential content includes items such as the basis for FASB dissension, summary, background information, and other, like content. Essential content includes items such as implementation guidance and the actual standard. Only essential content is codified. Nonessential content is located in an archived standard available by means of the left navigation bar of the Codification.

[2] FASB Pre-codification Statement of Financial Accounting Standards No. 162, "The Hierarchy of Generally Accepted Accounting Principles" (2008).

[3] Modified from the Codification Notice to Constituents, www.asc.fasb.org/ (2008).

FIGURE 4-1 | FASB ACCOUNTING STANDARDS CODIFICATION RESEARCH SYSTEM (CODIFICATION)

subtopics, sections, and subsections, as depicted in Figure 4-2. The coding will emulate these four main categories.

Presentation topics are assigned codes 205–299 and include items such as Comprehensive Income (220), Notes to the Financial Statements (235), and Segment Reporting (280). Financial Statement Accounts numbered from 305–705 are listed separately as their own topics: Assets, Liabilities, Equity, Revenue, and Expenses. Examples of items within the Financial Statement Accounts include Inventory (330), Contingencies (450), and Research and Development (730). Business Combinations (805) and Interest (835) are topics that affect more than one financial statement and are therefore considered

FIGURE 4-2 | CODIFICATION CODING STRUCTURE

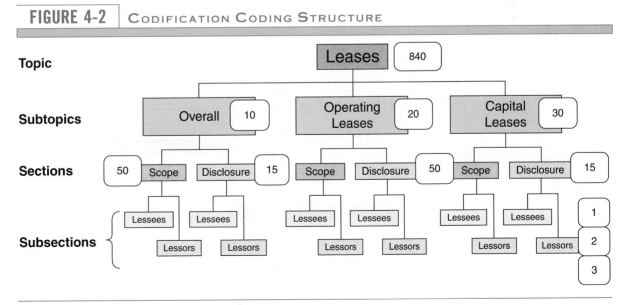

Modified from the *Notice to Constituents* in the Codification
Note: This is for illustration purposes only and does not include all topics, subtopics sections, and subsections.

transactions-oriented. The Broad Transactions topic is assigned codes 805–899. Lastly, unique accounting topics such as Development Stage Enterprises (915) are assigned to the Industries category with codes 905–999. If further refinement is required, unique coding numbers 00–99 will be assigned.

THE RESEARCH PROCESS

The Codification database enables researchers to obtain authoritative evidence to help solve their research questions more efficiently than they could using manual hardbound tools. Search processes in the Codification include using the topical category search, master glossary, and search inquiries. The location of each search process is shown in Figure 4-1, the Codification opening screen. The topical categories and master glossary entries are located in the left navigation pane and the search function is located in the right top pane.

As previously mentioned, the topical categories (Presentation, Assets, Liabilities, Equity, Revenue, Expenses, Broad Transactions, and Industry) are always displayed in the left navigation pane. As illustrated in Figure 4-3, to search within the topics, move the cursor over the topic of interest to open a new subtopic window. Keep moving the cursor to the right to open new windows until reaching the final area of interest, at which point clicking the left side of the mouse (left-clicking) will access the desired information in the center screen.

The master glossary is useful for browsing the Codification. A listing of key topics of the database's records is provided. To use the master glossary, left-click on the heading. The alphabet will appear in the center screen. (See Figure 4-4). Left-click the desired

FIGURE 4-3 | TOPICAL CATEGORY SEARCH

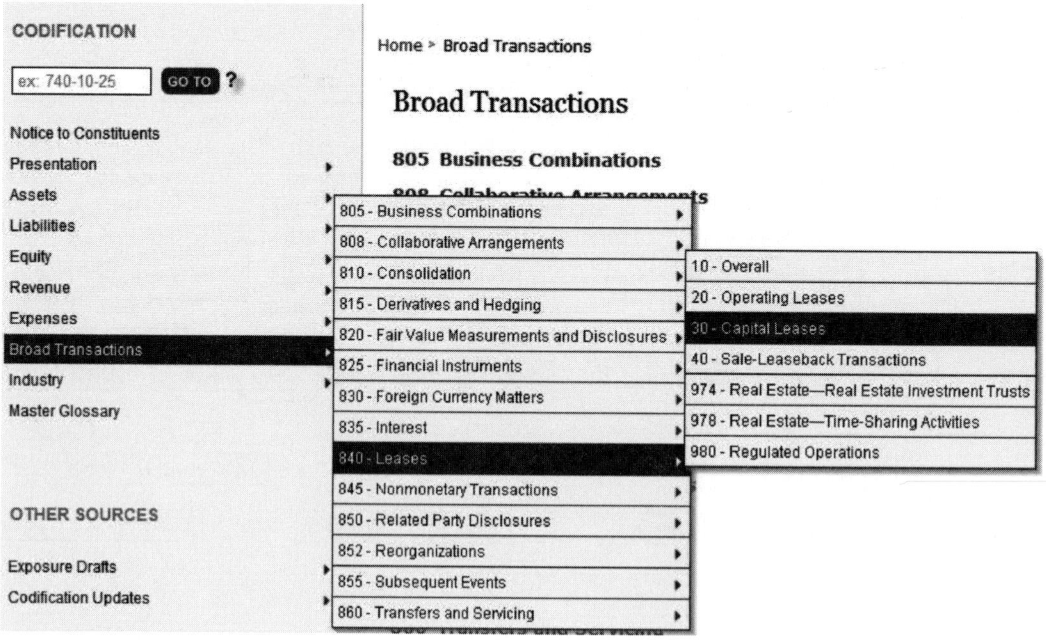

FIGURE 4-4 | MASTER GLOSSARY SEARCH

Glossary

Use the quick find feature at the end of this page, or use the alphabetic index to browse the terms beginning with that letter.

A | B | C | D | E | F | G | H | I | J | K | L | M | N | O | P | Q | R | S | T | U | V | W | X | Y | Z | View All

Glossary terms beginning with L

Land Development Costs

See Land Improvement Costs.

---

letter. Scroll down to the area of interest, and double-click the heading to produce the related literature.

A keyword search utilizes the search bar appearing at the top right of the database. Enter a single keyword or multiple keywords and click "Go." The search results appear in the center screen. Double-click the desired heading to produce the related literature. As illustrated in Figure 4-5, as a result of using the search term "accounts receivable," suggested subtopics to narrow the search appear in a window to the right of the screen.

An advanced search option is located beneath the search bar. This feature allows the search to be narrowed by exact phrases, Boolean operators, document titles, searches within specific topical areas, Codification citations, and the like. As with the simple search function, the search terms appear in the center screen with the suggested narrowing subtopics window to the right. Once a search is performed, the advanced search function appears below the potential results.

FIGURE 4-5 | KEYWORD SEARCH

Home > Advanced Search Results

Search Results

1 - 10 of 37 Results for: **accounts receivable**

Glossary Results: Monetary Assets and Liabilities, Carrying Amount   **>> more**

---

976 Real Estate—Retail Land > 310 Receivables > 50 Disclosure

General

... by entities with retail land sales operations shall include all of the following: Maturities of accounts receivable for each of the five years following the date of the financial statements Delinquent accounts receivable and the method(s) for determining delinquency The weighted average and range of stated interest rates of and the method(s) for determining delinquency The weighted average and range of stated interest rates of receivables

---

310 Receivables > 10 Overall > 50 Disclosure

General

...   This Subsection provides the following disclosure guidance for receivables:Loans and trade receivablesAssets serving as ... uncertainties Fair value disclosures. Loans and Trade Receivables 50-2 The summary ... include the following: The basis for accounting for loans trade receivables, and lease financings, including those classified as held for sale The ...

Narrow

By Related Term:?

- balance sheet
- fair value
- cash flow
- interest rate
- amortization
- long-term

By Area: ?

- ☐ Presentation(5)
- ☐ Assets(12)
- ☐ Revenue(2)
- ☐ Expenses(1)
- ☐ Broad Transactions (7)
- ☐ Industry(10)

For all searches, use the back arrow in the browser to move back to the previous search. Alternatively, the researcher can click on the larger topical area, and the previous search results will display. For instance, a search on "goodwill" results in the following topic and subtopic: "350–20 (Intangibles—Goodwill and other)." A further refinement results in subsection "05—overview and background" or "15—scope and exception." A researcher who clicks subsection 05 and then wants to go back to the previous search results could either click the back button in the browser or click subtopic 20 to list all subsections related to "goodwill."

To copy or print a particular record, click the Page Functions box appearing at the top center of the screen once a search is performed and there is text to print or copy. A drop-down window will appear. Choose "Printer-Friendly version" to print or copy the record to another program. Choose "Printer-Friendly with sources" to locate the corresponding archived standard.

In deciding when to stop the research, consider the distinction between primary and secondary authorities in accounting. Primary authorities in accounting are considered self-supporting. By themselves, they individually support a particular accounting principle within GAAP. Secondary authorities in accounting are not sufficient by themselves to support a particular accounting principle, but the researcher should use them in combination with other supporting authorities. A listing of primary and secondary authoritative support was provided in the previous chapter. Essentially, when one must rely upon nonauthoritative GAAP, the researcher should support the position with multiple sources. Thus, the researcher must perform more extensive research when struggling with an issue not answered by the authoritative level of GAAP. The researcher must recognize that many research questions lack clear-cut answers, so professional judgment is a key element in deciding when sufficient support exists to stop the research process.

LOCATING GAAP USING THE CODIFICATION

The Codification is the major source for finding essential GAAP authorities. The Codification includes all authoritative GAAP. For example, it incorporated the principles from FASB Statements and Interpretations and the predecessor AICPA ARBs and APBOs, FASB Technical Bulletins, AICPA SOPs that are cleared by the FASB, Abstracts of EITF Statements, FASB Staff Positions, and limited AICPA Audit and Accounting Guidance.

A mixture of authoritative and nonauthoritative GAAP authorities are located in the AICPA reSOURCE Online Library database (highlighted in Chapter 8). For instance, the full AICPA Industry and Audit Guides and the AICPA SOPs are available from the AICPA reSOURCE database. These guides are more fully discussed in the text concerning the auditing authorities. Similarly, the researcher can use the Codification or AICPA reSOURCE database to access the AICPA Practice Bulletins. Industry practices that are widely recognized and prevalent in the industry are left to the individual accountant's analysis, which one should document by using some of the accounting and business databases described in Chapter 6.

Nonauthoritative GAAP authorities, which one uses only in the absence of another source of established accounting principles, can come from a wide variety of locations. For example, the nonauthoritative GAAP level includes AICPA Technical Practice Aids, accessible from the AICPA reSOURCE database. The AICPA provides other electronically formatted publications as aids for the practitioner, but these aids are part of the nonauthoritative GAAP-level authorities.

Other nonauthoritative GAAP authorities include relevant journals and treaties available in the accounting, business, and legal databases discussed in Chapter 6.

These secondary sources on GAAP often help the researcher in quickly understanding the authority in an area of accounting. For example, the student researcher may use LexisNexis Academic to locate the Miller GAAP Guide (located under Business and Accounting). This guide is organized alphabetically by topic under GAAP and by accounting principles and specialized industry accounting concerns.

EXAMPLES USING THE CODIFICATION

The following provides a brief tutorial with screen shots in the use of the Codification for a research project on lease costs. The student is advised to access the author's Web site (www.weirich.wiley.com) for a link to the FASB's Codification online tutorial for further details of this essential database. Assume the researcher wants to determine whether certain costs qualify as lease costs, and, if so, whether to capitalize them or write them off. The researcher could first select the master glossary option located in the left navigation panel of the Codification opening screen, as shown in Figure 4-1.

RESEARCH TOOLS
ACL
AICPA reSOURCE
Codification
eIFRS
i2
Internet
LexisNexis Academic
RIA Checkpoint

To research lease costs, select the letter "L," as demonstrated in Panel A of Figure 4-6. Scroll down to "Leases." After left-clicking on "leases," lease results are displayed. Scroll down to section 840–10-25, "Leases—Overall—Recognition." The hyperlinks (subsections 1-69) in the database, as shown in Panel B of Figure 4-6, enable one to check the accounting authority for classifying leases. The first subsection (25-1) refers to the four capital lease criteria and subsequent subsections refer to real estate (25-19).

Assume the researcher has confirmed the lease as an operating lease and wants to know if the company can defer some initial costs, such as the broker's fee for finding the lessee. Using the Codification database, the researcher then performs an advanced

FIGURE 4-6	LEASE SEARCH USING MASTER GLOSSARY

PANEL A

Glossary

Use the quick find feature at the end of this page, or use the alphabetic index to browse the terms beginning with that letter.

A | B | C | D | E | F | G | H | I | J | K | L | M | N | O | P | Q | R | S | T | U | V | W | X | Y | Z | View All

Glossary terms beginning with L

Land Development Costs

See Land Improvement Costs.

↓

Lease

An agreement conveying the right to use property, plant, or equipment (land and/or depreciable assets) usually for a stated period of time.

Lease and Well Equipment

See Wells and Related Equipment and Facilities.

Lease Incentive

An incentive for the lessee to sign the lease, such as an up-front cash payment to the lessee, payment of costs for the lessee (such as moving expenses), or the assumption by the lessor of the lessee's preexisting lease with a third party.

Lease Inception

(continued)

FIGURE 4-6 | LEASE SEARCH USING MASTER GLOSSARY (CONTINUED)

PANEL B

Home > **Master Glossary Term Usage**

Glossary Term Usage

The glossary term is used in the following locations.

Lease

840 Leases > 10 Overall > 05 Background

- 840 Leases > 10 Overall > 05 Background > General, paragraph 05-2
- 840 Leases > 10 Overall > 05 Background > Lessees, paragraph 05-9
- 840 Leases > 10 Overall > 05 Background > Lessors, paragraph 05-10

840 Leases > 10 Overall > 10 Objectives

- 840 Leases > 10 Overall > 10 Objectives > General, paragraph 10-1

840 Leases > 10 Overall > 15 Scope

- 840 Leases > 10 Overall > 15 Scope > General, paragraph 15-3

840 Leases > 10 Overall > 25 Recognition

- 840 Leases > 10 Overall > 25 Recognition > General, paragraph 25-1
- 840 Leases > 10 Overall > 25 Recognition > Lessees, paragraph 25-28
- 840 Leases > 10 Overall > 25 Recognition > Lessors, paragraph 25-40

search with the keywords "leases initial direct costs." The search results reveal that the company, as a lessor, should defer the initial direct lease costs (840-20-25-16).

(Note: The citation styles for the Codification will vary in practice from those just citing the number sequence to those using ASC (Accounting Standards Code) followed by the numbers).

SEC ACCOUNTING FOR PUBLIC COMPANIES

SEC accounting is not the same as GAAP accounting. SEC sources follow the traditional legal hierarchy explained in more detail in the discussion of sources of tax law in Chapter 7. Securities laws generally appear under title 15 of the United States Code (U.S.C.). Because there are relatively few major securities laws, these are more commonly cited just by the name of the particular law, such as the Securities Exchange Act of 1934. These laws are widely available both on the Web and in legal databases, such as LexisNexis, described in the database chapter.

RESEARCH TIPS

For public companies, research relevant SEC rules and regulations.

The SEC has the statutory authority to establish accounting rules and regulations for public companies. For example, the SEC requires companies to make and keep books, records, and accounts, which, in reasonable detail, accurately and fairly reflect its transactions and the disposition of its assets. Issuers must devise and maintain internal controls sufficient to allow the preparation of financial statements in conformity with GAAP and to maintain the accountability of assets. Such corporations must file an annual Form 10-K report, quarterly Form 10-Q reports, and Form 8-K when significant accounting matters arise (for example, a change in auditors).

SEC REGULATIONS AND SOURCES

Regulations interpreting the statutory securities laws are codified in the Codification of Federal Regulations (CFR). Securities regulations issued by the SEC are placed under a different title number than the corresponding statutory law, CFR title 17. Securities regulations include:

1. **Regulation S-X, Form and Content of Financial Statements.** Describes the types of reports that public companies must file and the forms to use.
2. **Regulation S-K, Integrated Disclosure Rules.** Prescribes the requirements for information presented outside the financial statements required under Regulation S-X.

SEC's Published Views and Interpretations

Beyond regulations, the SEC administrative interpretations include various types of releases, which include the following:

1. **Financial Reporting Releases (FRRs)** prescribe the accounting principles that public companies must follow. FRRs update the SEC Codification of Financial Reporting Policies and Regulations S-K and S-X. A typical SEC Financial Reporting Release contains the following types of information:
    *   The background of the topic
    *   An evaluation of the comments received on the proposed rules
    *   A discussion of the final rules
    *   A discussion of transition provisions
    *   The text of new rules
2. **Accounting and Auditing Enforcement Releases (AAERs)** announce enforcement actions of the SEC's reporting and disclosure requirements. AAERs generally include a summary of the enforcement action, a discussion of the facts, the SEC's conclusions, and any orders issued (for example, an order to restrict practice before the SEC by the accountant involved for a specific time period).
3. **Accounting Series Releases (ASRs)**, predecessors to the development of FFRs and AAERs, were issued from 1937 to 1982. The SEC has codified non-enforcement-related ASRs that are still in effect. The SEC has published a topical index to enforcement-related ASRs.

> **QUICK FACTS**
> AAERs illustrate errors conducted by a registrant or its auditor.

All releases are identified with release numbers: a prefix indicating the applicable statute or special type of release and a sequential number that is assigned in the order of issuance. Here are some common prefixes and their applicable statute or special type of release:

Prefix	Applicable Statute or Special Type of Release
33	Securities Act of 1933
34	Securities Exchange Act of 1934
AS (ASR)	Accounting Series Release
FR (FRR)	Financial Reporting Release
ER (AAER)	Accounting and Auditing Enforcement Release

Some reference sources, however, replace the prefix with the applicable statute or special type of release. A release often has several release numbers because it applies to more than one statute. For example, Release Nos. 33-6483, 34-20186, and FR-14 represent the same release on an accounting matter that affects filings under the 1933 and 1934 Acts.

The Codification of Financial Reporting Policies is a compendium of the SEC's current published views and interpretations relating to financial reporting. It supplements the rules in regulations S-K and S-X by providing background and rationale for certain of those rules. Generally, the Codification of Financial Reporting Policies is updated only for the discussion of final rules. While that information is generally adequate in that it provides the important views of the SEC, accountants occasionally refer to the original release for more detailed background information.

SEC Staff Policy

SEC staff policy is published in Staff Accounting Bulletins (SABs), no-action and interpretative letters, correspondence about accountants' independence, and 1933 and 1934 Act Industry Guides. Technically, SEC Staff Policy is not approved formally by the commissioners, so it is not part of the official rules or interpretations of the SEC. However, SABs are unofficial interpretations of the SEC's prescribed accounting principles. SABs represent interpretations and practices followed by the SEC's staff in the Chief Accountant's Office and Division of Corporate Finance in administering the disclosure requirements of the federal securities laws. SABs relate to accounting and disclosure practices under the rules and regulations. The SEC has maintained a codification of SABs to make them more useful to users.

No-action and interpretative letters are published SEC staff responses to inquiries for interpretations of the application of statutes or rules and regulations to a particular transaction contemplated by a registrant or for a general interpretation of the statutes. The response may indicate that the staff will not recommend that the SEC take any action regarding the proposed transaction or that certain procedures must be followed regarding the transaction.

Given this extensive literature regarding SEC pronouncements, Figure 4-7 summarizes the hierarchy of the major SEC Authoritative Pronouncements and Publications.[4] Many of the previously discussed SEC administrative materials are available on its Web site (www.sec.gov). The SEC Web page on information for accountants is also helpful, as shown in Figure 4-8.

The SEC influences accounting standards set by the FASB and actions within the profession. In December 2001, the SEC sought to remind professionals that:

> the selection and application of the company's accounting policies must be appropriately reasoned. . . . [E]ven a technically accurate application of GAAP may nonetheless fail to communicate important information if it is not accompanied by appropriate and clear analytical disclosures to facilitate an investor's understanding . . .

This release suggested, as the U.S. courts have repeatedly stated, that compliance with the technical professional standards in GAAP are not enough. A professional must comply with the underlying intentions of the law and regulations for financial information.

---

[4] Paul B. W. Miller and Jack Robertson, *"A Guide to SEC Regulations and Publications: Mastering the Maze," Research in Accounting Regulation* 3 (July-August 1989): 239–249.

FIGURE 4-7 | HIERARCHY OF SEC AUTHORITIES AND PUBLICATIONS

Level 1: Statutes

i.e., 1933 Securities Act

1934 Securities Exchange Act

Level 2: Regulations and Forms

i.e., Regulation S–X

Regulation S–K

Level 3: Commission Releases

i.e., Financial Reporting Releases

Accounting and Auditing Enforcement Releases

Securities Releases

Exchange Act Releases

Level 4: Staff Advice

i.e., No-Action Letters

Staff Accounting Bulletins

ACCESSING SEC FILINGS AND REGULATIONS

SEC filings and regulations can be accessed using several methods: the SEC Web site (www.sec.gov), company Web sites, the SEC Next-Generation EDGAR System (discussed below), and commercial databases such as Commerce Clearing House, Inc. In most databases, SEC accounting sources are located in a different part of a database from FASB sources. However, as previously mentioned, some SEC authorities are located in the Codification, but in a separate part of the database.

The researcher can access company filings (for example, proxy statements, annual reports, 10-Ks, and 8-Ks) from several sources, including the SEC Web site, company Web sites, Lexis-Nexis Academic (discussed in a later chapter), and the SEC Next-Generation EDGAR System. The Next-Generation EDGAR system has replaced the SEC's EDGAR system, although older company filings are found in the EDGAR format and have been archived for retrieval.

The Next-Generation EDGAR system is a portal to SEC filings that allows the users (analysts, investors, and students) to extract data using customized searches. Documents can be retrieved in ACII, HTML, or XBRL. XBRL filings set the new system apart from other databases because the XBRL format and format viewer allow the researcher to extract desirable information for analysis directly from filings without having to retype. This removes human error in data extraction and retyping.

The researcher can link to the Next-Generation EDGAR system from the SEC Web site, as shown in Figure 4-8. Once hyperlinked to the Next-Generation search screen, the researcher can search by company or fund name, ticker symbol, central index key, file number, state, country, or sic. For best results, use the search syntax strategies suggested in the five-step research process discussed earlier in the chapter. A researcher may also subscribe to filing feeds (RSS or Really Simple Syndication). The RSS will alert the researcher when a new filing becomes available.

RESEARCH TOOLS
ACL
AICPA reSOURCE
Codification
eIFRS
i2
Internet
LexisNexis Academic
RIA Checkpoint

FIGURE 4-8   SEC WEB PAGE ON INFORMATION FOR ACCOUNTANTS

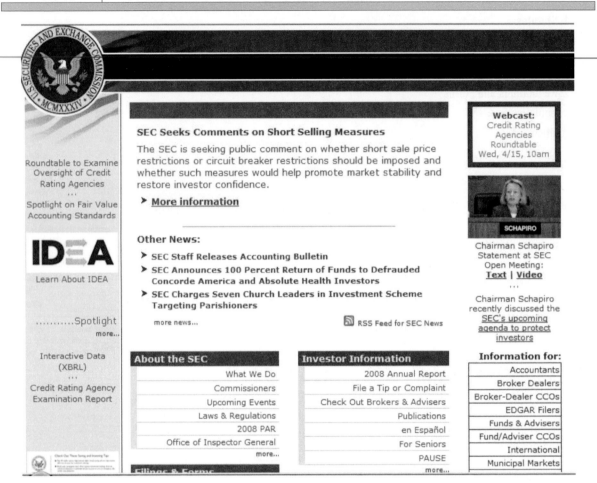

To access regulations, use the Codification for general guidance, the SEC Web site, or securities law service such as the Commerce Clearing House, Inc. (CCH) Federal Securities Law Reporter. A securities law service reprints the statutes, regulations, abstracts of selective administrative authorities, case abstracts, and helpful practice aids, such as forms used in practice to communicate with the SEC. Other commercial databases include a securities law service. For example, the Research Institute of America (RIA) Checkpoint® database has an SEC reference library. Chapter 6 explains several other databases that make searching SEC authorities more user-friendly.

CASES TO PRACTICE ACCOUNTING RESEARCH

Recall that leading academics have advocated learning from cases, particularly from real companies.[5] In the process of studying a case, one develops further analytical skills, enhances technological writing, and refines extemporaneous oral communication skills,

---

[5] W. Steve Albrecht and Robert J. Sack, "Accounting Education: Charting the Course through a Perilous Future," www.aicpa.org/edu/accteduc.htm.

particularly if a role-playing simulation is created. Case studies often enable the student to become more familiar with recent events in the profession.

Many cases exist that raise questions about the accounting or auditing practices. The primary sources of these cases are the Deloitte Trueblood Accounting & Auditing Cases (Trueblood Cases), the AICPA, and cases in publications such as *Issues in Accounting Education*.

Each year, Deloitte publishes ten new Trueblood Cases of one to four pages that present difficult intellectual and practical challenges requiring a broad array of skills and knowledge for their solution. These cases are now available (without the solutions) for viewing and downloading from the Deloitte Foundation's Web site (www.deloitte.com). Conduct a search for "Deloitte Foundation," and review the Trueblood Case Study Series. The cases are indexed among over twenty topics. That Web site also explains how professors can acquire access to the case solutions from the separate, password-protected part of the Web site. These solutions include more background information, a detailed discussion of the issues involved, and suggested solutions to the questions presented in each case study.

Issues in Accounting Education is the educational journal of the AAA, the leading professional organization for accounting professors. Each issue of the journal usually presents a few cases that professors could use in their accounting, tax, or auditing classes. The Pricewaterhouse/AAA case notebook (*Auditing/Accounting Teaching Cases and Exercises*) is freely available on the Web as a source of materials for assignment to students. However, the Web version omits the elements of each case that might compromise the usefulness of the case in the classroom. Faculty may purchase a suggested solutions manual based on the professional standards that were in effect when the cases were created.

Because of the rapid changes in tax laws, tax cases are more likely to become quickly outdated. Thus, one should use extra caution when considering a tax case because the age of the case increases the probability that some authority in the answer has changed. It is always advisable to perform the research of any suggested solution again rather than entirely trusting the source.

SUMMARY

Accounting research is challenging. The Codification has consolidated GAAP down to two levels, but there are still many sources. One needs to use the Codification to find relevant authorities. Thus, one must understand how the databases are structured, their contents, and search techniques. One sometimes needs to research SEC accounting rules and regulations for public companies and use other databases and Web sites to acquire those authorities. Practice developing research and analytical skills to meet the standards of the accounting profession and the public's expectations.

DISCUSSION QUESTIONS

1. What are the advantages of commercial databases compared to free Internet sources?
2. What are some tools to help in using a database?
3. What is the typical search process in a database?
4. What are the challenges to accounting research?
5. What are the four major topical areas that FASB Accounting Standards Codification Research System (the Codification) divides related guidance into?

6. Financial Statement Accounts is further divided into which topics?

7. Where can Original Pronouncements be found?

8. Does the Codification contain all GAAP authorities? Explain.

9. How are secondary sources on GAAP used to help the researcher?

10. Where does the researcher find:

    a. Authoritative GAAP sources?

    b. Nonauthoritative GAAP sources?

11. What are the SEC accounting authorities? Where are they located?

12. Does the Codification contain SEC authorities? If so, what authority does the Codification have over SEC content?

13. What makes the Next-Generation EDGAR system different from other research tools?

EXERCISES

Database Research Strategies

1. Prepare a search strategy for understanding a due diligence review of a company.

2. Propose a research strategy to investigate Natalie Churyk's suggestions for mastering the computerized CPA exam. Then implement the strategy and communicate the results (citing the relevant source).

The Codification

3. Use the topical categories in the left navigation bar of the Codification to identify the first three subtopics within the general topic of Presentation.

4. Company X-Co has a $10,000,000 gain from exercising stock options. What topic and subtopics would the researcher highlight in the left navigation panel to discover the relevant authority to resolve the issue?

5. Use the master glossary to find the definition of cash. Then use the printer-friendly version with sources to locate its associated archived standard.

6. Summarize one industry accounting issue related to the motion picture industry.

SEC and Its Authorities

7. Use either the SEC Web site or a database described in the next chapter and locate the following SEC sources. What does Rule 10(b)(5) discuss? (*Hint:* It interprets Sec. 10(b)(5) of the Securities Act of 1934.) What does SAB 99 discuss?

8. Use the Internet to acquire further understanding for explaining SEC actions to officers in a public company who ask you the following questions. What does the chief accountant for the SEC do? How should you prepare a client to handle an SEC investigation?

9. Use the Internet to access the SEC the Next-Generation EDGAR system. List the seven methods to search for a company.

10. Use the Next-Generation EDGAR system to find the most recent 10-K of a company of your choosing. Go to that company's Web site and view the same document. How do the two documents differ?

Finding Cases

11. Go to the Deloitte Foundation Web site (www.deloitte.com). Download a TrueBlood Case involving a joint venture or partnership. Write a sentence summarizing the issue in the case. Use the Codification database to find the authorities providing the answer to the issue presented. Identify those authorities.

12. Access the AICPA Web site (www.aicpa.org). Click the link for the Antifraud Resource Center. List the title of two fraud cases. Read one case and summarize the abstract of the case.

Using the Codification

13. Use the Codification to identify accounting authority governing each of the following:

   a. The accounting for prepaid advertising

   b. The accounting for negative loan amortization

   c. The accounting for accelerated depreciation

   d. The accounting for the range of an estimated loss contingency

   e. The accounting for a reporting period

   f. The accounting for factoring of trade receivables with recourse

14. Use the Codification to identify the accounting authority governing each of the following:

   a. The accounting for goodwill

   b. The accounting for start-up costs, sometimes referred to as organizational costs

   c. The accounting for installment receivable

   d. The accounting for subordinated debt

   e. The accounting for imputed interest

   f. The accounting for loss from operations

15. Use the Codification to locate archived FASB Interpretation 36.

   a. What does it discuss?

   b. How did you find that authority?

   c. What industry does that authority affect?

   d. What are the major organizational parts of that authority (placed in bold)?

16. Use the Codification to find which expenditures qualify as a research and development cost:

   a. The salaries of the research staff designing new products

   b. The commissions paid to sales staff marketing new products

17. Use the Codification to answer the following:

   a. What is a contingency?

   b. Precisely where in the authority did you find that definition?

   c. Under what circumstances are contingent losses recorded?

   d. Precisely where in the authority did you find the rule?

18. The Codification combines all relevant literature on a topic in one location. Identify the number of different issues/subparagraphs related to post-retirement benefits other than pensions. Provide citations for each.

19. Use the master glossary in the Codification to research the disclosure requirements for the post-retirement benefits other than pensions. Explain these requirements.

20. In some cases, preferred stock has some characteristics of a debt instrument.

   a. How should the accountant classify such debt in the financial statement?

   b. Reference relevant authorities from the Codification to support your answer.

21. Go to the SEC Web site (www.sec.gov).

   a. Access the Information for Accountant folder. Then go to the financial reporting information center. Determine how many accounting and auditing releases were issued in the current year.

b. Pre-codification SFAS No.115 establishes the accounting standard for investment securities. Search the relevant accounting interpretation and guidance for SFAS No. 115. What conflicts did the SEC resolve under SFAS No. 115?

APPENDIX

CPA Exam—Financial Accounting Simulations

Figures A4-1 through A4-4 provide an example of a financial accounting simulation on the CPA exam. Figure A4-1 provides the opening screen shot to the candidate regarding the instructions. Clicking on the research tab in Figure A4-1 provides the literature database to address the question presented in Figure A4-2. Clicking on the FASB literature at the left of the screen will open up the FASB literature, as depicted in Figure A4-3. Opening up the topical index and inserting "appraisals" as your search term provides the result in Figure A4–4 for review as to a possible solution. Navigating through the databases on the CPA exam is extremely important for success regarding the simulations.

FIGURE A4-1 | "SIMULATION DIRECTIONS TO CANDIDATES" SCREEN

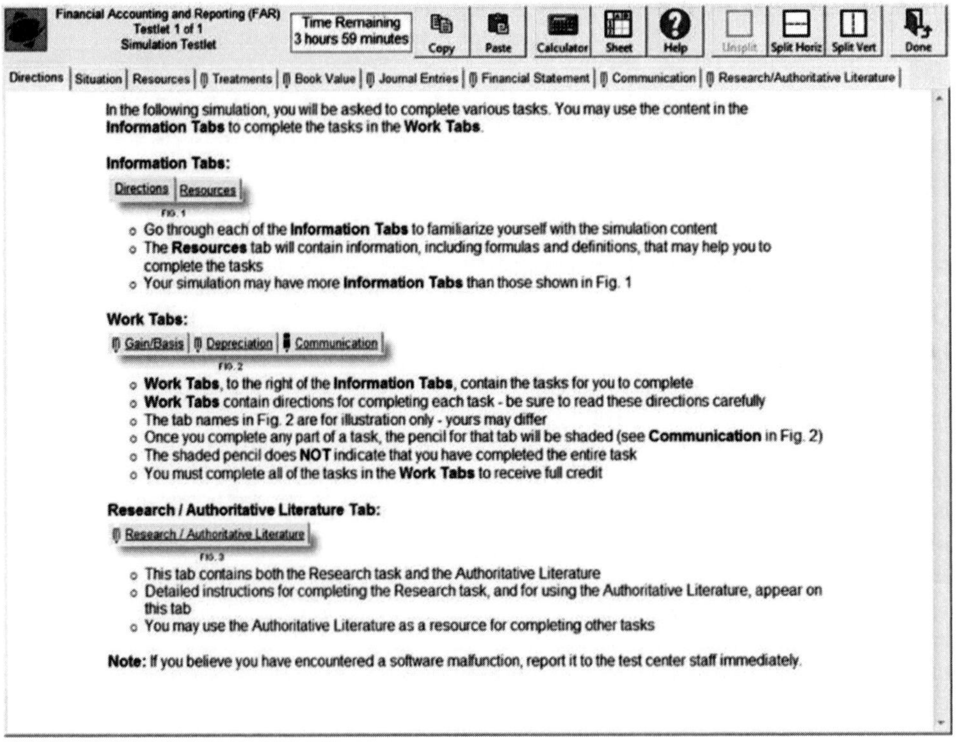

SIMULATION SCREEN FOR FINANCIAL ACCOUNTING AND REPORTING RESEARCH/AUTHORITATIVE LITERATURE

Financial Accounting and Reporting (FAR) Testlet 1 of 1 Simulation Testlet	Time Remaining 3 hours 59 minutes	Copy	Paste	Calculator	Sheet	Help	Unsplit	Split Horiz	Split Vert	Done

Directions | Situation | Resources | Treatments | Book Value | Journal Entries | Financial Statement | Communication | Research/Authoritative Literature

| VIEW DIRECTIONS | VIEW QUESTION |

Step 1 - Research Question

Included with the company's year 3 engineering study was an appraisal report that assigned a value to the machinery that exceeded its book value. The company's president asked you to determine whether the machinery could be written up to its appraised market value with future depreciation based on that amount. Find the proper citation in the Original Pronouncements that provides guidance in addressing the president's question.

Step 2 - Search

History | Search Result | Advanced Search | Help

[◀ BACK] [Home]

Search: [   ] [SEARCH ALL] [SEARCH WITHIN]

Table of Contents

📁 FASB Literature

Uniform CPA Examination Authoritative Literature

To access the Authoritative Literature:

Click on Table of Contents folders at left to locate and open appropriate documents

OR

Perform a search for a particular topic by entering text in the text box above. Use the buttons to the right and links above the text box to perform more detailed or advanced searches.

Step 3 - Answer

There are currently no choices available because no document has been selected. Use the pane to the left to navigate to a document that has choices.

| FIGURE A4-3 | OPENING SCREEN AFTER CLICKING THE "FASB LITERATURE" LINK IN FIGURE A4-2 |

| Financial Accounting and Reporting (FAR) Testlet 1 of 1 Simulation Testlet | Time Remaining 3 hours 58 minutes | Copy | Paste | Calculator | Sheet | Help | Unsplit | Split Horiz | Split Vert | Done |

Directions | Situation | Resources | (|) Treatments | (|) Book Value | (|) Journal Entries | (|) Financial Statement | (|) Communication | (|) Research/Authoritative Literature

| VIEW DIRECTIONS | VIEW QUESTION |

Step 1 - Research Question

Included with the company's year 3 engineering study was an appraisal report that assigned a value to the machinery that exceeded its book value. The company's president asked you to determine whether the machinery could be written up to its appraised market value with future depreciation based on that amount. Find the proper citation in the Original Pronouncements that provides guidance in addressing the president's question.

Step 2 - Search

History | Search Result | Advanced Search | Help

Search: [_____] [SEARCH ALL] [SEARCH WITHIN]

⬅ BACK   Home

Table of Contents
- ▶ 🗀 FASB Literature
- 🗀 Original Pronouncemer
- 🗀 Topical Index

Uniform CPA Examination Authoritative Literature

To access the Authoritative Literature:

Click on Table of Contents folders at left to locate and open appropriate documents

OR

Perform a search for a particular topic by entering text in the text box above. Use the buttons to the right and links above the text box to perform more detailed or advanced searches

Step 3 - Answer

There are currently no choices available because no document has been selected. Use the pane to the left to navigate to a document that has choices.

FIGURE A4–4 SCREEN AFTER CLICKING "APPRAISALS" IN THE TOPICAL INDEX

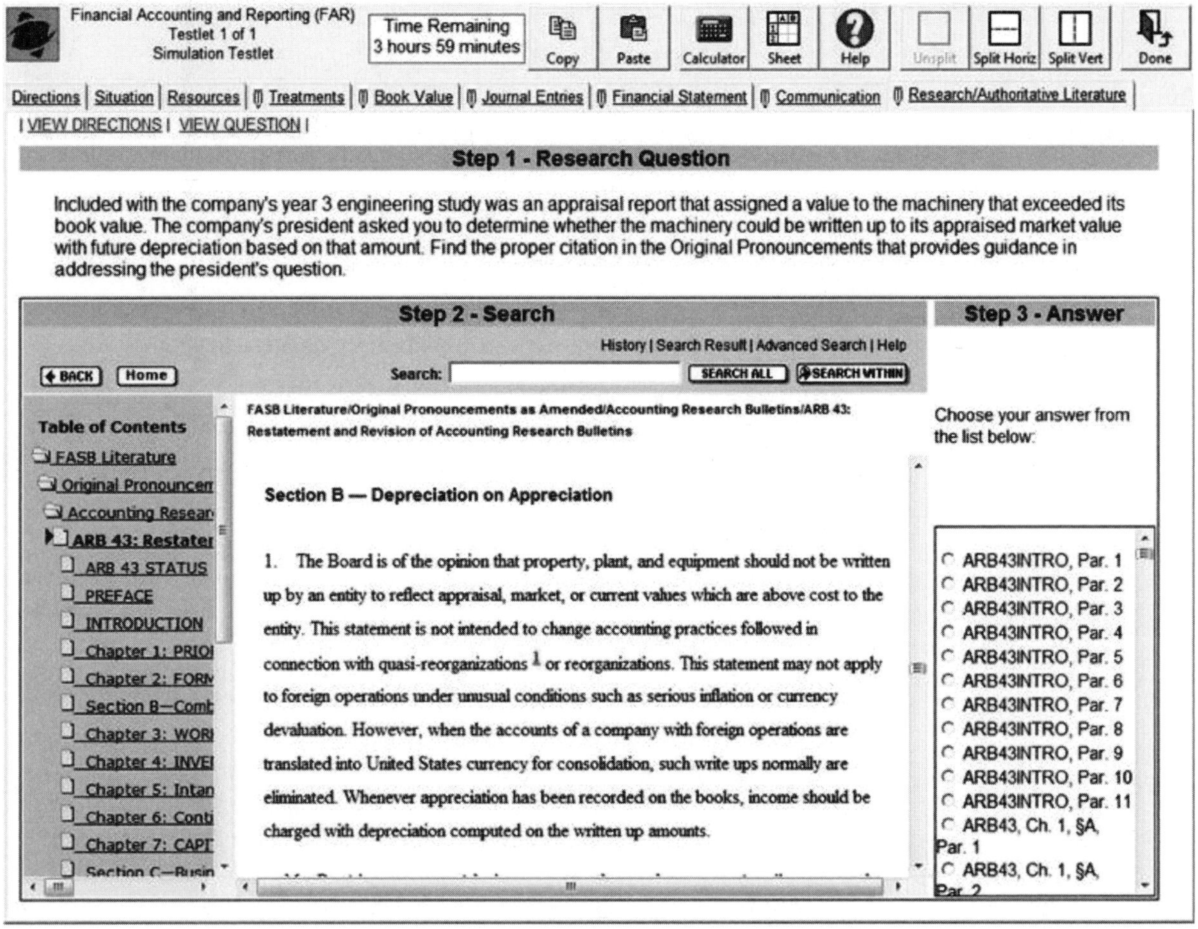

Financial Accounting and Reporting (FAR)
Testlet 1 of 1
Simulation Testlet

Time Remaining
3 hours 59 minutes

| Copy | Paste | Calculator | Sheet | Help | Unsplit | Split Horiz | Split Vert | Done |

Directions | Situation | Resources | (I) Treatments | (I) Book Value | (I) Journal Entries | (I) Financial Statement | (I) Communication | (I) Research/Authoritative Literature

| VIEW DIRECTIONS | VIEW QUESTION |

Step 1 - Research Question

Included with the company's year 3 engineering study was an appraisal report that assigned a value to the machinery that exceeded its book value. The company's president asked you to determine whether the machinery could be written up to its appraised market value with future depreciation based on that amount. Find the proper citation in the Original Pronouncements that provides guidance in addressing the president's question.

Step 2 - Search

History | Search Result | Advanced Search | Help

[← BACK] [Home]

Search: [_____] [SEARCH ALL] [SEARCH WITHIN]

Table of Contents

☐ FASB Literature
☐ Original Pronouncem
☐ Accounting Resear
▶ ☐ ARB 43: Restatem
  ☐ ARB 43 STATUS
  ☐ PREFACE
  ☐ INTRODUCTION
  ☐ Chapter 1: PRIO
  ☐ Chapter 2: FORM
  ☐ Section B—Comb
  ☐ Chapter 3: WOR
  ☐ Chapter 4: INVE
  ☐ Chapter 5: Intan
  ☐ Chapter 6: Conti
  ☐ Chapter 7: CAPI
  ☐ Section C—Busin

FASB Literature/Original Pronouncements as Amended/Accounting Research Bulletins/ARB 43: Restatement and Revision of Accounting Research Bulletins

Section B — Depreciation on Appreciation

1. The Board is of the opinion that property, plant, and equipment should not be written up by an entity to reflect appraisal, market, or current values which are above cost to the entity. This statement is not intended to change accounting practices followed in connection with quasi-reorganizations [1] or reorganizations. This statement may not apply to foreign operations under unusual conditions such as serious inflation or currency devaluation. However, when the accounts of a company with foreign operations are translated into United States currency for consolidation, such write ups normally are eliminated. Whenever appreciation has been recorded on the books, income should be charged with depreciation computed on the written up amounts.

Step 3 - Answer

Choose your answer from the list below:

- ○ ARB43INTRO, Par. 1
- ○ ARB43INTRO, Par. 2
- ○ ARB43INTRO, Par. 3
- ○ ARB43INTRO, Par. 4
- ○ ARB43INTRO, Par. 5
- ○ ARB43INTRO, Par. 6
- ○ ARB43INTRO, Par. 7
- ○ ARB43INTRO, Par. 8
- ○ ARB43INTRO, Par. 9
- ○ ARB43INTRO, Par. 10
- ○ ARB43INTRO, Par. 11
- ○ ARB43, Ch. 1, §A, Par. 1
- ○ ARB43, Ch. 1, §A, Par. 2

The Environment of International Research

LEARNING OBJECTIVES

After completing this chapter, you should understand:

- The international accounting environment.
- Global and domestic adoption of International Financial Reporting Standards.
- The International Accounting Standards Board and its structure.
- The standard-setting process, including due process and the Framework.
- How to utilize the electronic International Financial Reporting Standards to conduct research including the Standards hierarchy.

INTERNATIONAL ACCOUNTING ENVIRONMENT

International competition has forced many firms to look to new markets and investors to finance the expansion or modernization needed to remain competitive in world markets. Increasingly internationalized capital markets result in a need for internationally comparable financial statements and accounting standards. Accounting principles and reporting practices are the business world's communication and should move freely across national boundaries.

Different accounting principles grew out of the divergent economic and social environments of various nations and regions. Differences among national accounting and auditing standards become more disconcerting when trade barriers between nations were reduced due to international cooperation developments (for example, the North American Free Trade Agreement).

Efforts have increased during the past decade to move nations toward using international standards. The movement toward harmonization and convergence[1] has included the activities of supranational groups and individual scholars. Figures 5-1[2] and 5-2[3] depict the global and U.S. IFRS convergence efforts in recent years, respectively. Included in the global category are the International Federation of Accountants (IFAC), the International Accounting Standards Board (IASB), the Organization for Economic Cooperation and Development (OECD), and the European Union (EU).

> **RESEARCH TIPS**
>
> The AICPA Web site (www.ifrs.com) provides an abundance of IFRS information.

> **QUICK FACTS**
>
> Adoption of IFRS requires consideration of taxes, information systems, investor relations, compensation plans, reporting, and retirement plans.

---

[1] Harmonization moves toward reducing the overall number of alternatives but still allows for them as long as the alternatives do not conflict with IFRS. On the other hand, convergence moves toward adoption of one set of standards.

[2] Developed from dates listed in "IASB and the IASC Foundation: Who Are We and What Do We Do?" (www.iasb.org), and "International Financial Reporting Standards (IFRS): An AICPA Backgrounder" (http://www.IFRS.com).

[3] Adapted from "International Financial Reporting Standards (IFRS): An AICPA Backgrounder" (www.IFRS.com).

FIGURE 5-1 | GLOBAL IFRS TIMELINE

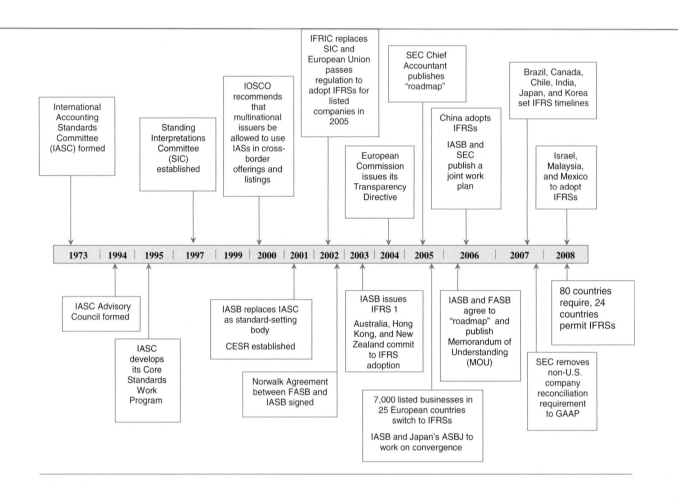

The IASB, through a due process procedure described later in this chapter, has issued a number of International Financial Reporting Standards (IFRSs) that incorporate the previously issued International Accounting Standards (IASs) by IFAC's International Accounting Standards Committee (IASC).

The IASB independently issues standards for presenting audited financial information, although it works closely with IFAC. IASB has received support from the International Organization of Securities Commissions and the World Trade Organization to create acceptable accounting standards for multinational securities and other international offerings.

U.S. convergence milestones with IFRS include the 2002 Norwalk Agreement and the subsequent reaffirmed Memorandum of Understanding and "roadmap,' as shown in Figure 5-2. The Norwalk Agreement was the first Memorandum of Understanding (MOU) between the IASB and FASB, whereby they agreed to work on both short- and long-term projects removing differences (convergence) between IFRS and U.S. GAAP and to continue coordinating activities. Reaffirmation of the MOU occurred in 2006 and 2008. In 2007, the SEC issued a "roadmap" to remove U.S. GAAP reconciliations for non-U.S. IFRS filers.

FIGURE 5-2 | U.S. IFRS TIMELINE

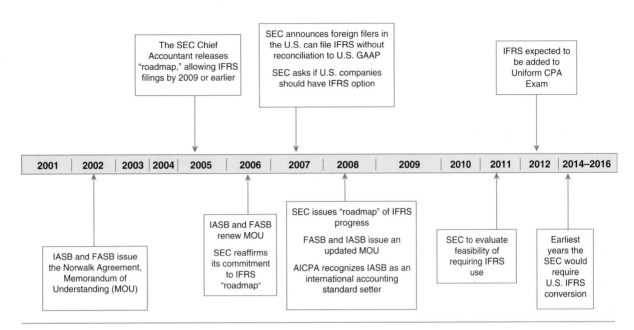

Research on accounting issues is conducted in a dynamic international environment. New professional standards are constantly issued. The updating of existing standards help to minimize the differences between national boundaries. Various constituents (for example, preparers, auditors, academics, investors, financial analysts, and regulators) influence the development of accounting standards. This chapter examines the adoption of IFRS globally and domestically in the United States; the IASB's standard-setting process, the IASB Board and committees, IFRS Standards, the Conceptual Framework; funding and regulation of IFRS; IFRS hierarchy; and research in electronic IFRS (eIFRS).

INTERNATIONAL ACCOUNTING STANDARDS BOARD (IASB)

The role of the IASB in today's world capital markets is to develop high-quality, enforceable, global financial reporting standards. The IASB's financial accounting standard-setting process is similar to the FASB's process in that it involves several entities, as noted in Figure 5-3.[4] The International Accounting Standards Committee Foundation's Constitution (the Constitution) describes the name, objectives, membership, and governance of each of the following entities or committees: the Monitoring Board, the International Accounting Standards Committee (IASC) Foundation, the Standards Advisory Council (SAC), the Board itself, and an International Financial Reporting Interpretations Committee (IFRIC). The Constitution was approved in 2000 and has been revised several times.

The Monitoring Board oversees the IASC Foundation by approving Trustee appointments to the IASC Foundation, reviewing the Foundation's annual written report

> **QUICK FACTS**
>
> The IASB and the Foundation have an objective to provide the world with a common financial reporting language.

---

[4] IASB, "IASB and the IASC Foundation: Who Are We and What Do We Do?" (www.iasb.org).

FIGURE 5-3 | How the International Accounting Standards Board (IASB) Operates

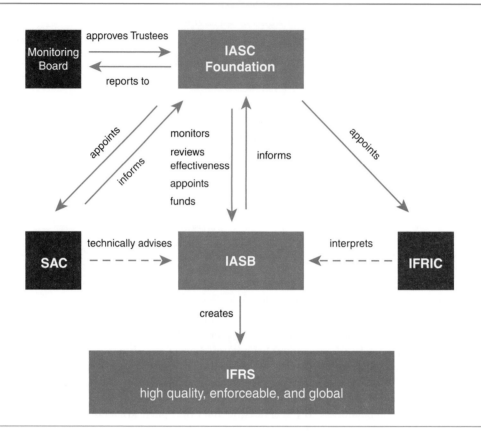

regarding its activities, and meeting with the Trustees of the Foundation at least on an annual basis. The Monitoring Board includes representation from regulators of major capital markets and leading global organizations. More specifically, the Monitoring Board is comprised of a member of the European Commission, the Commissioner of the Japan Financial Services Agency, the Chairman of the U.S. SEC, the Chair of the International Organization of Securities Commission (IOSCO) Emerging Markets Committee, the Chair of the IOSCO Technical Committee, and, as an observer, the Chairman of the Basel Committee on Banking Supervision.

The IASC Foundation's role is to develop a single set of global, high-quality standards; promote the use of those standards; consider its constituents (small to large and stable to emerging); and initiate convergence of IFRS with other national accounting standards. Empowered to carry out the tasks of the IASC Foundation are twenty-two financially knowledgeable Trustees: six members each from Europe, North America, and Asia/ Oceania and four from other geographic regions. The Trustees are responsible for appointing, monitoring, and reviewing the effectiveness of the IASB members. The Trustees also develop the IASC's strategy and budget, amend the Constitution, raise funds, and appoint members to the SAC and IFRIC (discussed later in this chapter).

The Standards Advisory Council (SAC) meets with the IASB three times per year to provide input on the IASB's technical agenda, project priorities, and individual projects.

The SAC also helps the IASB promote IFRS throughout the world by publishing articles and supporting IFRS at various professional meetings. The SAC is comprised of almost fifty members from geographically and professionally diverse backgrounds, such as preparers, auditors, academics, investors, financial analysts, and regulators. The SAC reports both its activities and those of the IASB to the Trustees.

The IASB was created by the IASC Foundation in 2001 to create a single set of high-quality global standards. The IASB holds public meetings during most months for a three- to five-day period, which are archived on the IASB Web site (www.iasb.org). Membership of the IASB is based on skill sets such that five members are auditors, five members are financial statement preparers, three members are financial statement users, and one member is an academician. The composition of the IASB ensures a broad geographical spectrum (nine countries) of fourteen individuals (twelve full-time and two part-time). By 2012, membership in the IASB will increase from fourteen to sixteen with no more than three part-time members. At that time, the IASB's membership must have at least four members from each of Europe, North America, and Asia/Oceania, as well as one from Africa and one from South America.

IASB Authorities

The IASB issues pronouncements, labeled International Financial Reporting Standards (IFRSs) and Interpretations of International Financial Reporting Standards (IFRICs), that interpret the IASB's own Statements. The IASB also recognizes predecessor authorities from the IASC entitled International Accounting Standards (IASs). As of 2009, the IASB has adopted the forty-one previous IASs and has issued eight new IFRSs. Most IFRSs contain:

> **QUICK FACTS**
> The IASB and the Foundation have an objective to provide the world with a common financial reporting language.

1. An introduction
2. A table of contents
3. An objective
4. A scope
5. Definitions
6. The actual standard
7. A list of the IASB members actually voting
8. The basis for a qualifying or dissenting vote of an IASB member
9. Appendices containing background information, a glossary of terms, examples of applying the standard, and other ancillary information

IFRSs are used as a basis for many companies, by the stock exchanges and regulatory authorities that allow presentation of financial statements using IFRSs, by supranational bodies to produce results that meet the needs of capital markets, by many countries having national accounting requirements, and as international benchmarks by countries that develop their own accounting requirements.[5]

The Standards Interpretations Committee (SIC) was established in 1997 to timely answer questions by financial statement preparers and users about issues not clearly covered by an existing set of authoritative pronouncements. As of 2009, eleven of its thirty-three interpretations are still followed.

---

[5] *AICPA Professional Standards*, international volume (June 1, 2003).

QUICK FACTS

The IFRIC provides guidance on unclear IFRS or on divergent practices.

The International Financial Reporting Interpretations Committee (IFRIC) replaced the SIC and has issued seventeen interpretations known as IFRICs. Chaired by the IASB's Director of Technical Activities, the IFRIC consists of highly knowledgeable individuals who are in a position to become aware of implementation issues before they become widespread and divergent practices regarding them become entrenched. The IFRIC can address industry-specific issues rather than those encompassing accounting and financial reporting as a whole. For example, IFRIC No. 15, "Agreements for the Construction of Real Estate," applies primarily to the real estate industry. To prevent divergence, clarification may be necessary, such as in IFRIC No. 12, "Service Concession Arrangements," which provides guidance on how to account for infrastructure, rights, and obligations arising from those arrangements.

RESEARCH TIPS

IFRSs, IASs, IFRICs, and SICs have the same level of authority.

When lack of consensus exists on an issue under consideration by the IFRIC, and the IFRIC decides that the problem merits further action, it will forward the file to the IASB for further deliberation. Conversely, if the IFRIC can reach a consensus on an issue, the IASB can usually infer that no Board action is necessary. Approved IFRIC interpretations have the same authority as IASB Standards. The Interpretations (IFRICs and SICs), along with the original pronouncements, are collectively known as IFRSs.

IASB Due Process

Given the importance of IASB Standards, an extensive due process was adopted in order to address transparency, accessibility, extensive consultation, responsiveness, and accountability. The IASB's six-stage due process, as depicted in Figure 5-4[6] and set out in the Constitution, is as follows:

1. Before a potential agenda item is set, the IASB receives input from working groups within the IASB, IFRIC, and SAC. The IASB considers the potential agenda item's relevance, existing accounting guidance, the possibility of increased convergence, the potential quality of any proposed standard, and the resources needed to examine the potential agenda item.

2. The IASB plans the research project to determine whether to work with other accounting standard setters, such as forming working groups comprised of staff and/or members from the various standard-setting bodies. The IASB's working groups are chaired by the Director of Technical Activities or Director of Research.

QUICK FACTS

Issuance of a discussion paper is not a mandatory stage of the IASB's due process.

3. Developing and publishing a discussion paper is not a mandatory stage, but the action is usually taken to obtain early feedback from constituents. If the discussion paper is omitted, the IASB will explain why. Typically, a discussion paper includes an examination of the topic, the alternative accounting treatments, the standard setters' views, and an invitation for comment. If another standard setter initiated the discussion paper, the IASB requires a simple majority vote before publication. If the IASB or one of its working groups initiated the research, the discussion paper is published because all IASB sessions are public. Analysis is performed on the comment letters received during the usual 120-day comment period, and the results are posted to the IASB Web site.

4. Developing and publishing the exposure draft (ED) is mandatory and is based on IASB staff research, discussion paper comments, SAC input, working groups, and other standard-setter input. Before the ED is issued for comment, a ballot takes place requiring approval by nine of the fourteen IASB members. ED periods are usually 120 days or longer for major projects; if a matter is urgent, the ED period is

---

[6] IASB, "IASB and the IASC Foundation: Who Are We and What Do We Do?" (www.iasb.org).

FIGURE 5-4 | Six Stages of IASB Standard Setting

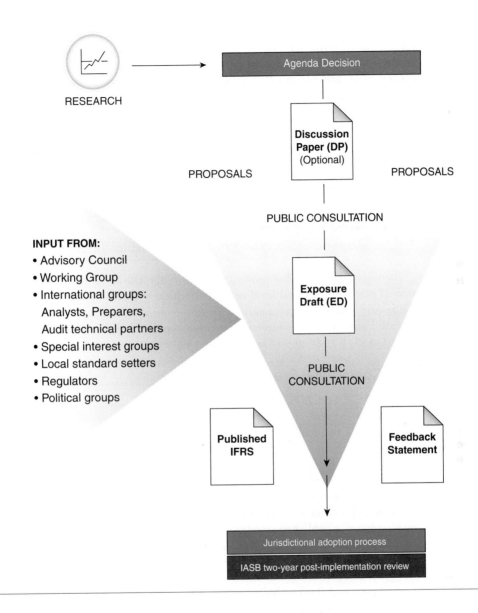

30 days. Once comments are received, they are summarized and posted to the IASB Web site.

5. The IASB then decides whether to draft an IFRS or publish a second ED. If the IFRS is drafted, the IFRIC reviews the draft before it goes to the IASB for a vote. A version of theIFRS draft is also posted for paid subscribers. An IFRS is issued only after any outstanding issues are resolved and the IASB members have voted in favor of the standard.

6. The IASB and its staff periodically hold meetings with constituents with respect to implementation guidance and any unforeseen standard shortcomings. The IASC

Foundation promotes educational seminars and events to ensure proper application of the IFRS.

IFRIC Due Process

IFRICs are issued to clarify IFRSs or prevent diverging viewpoints. A seven-stage due process is followed for issuing interpretations. During the process, the Committee ensures that its focus remains principle-based, it considers potential international convergence, and ensures that its guidance does not change or conflict with existing IFRSs or the Framework. The IFRIC due process is as follows:

1. A study is implemented to identify the issue.
2. The agenda is set.
3. IFRIC meetings and voting occur.
4. A draft interpretation is developed.
5. The IASB plays a role in the release of a draft interpretation.
6. A comment period is allowed.
7. An interpretation is approved by the IFRIC and the IASB.

> **QUICK FACTS**
>
> IFRICs require approval by the IFRIC and the IASB.

Having completed a due process procedure, the IASB's or IFRIC's final pronouncement is placed at an equal level in the IFRS hierarchy. All throughout the due process, IFRSs and IFRICs are summarized in non-technical language in the IASC's *Insight* journal. Final technical summaries are posted on the IASB Web site. The full standard is placed in eIFRS, discussed later in this chapter

IASB Conceptual Framework

> **RESEARCH TIPS**
>
> Use the Conceptual Framework for guidance when IFRSs do not apply directly the research question.

The IASB Conceptual Framework (the Framework) establishes objectives and concepts for the development of accounting standards. The Framework is also useful in the preparation of financial statements by listing the objectives and the qualitative characteristics of the financial statements and providing the definition and measurement concepts of the elements of financial statements and capital maintenance.

Ideally, the Board uses the Framework in the development of future standards. The Framework should also assist users and preparers in applying and interpreting standards and financial statements. For instance, preparers may need to look to the Framework in the absence of a published standard, and auditors may want to ensure clients' financial statements are in compliance with the IFRS to form an opinion on those statements. However, occasionally, a conflict arises between the Framework and previously issued IASs or IFRS. In conflict situations, the standards override the Framework.

The Framework itself includes objectives of financial reporting, assumptions of financial reporting, and qualitative characteristics of financial statements (understandability, relevance, reliability, comparability, and constraints such as cost-benefit and materiality). The Framework also conceptualizes the elements of the financial statements, measurement of these elements, and concepts for capital and capital maintenance.

Elements of financial statements include assets, liabilities, equity, income, and expenses. Assets are future economic benefits owned by the entity, resulting in resource inflows. Liabilities are current obligations as result of a past transaction resulting in resource outflows. Equity is the residual interest in an entity. Income is an inflow or economic benefit whereas an expense is a decrease in an economic benefit or outflow.

Capital maintenance refers to return on capital and return of capital. In the process of examining global firms, revaluations of assets and liabilities occur and would appear as capital transactions. Recall that the primary objective of IFRS financial statements is to provide information to users (for example, investors, employees, lenders, suppliers, customers, governments, and the public) that is useful for decision-making. Information is useful if it is understandable, relevant, reliable, and comparable. Relevant information predicts or confirms prior expectations and surpasses a materiality threshold. Reliable information is unbiased (neutral), representationally faithful (substance over form), and conservative. The last qualitative characteristic is comparability (through time and across firms). Timeliness and cost-benefit are constraints in examining the usefulness of information.

Although the Framework is quite extensive, it is not as comprehensive as the IASB or the FASB would like. Therefore, the IASB and the FASB have agreed to work jointly to publish a new conceptual framework that will provide a principles-based, consistent, converged framework for developing future accounting standards. As of 2009, the Boards are at various stages of due process on this new Framework. Issuances for constituent feedback include an ED entitled "Improved Conceptual Framework for Financial Reporting: The Objectives of Financial Reporting and Qualitative Characteristics of Decision-Useful Financial Reporting Information" and a discussion paper titled "Preliminary Views, Conceptual Framework for Financial Reporting: The Reporting Entity."

Principles-Based Accounting Standards

The IASB uses a principles-based approach to standard setting by focusing on the underlying principles of accounting transactions rather than on specific "bright-line" rules. For example, rather than rely on such criteria as the 75 percent economic life threshold to determine whether to capitalize lease transactions, accountants should focus on the underlying question: Do such transactions transfer the risks and rewards of a lease from the lessor to the lessee? To answer such questions, the IASB looks to the Framework to provide recognition, measurement, and reporting requirements and tends to limit application guidance, thereby encouraging professional judgment.

> **RESEARCH TIPS**
>
> Standards limit application guidance to encourage a principles-based approach.

IFRS FUNDING, REGULATION AND ENFORCEMENT

Long-term funding commitments to the Foundation and IASB from approximately thirty countries and/or organizations are shown on the IASB Web site. The Foundation's goal is to have broad-based funding that is open-ended (no strings attached), compelling (shared by all), and country-specific (measurement based on GDP). As of 2009, a majority of the Foundation's funding is voluntary.

The IASB and IOSCO have agreed to a list of necessary accounting issues to address in a core set of international accounting standards for use in cross-border offerings and multiple listings. Ideally, establishing a core set of international accounting standards should reduce the costs of doing business and help companies raise capital across borders, streamline internal accounting and auditing functions for multinational companies, increase the efficiency of market regulations, and decrease the costs of international financial statement analysis and investment.

The SEC has expressed three conditions for accepting international accounting standards for all public companies:

1. IASB standards should include a core set of accounting pronouncements that constitute a comprehensive, generally accepted basis of accounting.

FIGURE 5-5 | INTERNATIONAL LINKS TO IFRS

Organization	Link
Committee of European Securities Regulators (CESA)	www.cesr-eu.org
Business Europe (formerly UNICE)	www.businesseurope.eu
European Union (EU)	europa.eu
Federation of European Accountants (FEE)	www.fee.be
International Accounting Standards Board (IASB)	www.IASB.org
International Association for Accounting Education Research	www.iaaer.org
International Federation of Accountants	web.ifac.org
International Organization of Securities Commissions (IOSCO)	www.IOSCO.org
Organization for Economic Cooperation and Development	www.oecd.org
World Trade Organization	www.wto.org

2. IASB standards must have high quality, result in comparability and transparency, and provide for full disclosure.

3. Rigorous interpretations and applications must exist for IASB standards.[7]

Because local regulations govern the preparation and issuance of financial statements in most countries, differences of form and content persist among countries. Figure 5-5 provides a list of organizations impacting the international environment. One objective of the IASB is to harmonize interests and converge this diversity. Although the IASB does not have the authority to require compliance with IFRSs, the success of international accounting harmonization and convergence will depend upon the recognition and support of interested groups.

> **QUICK FACTS**
>
> The EU (twenty-seven European countries) has adopted IFRS.

The European Union (EU) consists of twenty-seven member states (Belgium, Germany, France, Italy, Luxembourg, the Netherlands, Denmark, Ireland, United Kingdom, Greece, Spain, Germany, Austria, Finland, Sweden, the Czech Republic, Estonia, Cyprus, Latvia, Lithuania, Hungary, Malta, Poland, Slovenia, Slovakia, Bulgaria, and Romania). Two of the EU's objectives are to create a single market for goods in the EU and to have the EU become a world power.

The EU has taken several measures to ensure consistency with IFRS. For example, roundtables are utilized, and the Commission has established two committees, the Committee of European Securities Regulators (CESR) and the European Securities Committee (ESC), to act as advisory groups. Roundtables identify potential IFRS application issues. The roundtable collects views from member states through the various audit firms, standard setters, and other interested bodies because membership includes the IASB, CESR, IFRIC, EFRAG, FEE, Business Europe (formerly UNICE), audit firms, national standard setters, preparers, and the SEC. If divergence from an IFRS is identified, the roundtable makes a timely recommendation to the IFRIC to eliminate the divergence.

> **QUICK FACTS**
>
> The CESR was created to advise the EU on IFRS convergence.

In 2001, the CESR and EOC were established. These organizations have assisted the EU in adopting IFRS. CESR provides opinions as to the progress non-EU countries are making toward IFRS conversions and on agreements with the IASB. For instance, Japan has made two agreements with the IASB, as depicted in Figure 5-1. The CESR filed a report in March 2008 stating it had no reason to believe that Japan's Accounting Board

---

[7] M. Houston and A. Reinstein, "International Accounting Standards and Their Implications for Accountants and U.S. Financial Statement Users," *Review of Business* 22 (Spring/Summer 2001).

(ASBJ) could not complete convergence in the time stated and that the EU should then consider Japanese GAAP as equivalent.

The SEC Office of International Affairs (OIA) works with a global network of securities regulators and law enforcement to promote cross-border regulatory compliance. The OIA advises the Commission with respect to SEC and non-U.S. initiatives on cross-border activities of U.S. issuers and U.S. financial service providers. The OIA also examines the impact of SEC rules on foreign market participants.

IOSCO regulates international markets through its working committees: the Technical Committee, for developed markets, and Emerging Markets Committee, for less-developed markets. Each IOSCO committee is further divided into the following functional groups: disclosure, regulation, enforcement, and investment.

INTERNATIONAL FINANCIAL REPORTING STANDARDS (IFRS) RESEARCH

International accounting research has a complex environment with numerous accounting standards, rules, and recommended practices. This chapter focuses solely on IFRS research. A sound understanding of the IFRS hierarchy and available databases is needed, as described below.

IFRS Hierarchy

A hierarchy exists among the standards issued within and related to IFRS. This hierarchy shows the researcher where to begin the search for a solution to a problem or issue under review. Although all IFRS pronouncements have the same authority, IFRS application is hierarchical and the researcher may find that an IFRS does not contain the needed information to address the question. International Accounting Standards (IAS) No. 8, "Accounting Policies, Changes in Accounting Estimates and Errors," establishes a hierarchy for choosing IFRS accounting policies.

1. Apply specific IFRSs and consider relevant implementation guidance. If specific IFRSs do not apply, choose the relevant and reliable accounting policy from the listed sources in the following order:

    a. Apply other IFRSs that involve similar or related issues.

    b. Apply the IFRS Framework.

    c. Apply pronouncements of other standard-setting bodies that are consistent with the IFRS Framework.

Electronic International Financial Reporting Standards (eIFRS)

The eIFRS database enables researchers to obtain authoritative evidence to help solve their research questions more efficiently than using hardbound books. The IASB offers two subscription services for eIFRS. The first package is a comprehensive service that combines CD-ROMs with printed publications as they are issued. The second package is an online service with the HTML available in English and the PDF version available in nine languages (English, German, Spanish, French, Greek, Dutch, Italian, Russian, and Slovak). KPMG sponsors full access to the IASB's eIFRS online version for International Association for Accounting Education and Research (IAAER) members. Thus, students joining the IAAER greatly benefit from low-cost access to this database.

In researching international issues, similar questions arise as in researching national issues:

RESEARCH TIPS

Look to IFRS first when researching authorities.

RESEARCH TOOLS

ACL
AICPA reSOURCE
Codification
eIFRS
i2
Internet
LexisNexis Academic
RIA Checkpoint

QUICK FACTS

eIFRS is produced in nine languages.

FIGURE 5-6 | LINKS TO IFRS MATERIALS

Firm/Organization	Available IFRS Resource
AICPA	www.ifrs.com
BDO Seidman, LLP	www.bdo.com/ifrs
Deloitte	www.deloitte.com/dtt/section_node/0,1042,sid%253D177677,00.html
Ernst & Young	www.ey.com/global/content.nsf/International/Assurance_-_IFRS
Grant Thornton LLP	www.grantthornton.com/portal/site/gtcom/menuitem.91c078ed 5c0ef4ca80cd8710033841ca/? vgnextoid=bb444cfadd5d3110VgnVCM1000003a8314acRCRD
International Accounting Standards Board	www.IASB.org
KPMG	www.kpmgifrg.com
McGladrey & Pullen, LLP	www.rsmi.com/Website/web.nsf/pages/ D0C917E473C1D707EB1802573B50046EAB8
PricewaterhouseCoopers	www.pwc.com/extweb/service.nsf/docid/c9788403273e7a62852573fc0075c82b

- Where does one start the research?
- What are the possible search strategies?
- How does one move around in the database?
- When can one stop the research?

When deciding where to start the search, one sometimes goes to a secondary source to acquire an overview of a topic and a greater understanding of basic terminology. There are many resources available to learn about international financial reporting. To start, the researcher may want to look at the links provided in Figure 5-6. Each Web site contains an extensive amount of IFRS content and links to useful resources. Referring back to Figure 5-6, the researcher can view the IASB Web site link as well as Web site addresses for other important international organizations and bodies impacting IFRS.

The opening screen of eIFRS is shown in Figure 5-7. The researcher has a choice whether to enter eIFRS or eIFRS Together with Educational Guidance. The latter is compiled by the IASC Foundation's education staff and not yet approved by the IASB. The navigation panel seen on the left of the screen remains the same throughout the eIFRS session.

The eIFRS database is an electronic version of the manual research materials issued by the IASB. The eIFRS database also includes changes since the last edition; an introduction; the IASC Foundation Constitution; the Framework; a preface to IFRS; IFRS, IAS, IFRICs, and SICs; a glossary; and the due process handbooks for IASB and IFRIC. These sources, except for the glossary, were previously discussed in this chapter.

The first method to search the eIFRS is to use its glossary. The glossary contains terms from each of the authorities and references them by standard and paragraph number. This is an excellent method to research a topic. For instance, if the researcher wanted to know what a guaranteed residual value is, the researcher would scroll down to the term, as shown in Figure 5-8, Panel A, to find the definition and click the IAS 17.4 hyperlink. This will link the researcher to the full definition, as shown in Panel B. From there, the researcher becomes aware of the standard number and can research further, if necessary.

The second way to search in eIFRS is to go directly to the desired section by left-clicking on the standard. For instance, if the researcher is interested in determining how to calculate earnings per share, the researcher would left-click on IAS No 33: Earnings per Share, revealing the screen shot in Figure 5-9, Panel A. The researcher would then click on the measurement option shown in Panel B to find guidance on calculating EPS. Results indicate for basic EPS:

RESEARCH TIPS

When entering eIFRS, the researcher is entering an electronic version of the hardbound standards.

FIGURE 5-7 | eIFRS OPENING SCREEN

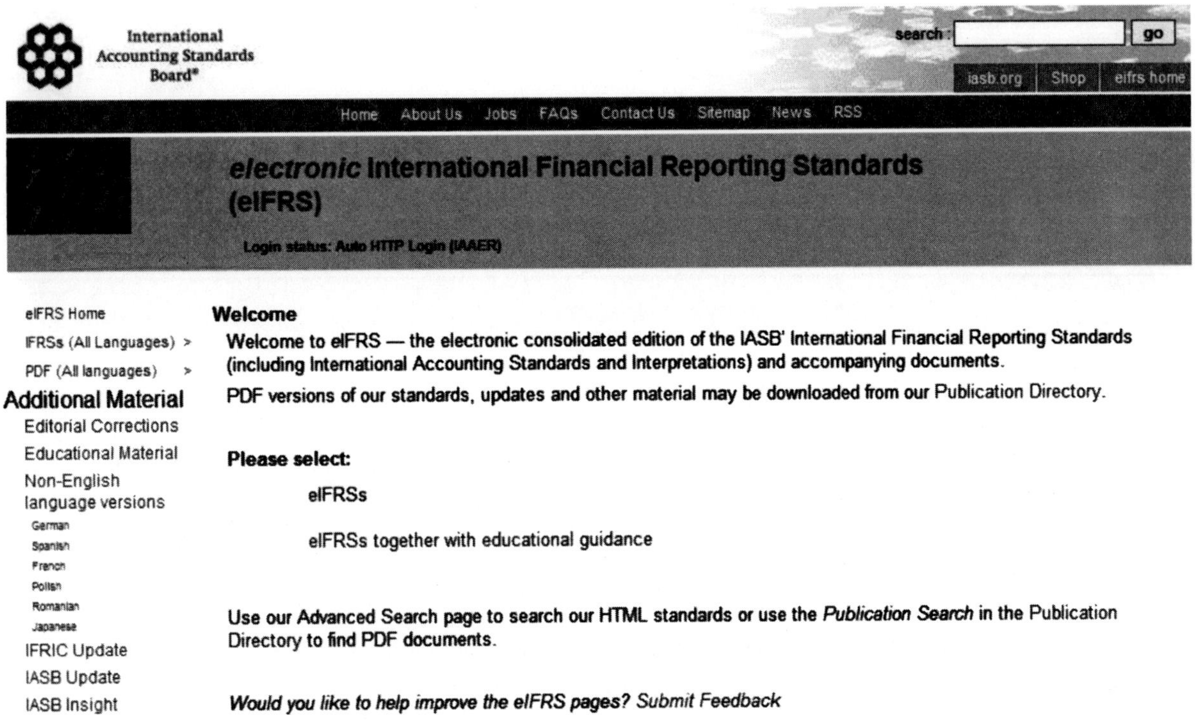

FIGURE 5-8 | GLOSSARY SEARCH

Panel A: Definition in Glossary

Guaranteed residual value is:

(a) For a lessee, that part of the residual value that is guaranteed by the lessee or by a party related to the lessee (the amount of the guarantee being the maximum amount that could, in any event, become payable); and

(b) for a lessor, that part of the residual value that is guaranteed by the lessee or by a third party unrelated to the lessor that is financially capable of discharging the obligations under the guarantee.

Panel B: After Clicking Hyperlink to Standard

Guaranteed residual value is:

(a) For a lessee, that part of the residual value that is guaranteed by the lessee or by a party related to the lessee (the amount of that guarantee being the maximum amount that could, in any event, become payable); and

(b) for a lessor, that part of the residual value that is guaranteed by the lessee or by a third party unrelated to the lessor that is financially capable of discharging the obligations under the guarantee.

Unguaranteed residual value is that portion of the residual value of the leased asset, the realization of which by the lessor is not assured or is guaranteed solely by a party related to the lessor.

Initial direct costs are incremental costs that are directly attributable to negotiating and arranging a lease, except for such costs incurred by manufacturer or dealer lessors.

| FIGURE 5-9 | IAS No. 33: Earnings per Share Search |

Panel A: Screen Shot after Clicking on IAS No. 33

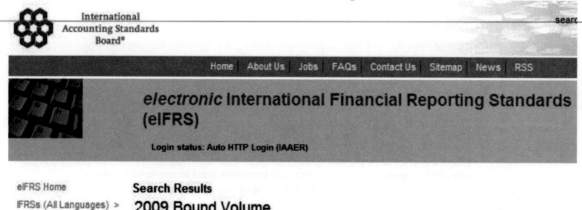

Panel B: Screen Shot after Clicking on IAS No. 33 Contents

Contents

FIGURE 5-10 | eIFRS ADVANCED SEARCH

Panel A: Advanced Search

All fields are optional

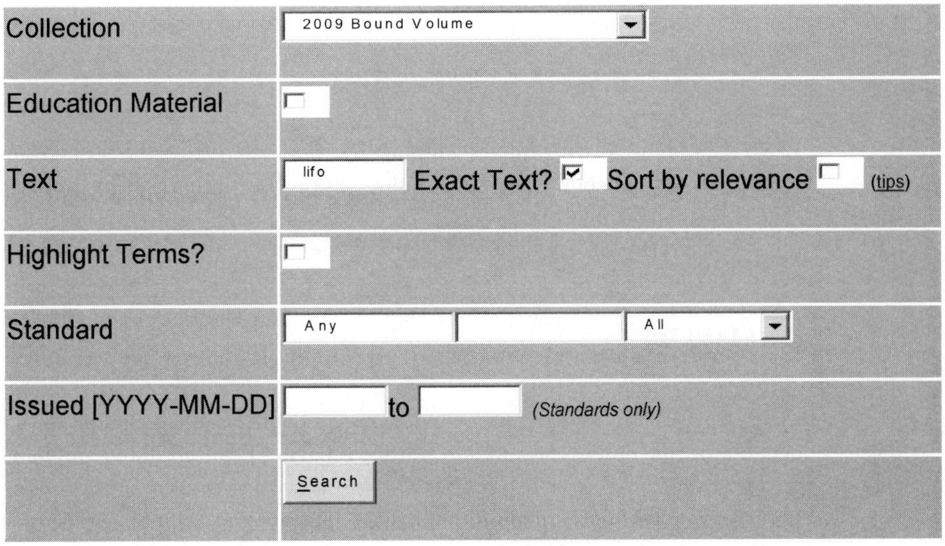

Collection	2009 Bound Volume ▾
Education Material	☐
Text	lifo Exact Text? ☑ Sort by relevance ☐ (tips)
Highlight Terms?	☐
Standard	Any All ▾
Issued [YYYY-MM-DD]	to (Standards only)
	Search

Search Tips for **Text** search (applicable to non-exact: match searches only)

- Enclose phrases in "double quotes"
- Sort by relevance only applicable when "text" is used also
- Use "+" to indicate words, phrases, or groups that must be present
- Use ">" to indicate important words
- Use "<" to indicate less important words
- Use "*" to indicate extensions to a word, that is, "financ*" matches "financial", "finance," and "finances"
- Use "('and')" to group subexpressions
- Searches are case-insensitive

Panel B: Results for LIFO Search

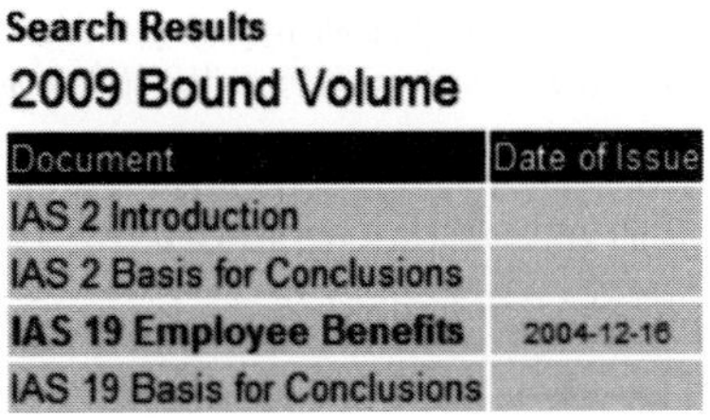

Search Results

2009 Bound Volume

Document	Date of Issue
IAS 2 Introduction	
IAS 2 Basis for Conclusions	
IAS 19 Employee Benefits	2004-12-16
IAS 19 Basis for Conclusions	

Basic earnings per share shall be calculated by dividing profit or loss attributable to ordinary equity holders of the parent entity (the numerator) by the weighted average number of ordinary shares outstanding (the denominator) during the period. (IAS 33, para. 10)

RESEARCH TIPS •

To limit search
results, use
quotations.

A third way to search within eIFRS is to use the advanced search function, as shown in Figure 5-10. The researcher can refine a search by volume, standard, issue date, relative importance of words by use of the > and < symbols, exact phrases by using quotations, or word stems by use of the * symbol. For instance, say a U.S.-based company is considering expanding into the U.K. market and would like to buy an already established business there. The U.S.-based company uses LIFO. Will that inventory method be permitted in the U.K.? The researcher types in "LIFO," and the results shown in Figure 5-10, Panel B, appear. Clicking on IAS 2 and scrolling down to paragraph 13 reveals that LIFO is not permitted under IFRS.

In deciding when to stop the research, consider the IFRS hierarchy. IFRSs, IASs, IFRICs, and SICs are primary authorities. If needed, use the Framework and other national GAAP in combination with other supporting authorities to support the research question when an answer does not exist within the highest levels. When the answer is not clear-cut, professional judgment is the key element in deciding when sufficient support exists to stop the research process.

SUMMARY

This chapter has presented an overview of the bodies that set standards in international accounting, the process of standard setting, the types of authoritative pronouncements, the meaning and hierarchy of IFRS, and IFRS research. Because the IASC's objectives include promoting a single set of high-quality standards and promoting convergence, IFRS is continuing to evolve. The IASB is carrying out the IASC's objectives by working on joint projects with various international standard-setting bodies, and accountants must research changes in pronouncements to keep abreast of current applications of principles.

DISCUSSION QUESTIONS

1. What is the predecessor Board/committee to the IASB? How many standards did the predecessor issue? What are the standards called?

2. Describe the due process procedures of the IASB in the establishment of a standard.

3. What is the IASB's Conceptual Framework? How is it used by the IASB? By a researcher? By a practitioner?

4. What level of authority does the Framework have?

5. Can the IASB enforce the use of its standards? If not, what entities can?

6. What is the Norwalk Agreement?

7. What is the IFRS hierarchy? Explain.

8. If you were a new country setting up an agreement with the IASB to converge to IFRS, which organization would examine whether you were in compliance with your agreement or not?

9. If a researcher could not find the answer to the research question in IFRS, where should the researcher look next?

10. What are the main goals/objectives of the IASC?

11. How are the IASC and IASB funded?

12. Explain the three conditions that the U.S.-SEC offered for accepting international accounting standards.

EXERCISES

1. Access the IASB Web site (www.iasb.org) and list three of its active projects.

2. Access the SEC Web site (www.sec.gov), click International Affairs, International Enforcement Assistance, and list the four types of enforcement cases.

3. Access the AICPA IFRS resource page (www.IFRS.com). What are two featured IFRS news items?

4. Access the IOSCO Web site (www. IOSCO.org), click the About IOSCO section, and list the working committees.

5. Access the European Union Web site (www.europa.eu). How many member states are present on the home page?

Using eIFRS

1. Open IFRS1: First Time Adoption of International Financial Reporting Standards.

   a. Which authority does this replace?

   b. Briefly summarize the introduction to paragraph 4.

2. How many IFRICs have been issued?

3. Open up an IAS or IFRS.

   a. What are the major organizational parts of the authority (placed in bold)?

   b. Compare your answer in (a) to the major organizational parts of an IFRIC or SIC.

   c. Are (a) and (b), for the most part, the same? If yes, how so? If not, how do they differ?

4. Use eIFRS to identify the accounting authority governing each of the following:

   a. Customer loyalty programs

   b. Operating lease incentives

   c. Operating segments

   d. Treasury share transactions

   e. Agriculture

5. Use eIFRS to determine how the accountant would conduct an impairment test for long-lived assets.

   a. Which authority describes the impairment test?

   b. What process did you use to find the authority?

   c. Briefly explain the impairment test.

6. Which authority discusses negative goodwill? How is it treated once identified?

7. Does IFRS have specific criteria (that is, bright lines) in determining whether to classify a lease as a capital lease?

8. Can the completed contracted method of revenue recognition be used under IFRS?

9. Use the glossary to locate the definition of a contingent liability.

   a. What is the definition?

   b. What standard is the definition found in?

10. Use the glossary to locate the definition of materiality.

    a. What it the definition?

    b. What authority can it be found in?

Other Research Databases and Tools

LEARNING OBJECTIVES

After completing this chapter, you should understand:

- Additional database research strategies.
- U.S. accounting search tools, especially commercial accounting databases.
- U.S. governmental accounting databases from GASB and FASAB.
- Financial research databases, especially S&P NetAdvantage and Mergent.
- Business research databases for business information, articles, and statistics.
- Massive legal databases, especially LexisNexis Academic.

This chapter begins by enhancing the five-step database research strategies as applied to many more databases beyond the Codification, IDEA, and eIFRS databases discussed in the previous two chapters. This chapter focuses on other databases and tools used by accountants and auditors for accounting, financial, business, and legal database research. The appendix provides a list of Web site addresses for the databases and Web sites mentioned in this chapter.

Caution: Database research presents challenges, but databases are constantly improving. Often, one does not have access to the best database to use for the desired information. When this is the case, use the best alternative database or source of information at your university. Although the databases presented are among the most popular at U.S. universities, these databases are licensed in many countries.

OTHER DATABASE RESEARCH STRATEGIES

Fundamental database research strategies for financial accounting research were presented in Chapter 4. This section builds on those strategies as applied to financial, business, and legal databases. Additional advice is presented for all the steps before the final step of communicating the research.

Step One: Define the Information Needed

Financial research searches may seek to acquire financial and operating ratios for a company and industry comparison. Accountants may need to help create an investment portfolio, review a company's earnings reports, explain part of an analyst report to a client, or understand a company's market share within an industry. Auditors might need to use a database to further develop analytical procedures to compare an audit client to other companies in its industry. Business information needs can arise for many reasons, such as the following:

RESEARCH TOOLS
ACL
AICPA reSOURCE
Codification
eIFRS
i2
Internet
LexisNexis Academic
RIA Checkpoint

- Understand the industry of a client to assess material risks to the business.
- Search for financial news that may affect the health of a business or determine which public companies have recently gone through reorganization.
- Inquire into the background of new corporate executives.
- Conduct research to better understand a company's new products and patents to assess their future financial health.

EXAMPLE: How does one identify the information needed for researching companies X.inc, Y.ltd, and Z.bv?

Discussion: The ending of companies' official names often gives one insight to the region or country of the company. For example, "inc" is commonly attached to U. S. companies, "ltd" is attached to British or Japanese companies, and "bv" is attached to Dutch companies. Inquire whether the company is a subsidiary of another company. If so, determine the structure of the related entities. Often, multinational companies have a more complex group structure and present a challenge in clarifying the chain of related organizations. It is sometimes helpful to examine the company's Web site. Most likely, one will need to use either a database having a directory of corporate affiliations or a hardbound reference treatise, such as *Who Owns Whom.*

If X.inc is a small company, one may need to check with the business registration in the appropriate state. Depending on the answers to these initial questions in identifying the companies, different informational needs and sources to search will arise.

Legal information is often sought by accountants on tax laws and likely regulatory changes or pending legislation. Subsequent chapters provide other examples of common searches by tax professionals and forensic auditors. Accountants may also use a legal database to find leading news sources to monitor important world issues, such as a Mideast crisis resulting in major oil price fluctuations.

Step Two: Determine the Sources to Search

Commercial databases have several advantages as compared to free Internet sources. The greatest advantage is subscription revenues to maintain and improve important database features, such as reliable sources of information, better search tools, helpful organizational structure, and more comprehensive retrieval systems to help the researcher search quickly through large amounts of data.

One often chooses the appropriate commercial database to use in financial, business, or tax law research by reviewing a database directory that describes the database parts. Consider the functionality of using the database as to its user-friendliness to retrieve relevant documents from a vast library or collection of data. Note that databases are often divided into many alternative products that are marketed for different target audiences. For example, country-specific products of a large database often exist.

Industry information can include such concerns as locating industry leaders, financial information and ratios, industry trends, and news about the industry. Major sources for analyzing large industries include government agencies and industry analyses. For newer and smaller industries, consider finding specialized databases, trade association material, or industry newsletters. To examine a specific industry, one may need the appropriate industry code; the North American Industry Classification System (NAICS), which became a six-digit code in 2007, or its predecessor, the Standard Industrial Classification (SIC). The SIC code is sometimes used, even though it was created years ago by the Office of Management and Budget. If necessary, visit the U.S. Census NAICS Web site to acquire industry codes.

Step Three: Use Search Techniques and Tools

Challenges in online research include finding all relevant authoritative sources, even if a document does not include the exact words specified in the search request. To assist the search, use powerful search tools. Such tools may include an advanced keyword search by segment searching or changing connector terms. Perform segment searching to restrict a search to a particular field, such as a headline, topic, or country. Employ connector terms to search for keywords within the same sentence, paragraph, or other specified region. Use a date restriction to help screen the search for relevant information.

Caution: For keyword searches, determine whether any limitations exist in the search engine. For example, check if the search engine merely reviews the abstract rather than the full text of the documents. Some databases will require quotation marks around any keyword phrase to limit the search. One might need to use a thesaurus or brainstorm to find alternative keywords in the documents having the same meaning as the original keywords. Often, one must try several keyword searches.

Reminder tools within a database include memory location, research history, and help tools. A memory tool for the database's precise location is often placed near the top of a search screen and displays the drill-down within the database to show one's precise location. A research history tool assists in recalling what prior searches were made in the database. A help tool is often invaluable to learn more or remind oneself about the particular database.

RESEARCH TIPS

Check for database search engine limitations.

Step Four: View the Results and Manage the Information

View the search results in citation, annotated or full text format. Search results on a company will sometimes merely provide an overview. Often, tabs on top or lists on the left side of the screen enable access to additional documents, such as detailed financial statements. Use diagnostic tools to view the data in different forms, such as descriptive graphics or charts. Manage the information by printing or downloading important results. If citations are downloaded, remember to reformat the citations used to the appropriate style.

Citation styles can differ depending on the particular profession or even journal. For business reports, use the APA citation style. In the text, cite the author's last name and publication year. In a list of references, the following basic format is used: author's last name and first name initial, (year), article title, journal, volume number (issue number), article pages. Minor style differences are common among various accounting and business journals. Observe the references used in example articles.

The citation typical for law review articles providing insights into tax or securities law concerns uses a very different approach. For example, law reviews are cited by author's full name, article title, volume number, abbreviated name of the journal, initial page number, and (year). The following example compares the APA style and law review citation style for the same article. Pay attention to details in a citation format, such as the punctuation and typeface used.

APA: Pearson. T. & G. Mark (2007). Investigations, Inspections and Audits in the Post-SOX Environment. *Nebraska. Law Review.* 86(1), 43–118.

Law: Thomas C. Pearson and Gideon Mark, *Investigations, Inspection/U and Audits in the Post-SOX Environment*, 86(1) NEB. L. Rev. 43 (2007).

RESEARCH TIPS

One often needs to reformat citations from a database to the appropriate style.

U.S. ACCOUNTING RESEARCH TOOLS

Research tools for accountants, as of mid-2009, consist mostly of commercial databases geared toward accounting needs and AICPA hardbound reference books. Commercial accounting databases provide access to authoritative and nonauthoritative accounting and auditing literature. The AICPA has a number of hardbound reference books, such as

Accounting Trends and Techniques, *Financial Report Surveys*, and the *Audit and Accounting Manual*.

Indices within a database are often helpful and convenient for finding nonauthoritative accounting literature, especially when it provides full text access to the articles. Thus, usage has declined for *Accounting and Tax Index*, a leading hardbound index of over one thousand publications on accounting or tax.

Commercial Accounting Databases

QUICK FACTS

Two commercial databases with accounting standards are RIA Checkpoint and CCH's Accounting Research Manager.

Two competing commercial accounting databases that can be used to enhance the effectiveness and efficiency of accounting and auditing research are RIA Checkpoint and CCH's Accounting Research Manager (ARM). RIA Checkpoint is primarily known as a tax database that has a financial research library available for a premium-cost subscription. In RIA Checkpoint, one can personalize the home screen. An example of a personalized screen for accountants is presented in Figure 6-1. Similarly, an example of the information provided for those in corporate finance is presented in Figure 6-2.

CCH's ARM provides insightful interpretations on GAAP, GAAS, and SEC rules and maintains one's currency in these topics. This database includes complete authoritative texts of major U.S. and international accounting standards, AICPA technical practice aids, and AICPA Audit and Accounting Guides for various industries. ARM's organization for the international accounting authorities is shown in Figure 6-3. ARM's organization under the table of contents search method is shown for international accounting authorities in Figure 6-4. An index of accounting topics is also available in ARM, as shown in Figure 6-5.

FIGURE 6-1 RIA CHECKPOINT FINANCIAL LIBRARY FOR ACCOUNTING & AUDITING (REARRANGED ORDER)

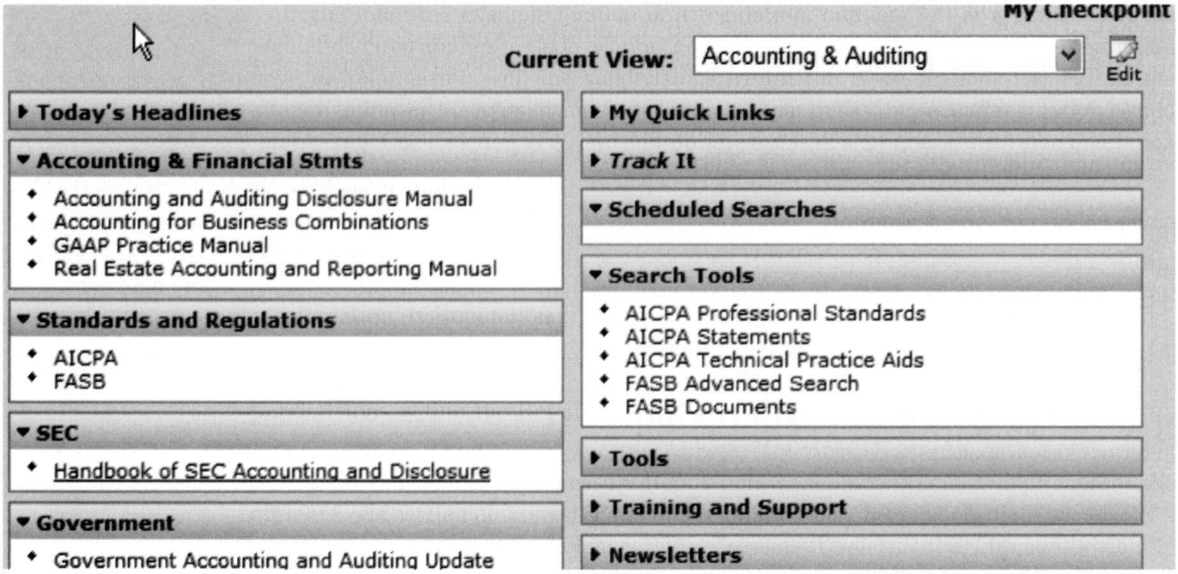

FIGURE 6-2   RIA CHECKPOINT FINANCIAL LIBRARY FOR CORPORATE FINANCE
(REARRANGED ORDER)

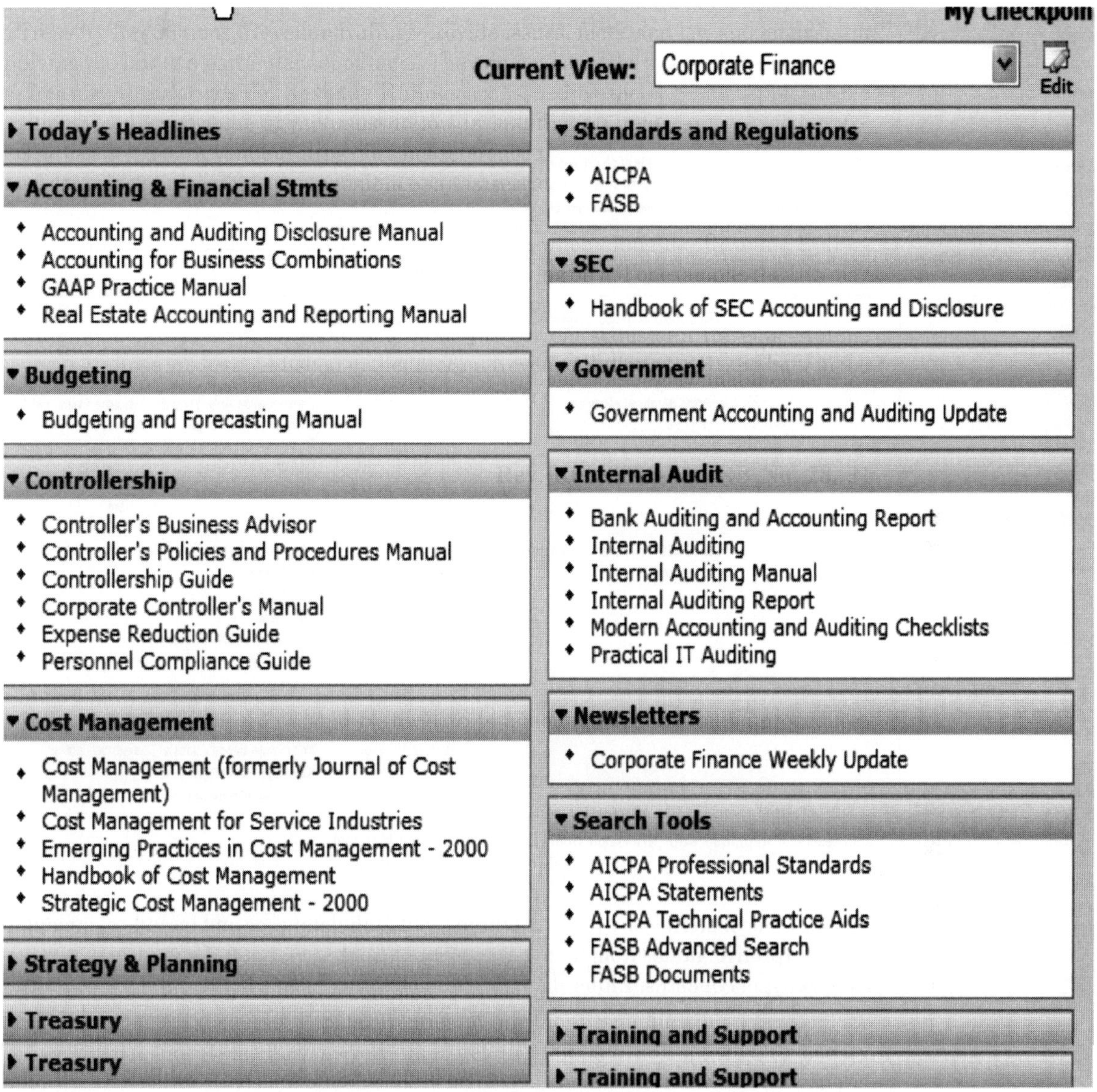

Current View: Corporate Finance ▾   Edit

My Checkpoint

▸ **Today's Headlines**

▾ **Accounting & Financial Stmts**
* Accounting and Auditing Disclosure Manual
* Accounting for Business Combinations
* GAAP Practice Manual
* Real Estate Accounting and Reporting Manual

▾ **Budgeting**
* Budgeting and Forecasting Manual

▾ **Controllership**
* Controller's Business Advisor
* Controller's Policies and Procedures Manual
* Controllership Guide
* Corporate Controller's Manual
* Expense Reduction Guide
* Personnel Compliance Guide

▾ **Cost Management**
* Cost Management (formerly Journal of Cost Management)
* Cost Management for Service Industries
* Emerging Practices in Cost Management - 2000
* Handbook of Cost Management
* Strategic Cost Management - 2000

▸ **Strategy & Planning**

▸ **Treasury**

▸ **Treasury**

▾ **Standards and Regulations**
* AICPA
* FASB

▾ **SEC**
* Handbook of SEC Accounting and Disclosure

▾ **Government**
* Government Accounting and Auditing Update

▾ **Internal Audit**
* Bank Auditing and Accounting Report
* Internal Auditing
* Internal Auditing Manual
* Internal Auditing Report
* Modern Accounting and Auditing Checklists
* Practical IT Auditing

▾ **Newsletters**
* Corporate Finance Weekly Update

▾ **Search Tools**
* AICPA Professional Standards
* AICPA Statements
* AICPA Technical Practice Aids
* FASB Advanced Search
* FASB Documents

▸ **Training and Support**

▸ **Training and Support**

Various libraries exist in ARM. The SEC library includes such issuances as SEC rules and regulations, financial reporting releases, staff accounting bulletins, SEC practice guides, background materials, and SEC forms. Figure 6-6 shows a partial list of standards through SEC regulations. The government library includes government accounting literature, such as GASB statements and interpretations for state and local government accounting, and auditing materials, such as the General Accountability Office's "Yellow Book" auditing standards for federal entities and government contracts.

FIGURE 6-3 CCH ACCOUNTING RESEARCH MANAGER (OPENING SCREEN)

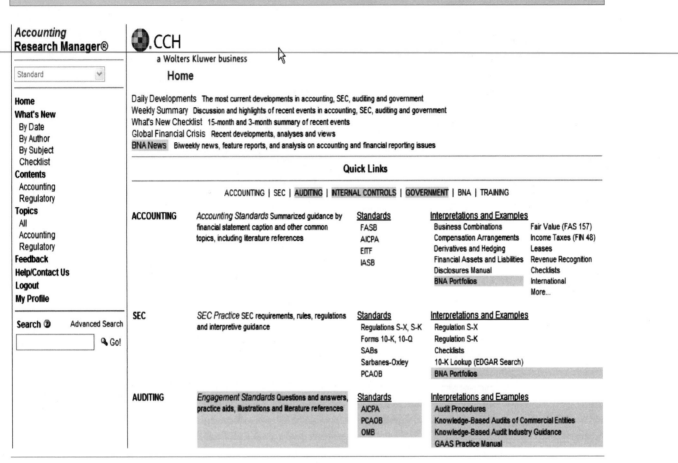

Reference materials are provided throughout both databases and include commentary and interpretive guides from financial reporting experts. Figure 6-7 shows an example of a checklist of concerns. Either database promotes currency not only through a news area in the database, but also by a weekly or daily e-mail newsletter to subscribers highlighting key developments. For example, ARM highlights key developments, new authorities, and proposals from the FASB, AICPA, SEC, EITF, IASB, PCAOB, IIA, COSO, GASB, GAO, and OMB. Figure 6-8 illustrates the new development tool in the context of the PCAOB in April 2009.

AICPA's Reference Books

Accounting Trends and Techniques shows current practice on a particular accounting issue and how companies of various sizes in a wide range of industries have complied with professional standards for financial reporting purposes. This information arose from an annual survey of accounting practices. Reporting practices of selected companies are presented, along with significant trends in reporting practices. This AICPA treatise was more important under old U.S. GAAP, when accounting practices occupied level D of the five-level GAAP hierarchy. However, *Accounting Trends and Techniques* is expected to adjust to FASB's new codification and still provide value in the form of nonauthoritative examples.

QUICK FACTS

Commercial accounting databases enhance the effectiveness and efficiency of accounting and auditing research.

FIGURE 6-4	CCH ACCOUNTING RESEARCH MANAGER, EXAMPLE OF TABLE OF CONTENTS FROM THE IASB

Accounting
Research Manager®

[Standard ⌄]

Home
What's New
  By Date
  By Author
  By Subject
  Checklist
Contents
  Accounting
  Regulatory
Topics
  All
  Accounting
  Regulatory
Feedback
Help/Contact Us
Logout
My Profile

Search ⑦   Advanced Search
[   ] 🔍 Go!

⬤.CCH
a Wolters Kluwer business

Contents - Accounting

    🔖 Expand All   🔖 Collapse All   ⬆ Page Up

⊞ **Accounting Research Manager**
⊞ **AICPA - American Institute of Certified Public Accountants**
⊞ **EITF - Emerging Issues Task Force**
⊞ **FASB - Financial Accounting Standards Board**
⊟ **IASB - International Accounting Standards Board**
    ⊞ **Framework of IAS Financial Statements**
    ⊞ **International Financial Reporting Standards**
    ⊞ **International Financial Reporting Standards - Issued But Not Yet Effective**
    ⊞ **International Financial Reporting Interpretations Committee**
    ⊞ **International Financial Reporting Interpretations Committee - Superseded**
    ⊞ **International Accounting Standards**
    ⊞ **International Accounting Standards - Issued But Not Yet Effective**
    ⊞ **International Accounting Standards - Superseded**
    ⊞ **SIC - Standing Interpretations Committee**
    ⊞ **SIC - Standing Interpretations Committee - Superseded**
    ⊞ **Staff Implementation Guidance**
    ⊞ **Staff Implementation Guidance - Superseded**
    ⊞ **Proposal Stage Literature**
    ⊞ **Newsletters and Releases**

The list above is limited to 200 lines. Use the Page Up and Page Down butt

    🔖 Expand All   🔖 Collapse All   ⬆ Page Up

Financial Reporting Surveys by the AICPA provided a continuing series of surveys that supplemented the overview that *Accounting Trends and Techniques* provided. The surveys show in detail how companies in a wide range of industries disclose specific accounting and reporting questions in their financial reports.

The AICPA *Audit and Accounting Manual* provides guidance and extensive examples for conducting an audit. The manual explains and illustrates the procedures for an audit engagement. Auditing topics in the manual include engagement planning, audit approach, and internal control structure. Administrative guidance includes supervision, correspondence, working papers, and quality control aids. Accountants' reports are covered as well as compilations and reviews. The staff of the AICPA has authored the manual and provided reference to the AICPA's pronouncements. As audit software programs continue to improve, however,

QUICK FACTS

AICPA reference books provide examples addressing specific accounting and reporting issues.

FIGURE 6-5   CCH ACCOUNTING RESEARCH MANAGER, EXAMPLE OF TOPICS IN ACCOUNTING

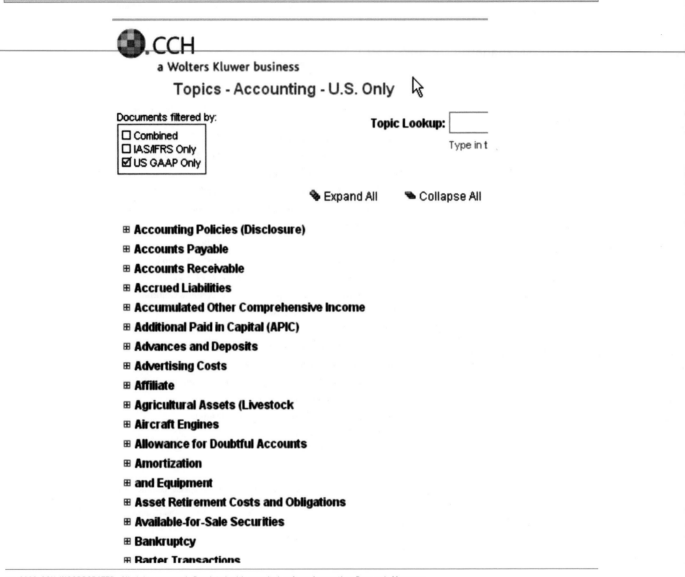

software guidance on audits has begun to serve as an alternative to this historically valuable manual.

U.S. GOVERNMENT ACCOUNTING DATABASES

Use the Government Accounting Research System (GARS) for researching U.S. accounting issues for state and local governments. When researching U.S. federal government entities' accounting issues, use the codification of authorities by the Federal Accounting Standards Advisory Board (FASAB). As of 2009, both sources of government accounting continue to use a hierarchy of authorities that the accounting researcher must understand.

FIGURE 6-6 | CCH ACCOUNTING RESEARCH MANAGER, EXAMPLE OF SEC REGULATIONS

Print View ⑦ Linkages ⑦ Show URL ⑦ What's New ⑦

.CCH
a Wolters Kluwer business

Accounting Research Manager ® - Standard

Accounting Research Manager
  SEC Practice\07. SEC Rules, Regulations and Releases
  Contents

Table of Contents

<u>Link</u>	<u>Title</u>
▢	Regulation A - Conditional Small Issues Exemption
▢	Regulation AB - Asset-Backed Securities
▢	Regulation AC - Analyst Certification
▢	Regulation BTR - Blackout Trading Restriction
▢	Regulation C - General Requirements of 1933 Act Registrants
▢	Regulation D - Limited Offer and Sale of Securities Without Registration
▢	Regulation FD - Fair Disclosure
▢	Regulation G
▢	Regulation S-B - Small Business Disclosure Requirements
▢	Regulation S-K - Non Financial Statement Requirements
▢	Regulation S-T - Electronic Submission Rules (EDGAR)
▢	Regulation S-X - Financial Statement Requirements
▢	Regulation S - Offshore Offers and Sales
▢	Regulation 12B - Registration and Reporting - 1934 Act

GASB's Government Accounting Research System (GARS)

GARS provides comprehensive information for state and local government accounting. While a summary of GASB's accounting standards is freely available on the Web, access to the GARS database is limited to subscribers. Individual standards, however, are available for purchase at the GASB Web site.

A GARS database demonstration is available at the GASB Web site (under Publications). The GARS demonstration opening screen is shown in Figure 6-9. Several major InfoBases are provided in GARS, including original pronouncements, current text, EITF abstracts, staff implementation guides by the GASB staff, and a topical index. Although GARS' current text provides GASB's codification of accounting standards, as shown in Figure 6-10, a hierarchy of authorities continues to exist for state and local accounting.

RESEARCH TIPS

The GARS database is structured similarly to the old FARS database, with Original Pronouncements and current text, but also includes government accounting materials.

FIGURE 6-7 | CCH ACCOUNTING RESEARCH MANAGER, EXAMPLE OF SECONDARY SOURCES (CHECKLISTS)

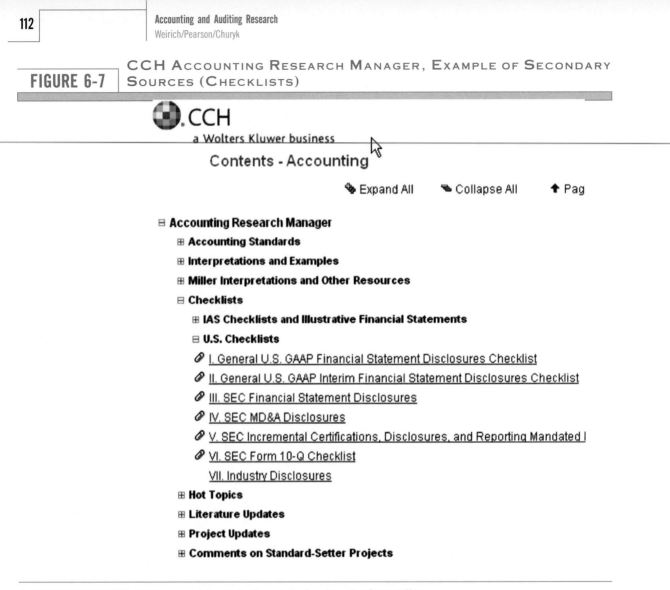

● **CCH**
a Wolters Kluwer business

Contents - Accounting

🐾 Expand All   🐾 Collapse All   ⬆ Pag

⊟ **Accounting Research Manager**
   ⊞ **Accounting Standards**
   ⊞ **Interpretations and Examples**
   ⊞ **Miller Interpretations and Other Resources**
   ⊟ **Checklists**
      ⊞ **IAS Checklists and Illustrative Financial Statements**
      ⊟ **U.S. Checklists**
          ⌗ I. General U.S. GAAP Financial Statement Disclosures Checklist
          ⌗ II. General U.S. GAAP Interim Financial Statement Disclosures Checklist
          ⌗ III. SEC Financial Statement Disclosures
          ⌗ IV. SEC MD&A Disclosures
          ⌗ V. SEC Incremental Certifications, Disclosures, and Reporting Mandated I
          ⌗ VI. SEC Form 10-Q Checklist
          VII. Industry Disclosures
   ⊞ **Hot Topics**
   ⊞ **Literature Updates**
   ⊞ **Project Updates**
   ⊞ **Comments on Standard-Setter Projects**

FASAB Codification of Authorities

A codification of authorities exists for U.S. federal accounting, including concepts, standards, interpretations, and technical releases. As of 2009, the FASAB's Codification consists merely of a non-searchable text document. The FASAB Codification is freely available at its Web site. The table of contents for the FASAB Codification's is illustrated in Figure 6-11.

The FASAB's discussion of authorities first presents concepts to guide the FASAB as it deliberates on specific issues for new standards. Presented next are the standards, the Original Pronouncements. FASAB's Interpretations clarify the original meaning of the standards, add definitions, or provide other guidance that is generally narrow in scope. These FASAB authorities are organized similarly to GARS for state and local accounting, including a current text and other information, such as exposure drafts.

A four-level hierarchy of accounting authorities is still used for federal GAAP, as of 2009. Level A, the highest level of federal GAAP, arises from FASAB statements and interpretations. Historically, the researcher needed to use the FARS database to access

QUICK FACTS

U.S. government accounting continues to use a hierarchy of authorities.

| FIGURE 6-8 | CCH ACCOUNTING RESEARCH MANAGER, EXAMPLE OF "WHAT'S NEW" (PCAOB) |

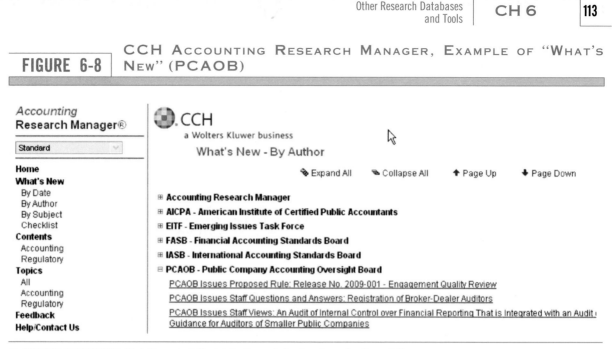

most Level B authorities, FASB authorities specifically made applicable to federal entities by the FASAB. In 2009, the FASAB is scrambling to codify that information into its own database. Additional Level B authorities arise from the FASAB technical bulletins and external sources, as determined by the FASAB.

The lowest two levels of authorities for federal GAAP are less used. Level C includes the FASAB technical releases, created by its Accounting and Auditing Policy

| FIGURE 6-9 | GARS TUTORIAL OPENING SCREEN |

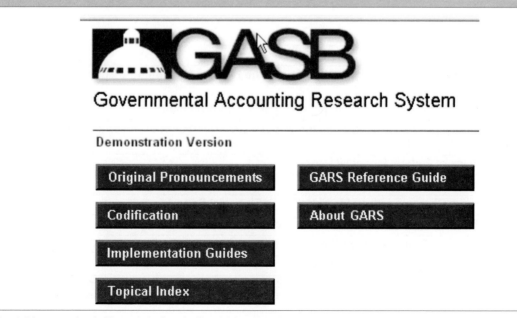

FIGURE 6-10   GASB ORIGINAL PRONOUNCEMENTS

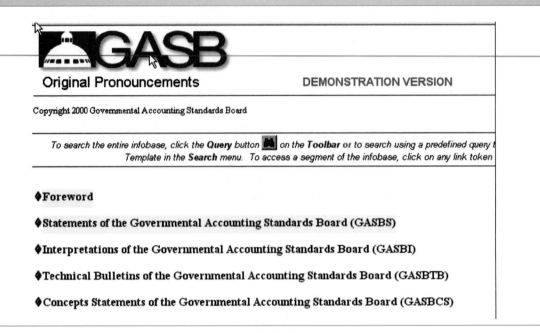

GASB

Original Pronouncements   DEMONSTRATION VERSION

Copyright 2000 Governmental Accounting Standards Board

*To search the entire infobase, click the **Query** button 🔍 on the **Toolbar** or to search using a predefined query Template in the **Search** menu. To access a segment of the infobase, click on any link token*

◆**Foreword**

◆**Statements of the Governmental Accounting Standards Board (GASBS)**

◆**Interpretations of the Governmental Accounting Standards Board (GASBI)**

◆**Technical Bulletins of the Governmental Accounting Standards Board (GASBTB)**

◆**Concepts Statements of the Governmental Accounting Standards Board (GASBCS)**

GARS material was reproduced with permission from the Financial Accounting Foundation.

FIGURE 6-11   FASAB PRONOUNCEMENTS AS AMENDED, AS OF JUNE 30, 2008, TABLE OF CONTENTS

Table of Contents

Contents

Executive Summary

Federal Financial Reporting and the Role of the Federal Accounting Standards Advisory Board

The Federal Accounting and Financial Reporting Environment

Accountability and Users' Information Needs—the Foundation of Governmental Financial Reporting

Objectives of Federal Financial Reporting

Balancing Costs and Benefits in Recommending Standards

Qualitative Characteristics of Information in Financial Reports

How Accounting Supports Federal Financial Reporting

How Financial Reporting Supports Reporting on Operating Performance

Appendix A: Basis for Conclusions

Appendix B: Users' Information Needs Addressed by Federal Financial Reporting

Committee. Level C also contains approved materials from the AcSEC Practice Bulletins, available from the AICPA ReSOURCE database. Level D consists of all other accounting literature on federal GAAP, which arises from a variety of sources.

FINANCIAL RESEARCH DATABASES

Accountants regularly perform financial research, sometimes as investment or business advisors. They investigate such concerns as:

- The consolidation policies used to account for less than 100 percent-owned subsidiaries.
- The balance sheet presentation of unfunded pension liabilities.
- Examples of dual-dated audit reports.
- The size ranking of a company, used for executive compensation studies.
- Pending government investigations against a company.
- Information to prepare for vendor or partner negotiations.
- Ratio analysis for credit ratings.
- Opportunities and financial issues arising from patents.

This chapter's discussion on databases focuses mostly on the unique advantages of several popular major databases for financial, business, and legal research. Financial research databases include S&P NetAdvantage, Mergent Online, and Thomson Research. Some databases provide better access to data on such items as private companies, bonds, daily stock prices, financial ratio analysis, industry comparisons of companies, or foreign companies. Other databases may excel in investment analyst reports, historical corporate data, corporate histories, mutual funds, or financial press news.

U.S. public company data and information is widely available. However, the depth of coverage of public companies varies by database. For example, some show segmental information on public company financials and other such items as business property, subsidiaries, long-term debt, and bond ratings. Results from searching public companies in a financial database usually initially provide summary financial information.

Caution: Examine whether the database also offers an option to view the complete financial information. The number of years for viewing the financial information in a database may vary, with three to five years as the most typical.

Standard & Poor's (S&P) NetAdvantage

The opening screen of S&P's NetAdvantage provides a handful of guides on the bottom right to using the database. Most of the screen features separate news on the market, bonds, the economy, and industries. The right side of the opening screen has quick links to industry surveys, investment publications, investment advisory reports, and S&P indices. Investment publications include bond reports, fund reports, security dealers, and others shown in the drop-down box.

An example of a S&P index is S&P's 500, which represents stocks selected by S&P as leading companies in various industries and is often used as a benchmark for judging money managers. From the S&P overview of the S&P 500, one is provided with various choices on the left side of the screen, such as viewing S&P 500 vital statistics.

Private companies are those not listed on a stock exchange, so they do not need to file with the SEC. Private company information is extensively provided in both S&P's NetAdvantage, as well as the legal database LexisNexis. S&P's NetAdvantage also provides information on public companies, market news, investment analyst reports, industry surveys, and more, as shown in its opening screen. The database includes a dozen financial and investment publications providing insight for company research and analysis, such as the *Bond Guide*, *Mutual Fund Report*, *Dividend Record*, and *S&P's Corporation Records*. Use the tabs near the top of the screen in S&P's NetAdvantage to go to the type of investment at issue, such as company research.

EXAMPLE: Acquire financial information about Cargill, a private company headquartered in Minnesota.

Discussion: Select the tab for company research in S&P's NetAdvantage. In the box for company profile, select "register private company." Enter "Cargill" in the blank box and search. The search results display five companies that include the name Cargill. Check the most logical choice (Cargill Incorporated), and verify that its headquarters are in Minnesota. Notice that the summary data displays such items as sales, employees, the primary and secondary NAIC codes, and an extensive list of officers. Notice that the left side of the screen provides choices for more detailed information, such as financial information. Do not stop at the summary information.

Powerful search functions exist in S&P's NetAdvantage that assist in more fully using the database. Search across multiple databases simultaneously to identify companies that meet specific criteria for analysis. Select from hundreds of database reports and charts. Make comparisons within the industry by choosing from various comparative reports. Find statistics for companies in the portfolio. Create public information books to customize the content desired in a report. Although S&P NetAdvantage is relatively easy to use, view the online help to learn more about reporting, charting for comparisons to major stock indices, and other specialized activities.

EXAMPLE: Determine what major private companies in Honolulu are audited by KPMG, in order to prepare for a job interview in Hawaii.

Discussion: Under the advance search option in S&P's NetAdvantage, identify the company city as Honolulu. For the accountant, enter "KPMG" and change the connector to "begins with," knowing that KPMG might have a different official name, such as KPMG LLP. The search results reveal the names of six major private companies in Honolulu having KPMG as their auditor. *Caution:* Before starting a new search, select the Clear button.

Bond information is available in S&P NetAdvantage in spreadsheet format. The descriptive information on each bond includes the type of bond issuance, its rating, and whether it's callable. The numerical data usually includes coupon rate, yield to maturity, sales price, and more.

EXAMPLE: Examine the bonds for General Motors to determine to what extent bondholders can convert the bonds to equity.

Discussion: On the right side of the opening screen, go to the drop-down box for Publication and select "Bond Report." Change the search drop-down box from ticker (stock market abbreviation) to company name. (If you know that the ticker for General Motors is GM, enter the requested name.) Select the arrow across for go. Examine the spreadsheet information, looking primarily under the "callable" column. One can acquire additional information about the particular bond such as a chart of the bond as compared to the S&P index for bonds, the issuance profile, key statistics, and the name of the underwriter.

Mergent Online

Public company snapshot information in Mergent Online is rather brief. However, notice that the tabs on top of the results screen provide access to specialized information, such as company financials, company history, joint ventures, and property locations. The company financials have important drop-down boxes allowing you to select from three to fifteen years of annual and quarterly financial information, the particular financial statement of interest, and alternative currencies with which to view the financial statements. A help option in the upper right of the screen addresses just the particular tab selected rather than providing options as to how to maximize use of the database.

Daily stock prices of public companies for the most recent day of trading (close, high, and low) and the yearly high and low are presented in Mergent Online after you select a company and choose quotes on the left side of the screen. Many other databases also provide current daily stock price information, such as S&P NetAdvantage, Factiva, and Thomson Research. Financial software also exists to assist in collecting data on stock prices and tracking an investment portfolio. Historical stock price information is available in the academic database Wharton Research Data Services (WRDS) in its Center for Research in Security Prices (CRSP) database. CRSP provides historical monthly and daily stock prices, as well as various market and benchmark indices.

Financial ratio analysis on companies is best provided in Mergent Online, LexisNexis Academic, or Factiva. Ratio analysis is often performed to determine profitability, liquidity, and solvency. Profitability ratios measure a company's success in using its assets and investors' equity. Liquidity ratios measure the company's ability to supply the cash necessary to pay maturing debt and meet other business needs. Solvency ratios measure whether a business can survive long term. If you are rusty on financial ratios, review this important topic. Unlike some databases, Mergent Online places the ratios under categories, such as profitability, liquidity, debt management, and asset management. However, Mergent Online provides only about twenty ratios, far fewer than some databases, such as the legal database LexisNexis Academic.

Industry comparisons of companies are generated in a customized report in Mergent Online. To perform such a comparison, on the research screen identify all companies, either by name or stock ticker symbol, separating them with commas. The search results will display basic information about each company, such as the SIC code for its industry classification. After confirming that these are the desired companies for comparison, open the analyst list and select "Create Company Report." Report criteria selections for categories and subcategories appear in drop-down boxes. Add the desired items to the report and select the years for the report before finishing by choosing "Create Report." Either print or download the comparison in order to place it into a spreadsheet.

Foreign companies (non-U.S. companies) included in Mergent Online actually outnumber U.S. companies. The twenty thousand foreign companies included represent 95 percent of non-U.S. global capital markets. However, if you are not able to check the box for private companies, then your library subscription is limited to just public companies. "Listed companies", rather than public companies, is the term for companies listed on a stock exchange in some countries. Two alternative databases from which to obtain significant foreign company information are S&P NetAdvantage and Thomson Research.

Thomson Research

Analyst reports included in Thomson Research historically provided the database with a competitive advantage. However, in 2008, major investment firms restricted access to their analyst reports. Analyst reports provide more comprehensive review of a company

RESEARCH TOOLS
ACL
AICPA reSOURCE
Codification
eIFRS
i2
Internet
LexisNexis Academic
RIA Checkpoint

RESEARCH TIPS

Use Mergent Online for daily stock prices, financial ratio analysis, industry comparisons of companies, and foreign company information.

than financial ratio comparisons. They closely examine other parts of the SEC filings on a company, such as financial statement footnotes and management discussion and analysis. The reports analyze the implications of new developments in the company, such as a change in management or the release of a major new product. Alternative databases to obtain some free analyst reports include Morningstar, Business and Company Resource Center, and LexisNexis Academic, all discussed shortly.

Historical corporate data, back to 1962 in some cases, is the real unique advantage of Thomson Research. Most databases start their corporate records in the mid-1990s when the SEC first required companies to submit electronic filings. Thomson Research provides an in-depth analysis on about one thousand companies that includes ownership data and identifies institutional investors. The earnings section has records for thirty thousand or more active companies. The content profile presented for a company usually includes financial data, SEC filings, the auditor's report, accounting practices, and financial ratios. The database includes some private companies from both the United States and more than fifty countries.

Nonfinancial information in Thomson Research include such topics as an overview of markets and technology, companies' joint ventures, licensing agreements, personnel changes, product announcements, and reports from Worldscope. Thomson Research offers such time-saving functions as spreadsheet-ready financial information and project tracking.

Caution: This publisher has a history of changing names for its databases and altering content for university subscriptions.

Other Financial Databases and Sources

Business and Company Resource Center Extensive corporate histories, insider buying and selling activity, and business journal news and analysis are among the items that stand out in this database. About three thousand company histories and fifteen hundred company chronologies are available for the more prominent global businesses. Listings for 465,000 U.S. and international companies are provided in the Resource Center, using financial content from Thomson. Extensive essays are provided for about one thousand industries. The database also includes industry statistics, market share reports, and company rankings.

Company comparisons based on asset or revenue size is often used for determining appropriate executive compensation for similarly sized organizations. The most famous ranking is the Fortune 500 companies. The Resource Center provides an option for the rankings of each company. Comparisons are also commonly used for trend analysis, which analyzes information over time. The database is more geared toward business students. For example, the Resource Center also helps one prepare a SWOT (strengths, weaknesses, opportunities, and threats) analysis of a company.

Hoover's Online Corporate group structures, industry information, and market intelligence are especially noteworthy in Hoover's Online. Histories for private and public companies are also available. Hoover's can also help match a specific product to a company. Hoover's Online attempts to provide objective information on companies by not relying on issuances from a company's corporate staff. Hoover's is a subsidiary of Dun & Bradstreet. The database Web site provides a weaker free sample version that doubles as a sales tool for individual purchases of Hoover's Reports. Note that some financial data from Hoover's is provided in LexisNexis Academic, discussed later with the legal databases.

Morningstar Investment Research Center Mutual fund data is the historical advantage of Morningstar. In Morningstar, complete reports are offered on about two thousand mutual funds and summary reports on over ten thousand. Alternative databases for mutual fund information are S&P's NetAdvantage, WRDS, and Value Line. Although Value Line offers the advantage of selecting mutual funds based on investment objectives, universities are less likely to subscribe to it than to Morningstar. All of these databases also provide information on public companies. Insider trading information, charts, and some analyst reports are also provided in Morningstar.

A glossary or dictionary is a common search tool in many databases. It often helps to understand various terms and abbreviations commonly used in the database, such as *beta*, a measurement of funds sensitivity to changes in the market. The glossary sometimes provides insight into common phrases, such as *due diligence*. Using the right terminology in accounting is particularly important.

Factiva Financial press news from leading publications, such as the *Wall Street Journal* and *Financial Times*, are provided in Factiva. This database offers the advantage of a Google-like search. Other advantages are its wealth of foreign language newspapers, as well as a large quantity of searchable newspapers. The Company and Industry sub-database provides a quick company overview with comparison reports. The Historical Market Data Center provides over twenty-five years worth of pricing on stocks, bonds, mutual funds, and global market indices.

Other well-regarded financial databases exist. These include Dialog, ORBIS, and country-specific databases. However, these databases are often not available through university subscriptions.

RESEARCH TIPS

Factiva is useful in providing the financial press and many foreign language newspapers.

Financial Research Challenges

Physically visiting the library and using various valuable hardbound sources is a challenge to overcome in the Electronic Age. Examine notable hardbound business services. Internationally, Dun & Bradstreet, Moody's (now Mergent) and Standard & Poor's (S&P) are the leading publishers of such reference books. For example, S&P offers Value Line Investment Service, which shows a list of major companies in an industry and provides an analysis of each company. Dun & Bradstreet has the Million-Dollar Directory to check a listing of U.S. companies.

Hedge fund and private equity financial data is hard to acquire because it is generally not released to the public. Hedge funds and private equity funds are important because one-third of the transactions on leading stock markets are estimated to arise from these investment vehicles. As of 2009, hedge funds and private equity firms rarely need to provide financial information. Thus, the limited databases that include data on many hedge funds and private equity firms are still very expensive.

Mergers and acquisition (M&A) data also requires specialty databases that few universities can afford. However, the legal databases provide some M&A information. One can find articles on M&A and other important topics in the financial press, as discussed shortly. One should also search the Web for government, industry, and private studies on these complex topics.

RESEARCH TIPS

Specialized financial research may require access to other, expensive databases.

Academic accounting research presents challenges, but database and Web sources exist to help. WRDS for academia provides a combination of databases relevant for conducting empirical research academic studies for accounting, finance, banking, or economics. For example, the WRDS database includes Compustat, a database that segments items in the quarterly and annual financial statements back to the 1960s or 1980s, depending on the data. The Accounting Research Network, part of the highly respected Social Science Research Network on the Web, provides abstracts of the latest academic research from leading academic researchers. Financial Web site information geared for academics is available via a Web site at Ohio State University.

To analyze professional accounting concerns, two databases in WRDS (Audit Analytics and Risk Metrics) are particularly relevant. Audit Analytics provides data on such items as financial restatements, internal control disclosures, auditor changes, and auditor fees. It provides specialized data, such as all auditor reports for benefit plans as found in 11-K filings with the SEC. Risk Metrics provides data related to such topics as corporate governance, proxy voting, and corporate responsibility issues.

Specialized research often requires additional knowledge about the topic for successful research, such as credit information on companies, bankrupt companies, or UCC filings on business assets. Credit report information on a business is available through Skyminder's Web site. Information on bankrupt companies, or those that have merged out of existence, is provided in Mergent Online's company archives. Alternatively, for bankrupt companies, use either Hoover's Business Boneyard for premium subscribers or a hardbound reference reporter. UCC filings are made to place liens against a business' personal property. UCC filings are available in each state, often under the secretary of state's office. Use of the UCC information helps banks determine whether to extend credit to a small business.

BUSINESS RESEARCH DATABASES AND TOOLS

Business research databases can assist the accountant in various ways, such as finding relevant articles on a business topic, discovering international business sources, acquiring statistical information, or conducting specialized research.

RESEARCH TOOLS
ACL
AICPA reSOURCE
Codification
eIFRS
i2
Internet
LexisNexis Academic
RIA Checkpoint

Article Index Databases

Several article index databases exist to help find relevant but nonauthoritative analysis on a topic. Note that some article index databases have also expanded to provide company information. Also, other types of databases can outperform article index databases in specialized areas, such as financial research database Factiva and legal research database LexisNexis Academic.

Full-text access to about twenty-three hundred business and management periodicals is the strength of Business Source Premier. Almost half of these periodicals are scholarly business journals covering accounting, finance, and other business areas. The database also indexes more than three thousand other journals and provides brief company profiles. The database is a subset of the much larger EBESCO Host database.

Fewer accounting professional publications are provided in the article index database ABI/Inform Global. However, the database includes access to the *Wall Street Journal* and the *Financial Times*. This database indexes various international professional publications, academic journals, and trade magazines, with full-text access to about three thousand. Alternative databases for substantial article indices are Factiva and the legal databases discussed later in this chapter.

Country or regional article index databases are often valuable, such as Nikkei Telecom 21. This database is the largest online source on Japanese business, but available only in Japanese. It provides full-text search of major Japanese newspapers and profiles of 1.2 million public and private companies. A more limited English language alternative for an article index database on Japan is Proquest Asian Business and Reference.

RESEARCH TIPS

The Wall Street Journal and the *Financial Times* are available through ABI/Inform Global and Factiva databases.

International Business Sources

For international business, start with the web directory GlobalEDGE's resource desk. This Web directory was originally created by the Center for International Business

Education and Research at Michigan State University. The directory provides guidance to major international business sources on such topics as trade issues, money, statistics, and current topics.

Government agencies or well-respected international organizations generally provide reliable information. Thus, take advantage of reports written by such U.S. agencies as the SEC, Department of State, Central Intelligence Agency, Export-Import Bank, and International Trade Administration. A special Web site by the U.S. government printing office for U.S. government documents sometimes helps locate relevant information. Leading international organizations include the World Bank, the International Monetary Fund, and the Organization for Economic Cooperation and Development.

Foreign databases provide valuable source for international business research. Investigate foreign databases for a particular country of interest, such as China Data Online, which provides financial indicators for more than five hundred industries, as well as economic statistics on China. Global databases such as Kompass often create country-specific databases. Kompass is a business database created in Switzerland covering over seventy countries, 2 million companies, 860,000trade names, 23 million product references, and 3.6 million executives' names. Limitations often apply to foreign databases when they are not geared for an English reading audience.

Trade associations exist for most industries. Trade association materials are not always released to non-members, but usually some information is available on their Web site, such as statistical data about the industry. To find relevant trade associations, use the Web site Associations Online or a hardbound comprehensive trade directory. Valuable books still exist for many business topics, such as for doing business in various countries. Thus, visit a university library, its business librarian, and reference books, especially for international business research.

Statistical Sources

Statistical data is especially useful in preparing for strategic business decisions. Stat-USA provides current and historical statistical data on business, international trade, and the economy from the U.S. Department of Commerce. Use Global Business Opportunities to acquire daily trade leads. Use the National Trade Data Bank to exploit the U.S. government's most comprehensive source of international information, market research reports, and other documents.

Commercial guides on countries, which are provided in Stat-USA, discuss economic trends, trade regulation, the foreign investment climate, and more. Use the International Trade Library to access over forty thousand documents related to international trade. An alternative database for statistical data from federal agencies and intergovernmental organizations is LexisNexis Statistical. The U.S. government, as the world's largest publisher, has such notable statistical publications as the *Federal Reserve Bulletin*, various types of census reference books, and *Survey of Current Business*.

Major statistical hardbound sources, which may start to appear online, provide various statistics on economic concerns. These sources include *S&P's Statistical Service*, *Handbook of Basic Economic Statistics*, and the *Statistical Abstract of the United States*. To acquire international statistical information, use such services as the Index to International Statistics or Worldcasts. Many state and local governments also publish valuable statistical data related to their geographical area.

Specialized Research

Nonprofit entities' financial information is best acquired by examining their tax returns (Form 990). The Web database Guidestar provides searchable access to the tax returns of more than a half-million nonprofit entities. The revision of IRS Form 990 beginning in 2009 provides a real wealth of information on nonprofit entities. Various Web sites provide specialized information on specific types of nonprofit entities, such as the Foundation Center Library on nonprofit foundations.

Patent research is complex and often transferred to specialists. There are many reasons to conduct patent research, such as examining patent filings, which can offer a wealth of business information. Remember that patents are sometimes highly valuable intangible assets that are usually not on the financial statements. Online patent databases exist for patents, such as LexisNexis TotalPatent, but patent databases are often cumbersome to use, and only patent abstracts are usually examined. To conduct patent research effectively, one must cycle through such materials as a classification index, a manual of classification, and classification definitions. The researcher should also learn to understand the law protecting patents by using a specialized database, such as BNA Intellectual Property Library. The novice researcher might begin by examining the Web site for the U.S. Patent and Trademark Office.

MASSIVE LEGAL RESEARCH DATABASES

Massive legal research databases originally focused on law, which is important for accountants in such areas as taxation, securities, contracts, and bankruptcy. Auditors need to understand the regulatory issues of the industries they audit. For the university community, both LexisNexis and Westlaw offer more limited versions of their databases, such as LexisNexis Academic. Specialized legal databases are also widely used by accountants, especially with tax law.

LexisNexis

Over 3.5 billion records are available in LexisNexis, including company information, news, and public records. LexisNexis has expanded from its legal origins in the 1970s to cover many subjects and information from all over the world. Over thirty-two thousand database sources are in LexisNexis. Often, a source consists of one publication over a period of time, such as the *New York Times*. While the *New York Times* is available on the Web, access to the extensive archives in LexisNexis is the reason to use the database. Use either the More Sources link or LexisNexis' searchable directory of online sources to understand the contents of the database sources in LexisNexis.

Company information on U.S. and foreign companies is provided in LexisNexis, through keyword searches and drilling down in the database. The Accounting, Tax & Financial Library includes not only numerous tax law sources, but also thousands of corporate annual reports. That library also has bankruptcy and securities laws and pronouncements from various standard setters in accounting and auditing. The Company and Financial folder in LexisNexis includes such items as SEC filings and M&A. To find relevant M&A information within this folder, use a segment search that is based on the type of offer or deal, as well as the industry. Premium cost enhancements include the LexisNexis Company Dossier, a report that includes such items as subsidiary listings, the company's legal counsel, and more.

News, professional publications, and other insightful secondary sources are included in LexisNexis. News on world events, business, and finance is taken from newspapers, newswires, and other sources. Publications include professional accounting journals, which provide short articles on a topic and law reviews that often contain a lengthy analysis of a narrow topic. Secondary source materials are primarily from leading professional publishers such as Warren, Gorham and Lamont; Thomson; and Tax Analysts.

Public records can reveal the financial affairs of a business or individual. Public records related to real estate include property tax assessment, deed transfer, mortgage records, and lien filings. Public records can also include such items as business locators, professional licenses, and state court judgments. Access various public records through LexisNexis. Alternatively, visit the source of the document and determine if Web access exists, such as the county for property tax assessment records.

LexisNexis Academic

Breadth of information at an affordable price is the reason many universities subscribe to the more limited legal database LexisNexis Academic. As of 2009, the five general folders in this database were General, News, Legal, Business, and People. Notice that the opening screen, as shown in Figure 6-12, has a choice of tutorials on the left side. Take advantage of LexisNexis Academic's tutorials to most effectively use the database.

Search engine limitations in LexisNexis Academic and the method of selecting specific sources in the database deserve some explanation. Until the particular folder of interest and sources are selected, avoid using the search engine in LexisNexis Academic as the search engine on the opening screen does not search the entire database. Note that sometimes the method of selecting specific sources is a drop-down box. To better understand the contents of a source, select the icon next to it.

FIGURE 6-12 | LEXISNEXIS TUTORIAL OPENING SCREEN ON SELECTING SOURCES

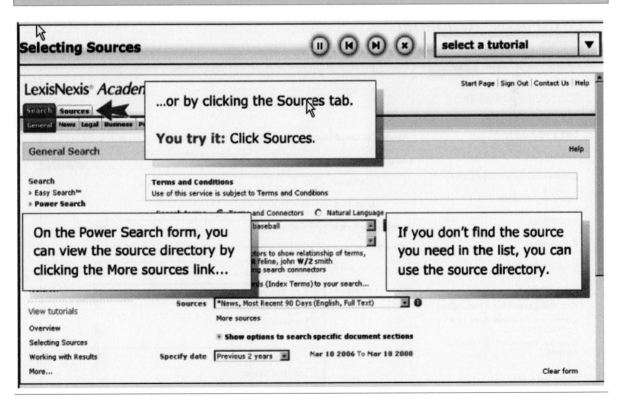

Company information under the Business folder in LexisNexis Academic has several options, such as company dossier, comparing companies, company profiles using various sources, and accounting. During 2008, LexisNexis Academic significantly improved its company information to compete with the best financial research databases.

Company dossier results for a company will first present a snapshot. Introductory nonfinancial information shows contact information for the corporate headquarters, industry classification, business description, and current news. The snapshot's financial information includes financial summary (net income, net sales, total assets, and total liabilities), current stock quotes and charts, and stock outstanding. The people and firms listed in the snapshot are major executives, board of directors, key competitors, and the auditor.

Important additional selections that provide more detail on the company are provided on the left side of the snapshot screen of the company dossier in LexisNexis Academic. Select the financial information to view five years of financial statements, financial ratios, growth estimates, insider trading activity, and analyst reports. Other parts of the dossier include recent news, intellectual property information, legal information, and references.

RESEARCH TIPS

LexisNexis Academic provides company dossiers that present extensive financial information on companies, including financial ratios and analyst reports.

EXAMPLE: Pull up Barnes and Noble, find recent intellectual property, and examine whether the financial ratios in LexisNexis Academic consider the intellectual property assets.

Discussion: Select the business folder and go to the company dossier, as shown in Figure 6-13. The result shows a handful of companies. Select the public parent

FIGURE 6-13 | LexisNexis Business Folder's Company Dossier

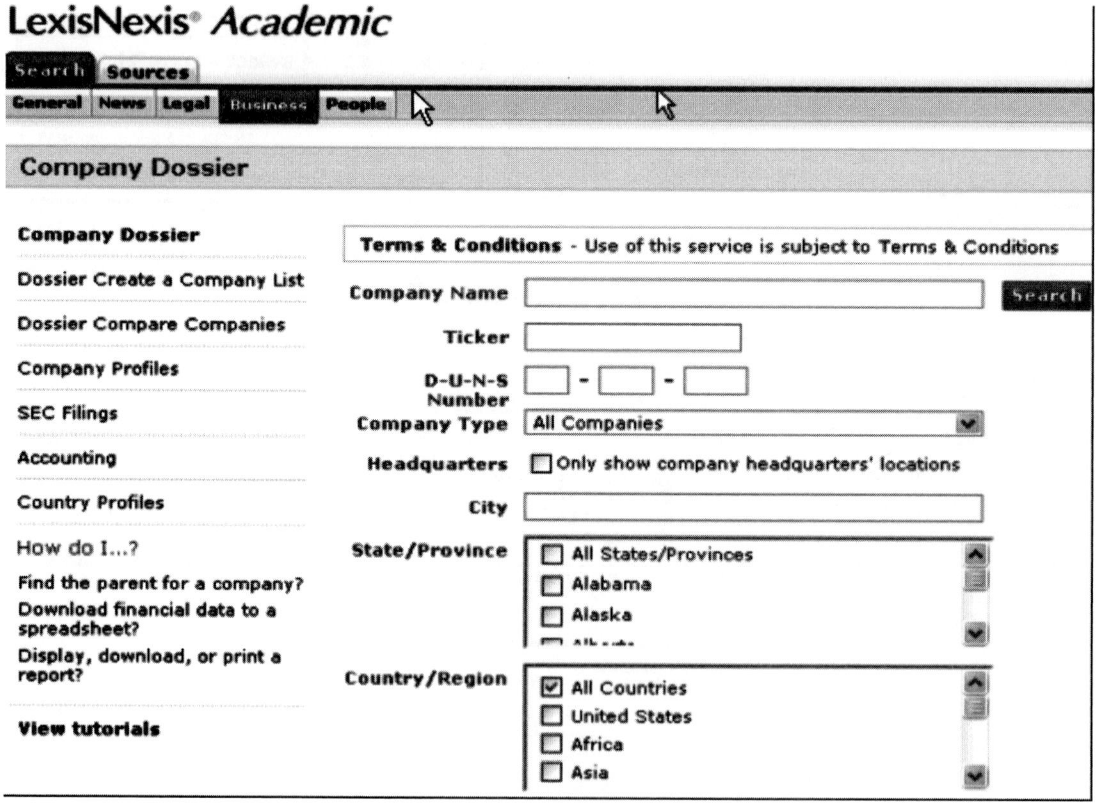

company headquartered in New York: Barnes and Noble, Inc. The search results then display the company snapshot. Select the intellectual property on the left side of the snapshot screen. Note the categories for patents, trademarks, and copyrights divided by the U.S., EU, and Japan. Selecting each patent item reveals no results for Barnes and Noble, unlike trademarks and copyrights.

The more than seventy financial ratios from the detailed financial information do not consider the value of the intangibles. The references reveal that the company dossier has used a variety of notable sources for each category. For example, the competitive positioning part of the report is from Hoover's and the Directory of Corporate Affiliations.

Accounting information under the Business folder in LexisNexis Academic is very weak compared to CCH's Accounting Research Manager. Primarily, nonauthoritative accounting sources are provided in LexisNexis Academic. Furthermore, the database presents an alphabetical mismatch of sources to select, such as the AICPA's *Journal of Accountancy*, SEC's financial reporting releases, and Wiley publications. LexisNexis Academic explains that the AICPA's Statements of Auditing Standards are reprinted in the *Journal of Accountancy*. However, one might use the PCAOB Web site and access its interim auditing standards, which are based on the AICPA's Statements of Auditing Standards.

Tax law is the primary reason accountants conduct legal research. LexisNexis Academic attempts to make tax law materials more accessible through a Web page on the subject, as shown in Figure 6-14. However, the tax law materials are poorly presented through an

FIGURE 6-14 | LexisNexis Legal Folder's Tax Page

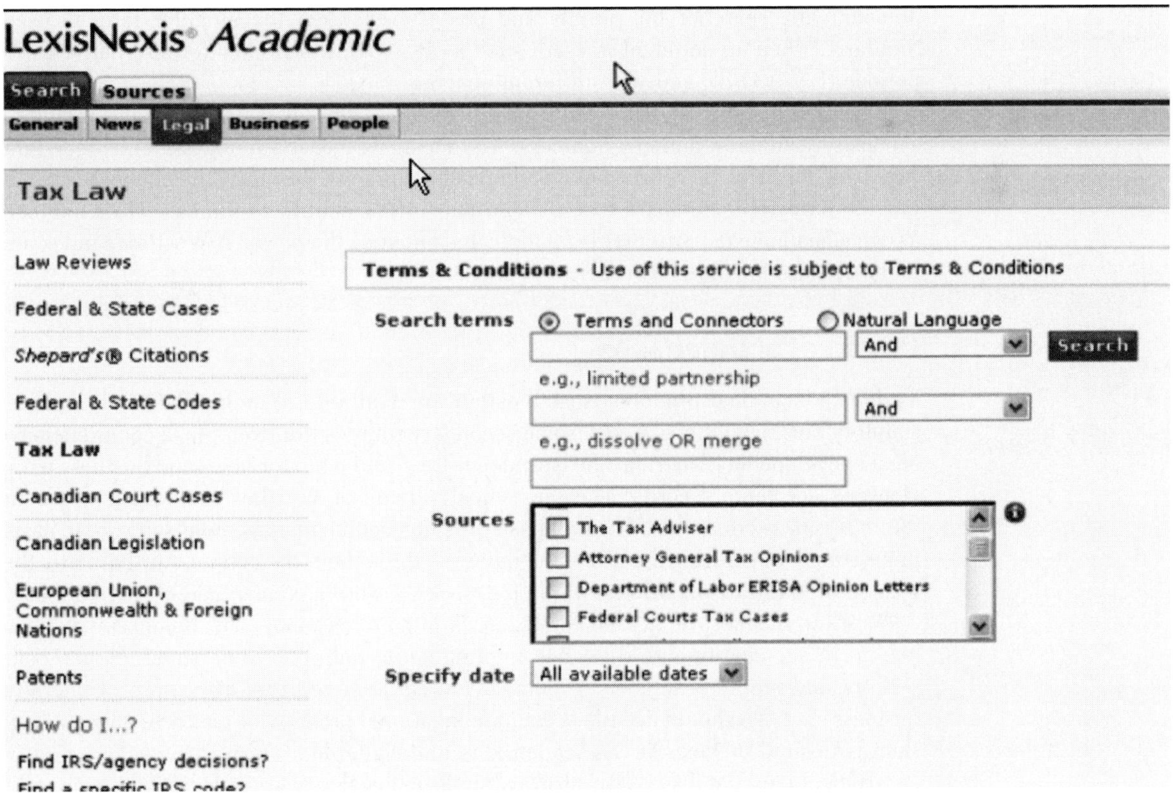

alphabetical mismatch of primary tax law sources and secondary sources. However, an advantage of LexisNexis Academic is that one can also research tax law in some other countries, such as Canada. Depending on the university's particular subscription to LexisNexis Academic, one might not have access to some sources. Consider using a specialized legal database in tax, such as RIA Checkpoint, discussed in the next chapter, on tax research.

The display of search results in LexisNexis Academic for legal research has strengths and weaknesses. One strength is that the order of the search results theoretically considers the relevance of the document. Another strength is that the left side of the screen shows the number of search results grouped by type of publication. One weakness is that some search results are still presented alphabetically rather than logically by their strength of authority. Thus, little guidance is provided for the novice researcher in distinguishing between authoritative sources and nonauthoritative materials. Another weakness in LexisNexis Academic is that the results displayed may look cumbersome with the extended view shown. Change the display to list view by selecting the drop-down box entitled Show.

Westlaw

Use Westlaw as an alternative to LexisNexis, especially for legal materials. The database also includes company profiles that overview a business and its operations. Helpful secondary source materials are provided for such areas as tax and internal audit.

Search tools in Westlaw facilitate keyword searches. Universal characters such as an asterisk (*) serve as placeholders for variable characters to expand on a root word. For example, searching for "document*" would also search for "documentation." Westlaw automatically searches for plurals and possessives when the singular term is used. Similarly, when an acronym is used, such as PCAOB, it searches for alternatives with periods (P.C.A.O.B.) and with different spacing.

Research tools in Westlaw are especially noteworthy for court cases and include a synopsis, headnotes, and key numbers. A synopsis for a case summarizes the procedural history of the case, the court's holding, and the major legal points by the court. Headnotes provide paragraph summaries of a single part of law central to the case. Key numbers assign a headnote to particular legal topic and enhance the power of Westlaw's index and its usefulness for the researcher.

Other Legal Databases

Various educational products from Westlaw are available. Campus Research includes statutory law, regulations, cases, some secondary sources (for example, a comprehensive legal encyclopedia [American Jurisprudence 2d]), and a tab for news and business using Hoover's corporate records. The law school version of Westlaw provides a vision for future business education. The database provides course management software to assist professors in integrating the use of the database throughout the course. Furthermore, this version of Westlaw provides rewards for students who maximize use of the database.

Westlaw Business is geared for business law professionals. Its Business Citator is helpful in aggregating due diligence information to help one understand clients, competitors, and suppliers and use the company information for legal disclosures. Generally, business students should use the Westlaw educational product for business only if a legal slant is desired or LexisNexis Academic is not available.

Article index databases are also available in legal research. HeinOnline provides full-text access to about twelve hundred law reviews. Wilson Web covers business as well as the legal literature. Its interface language choices appeal to many users outside of the United States.

SUMMARY

Database research on a particular accounting issue, company, or business topic is expected of today's professionals. Follow a research strategy to determine the information needed: the best sources, and helpful search tools. After viewing the results and organizing them, communicate the research results and cite your sources.

Extensive information on companies is available in financial research databases, but also to some extent in business databases and the massive legal research databases. The explosion of information has made it a necessity to understand databases and helpful hardbound reference sources. Many research tools are provided in databases to help the user conduct practical accounting research more efficiently. The future professional should practice using such databases as Accounting Research Manager, S&P's NetAdvantage, Mergent Online, Thomson Research, LexisNexis Academic, and other databases of value to accountants. See the appendix to this chapter for Web addresses to acquire more information on these databases and Web sites.

DISCUSSION QUESTIONS

1. What is included in the Accounting Research Manager?
2. How does one research government accounting?
3. What are the advantages of S&P's NetAdvantage?
4. When would one use Mergent Online?
5. What does the Thomson Research database cover?
6. When would one use the Factiva database?
7. What insight is offered by the Business and Company Resource database?
8. How is Hoover's Online distinguishable from other databases providing corporate information?
9. When would a researcher use Business Source Premier or ABI/Inform Global?
10. What is the major source of information in Stat-USA?
11. Explain how to conduct international business research.
12. Where are financial ratios found in LexisNexis or LexisNexis Academic?
13. What are the five general areas of coverage in LexisNexis Academic?
14. How does the LexisNexis Academic database compare to the LexisNexis database?
15. Explain the advantages of using Westlaw instead of Westlaw Business or Campus Research.

EXERCISES

1. What exposure drafts are available from the FASAB?
2. Given that GASB is related to FASB through their common oversight board, research GASB's plans for its hierarchy of accounting sources. Identify where you found that information.
3. Determine the major accounting provisions affecting the financial statement's presentation of unfunded pension liability. What database helped you find an answer?

4. Review Microsoft Corp.'s financial reports for the last three years and perform a ratio analysis of them. In one paragraph, discuss the company's financial situation. What databases and sub-databases did you use to find the answer?

5. Find the company Alexander & Baldwin. Write a one-sentence explanation describing Alexander & Baldwin's business. Identify the company's top competitors. Identify the databases and sub-databases that you used.

6. Conduct research to describe two major financial frauds that were discovered in the first quarter of 2009. What database and sub-database did you use?

7. What financial ratios are provided in the Mergent database? Compare and contrast this result to the financial ratios presented in S&P's NetAdvantage.

8. Find the profitability ratios for the bank Wells Fargo for 2008. Provide an analysis of what these ratios indicate for Wells Fargo's operations and use of its assets. How has Wells Fargo performed since 2008?

9. Use the topic guide in an article index database or legal database. Research Google Inc.'s Gmail system. What was the most controversial issue concerning the system when it was first released?

10. Use a commercial database to examine IBM&Apos;s first footnote in its financial statements for 2007. Compare and contrast the advantages or disadvantages in assessing IBM from a commercial database as compared to using the SEC Web site with its IDEA database.

11. Find the name of the major accounting journal published by the AICPA. Locate the two most recent articles in this journal using the keyword "derivatives." Give the citation for these articles using APA style. Summarize each article in a sentence.

12. Conduct a search to find the federal laws and regulations concerning the environmental liability disclosure requirements for Chevron. List the major items. What database and parts of the database did you used to locate the information?

13. Find 2008 stock prices on one of the largest private equity firms, the Blackstone Group. How much did their stock price drop during that year? Explain why. What sources of information did you use to find this answer? Why is information on this private equity firm more readily available than information for most private equity firms?

14. Find the IRS's market segment specialization program, which provides insightful audit information concerning more than sixty industries. Provide its Web site address. In one paragraph, identify the major issues in the automobile repair industry.

15. Examine the private company HCA, headquartered in Nashville, Tennessee. Summarize the corporate history of HCA. What legal concerns does this company face? Where did you find this information?

16. Using an appropriate database available to you, summarize the key financial ratios that you can find on the acquiring insurance company of Reliastar. Compare that information to any information provided on the company's Web site.

17. Find the growth rate for Yahoo from 2007 to 2008. What helps to explain the change in the company's stock price that year?

18. Examine an analyst report on Ford Motor Company. Who wrote the report? Outline the major contents of that analyst report. Where did you find this analyst report?

19. Access Stat-USA. Find out how much steel the United States traded internationally in 2007. Where in the database did you look?

20. Identify what other significant accounting and business databases your library provides. Select one valuable database for accountants, business advisors, or economists not discussed in this text. Provide a few PowerPoint slides and a research example explaining it.

Accounting Research Tools

21. Use the ARM database to find the title of GAAP Concept Statement No. 5. What is the purpose of the reporting discussed in the Concept? When was this Concept Statement last modified?

22. Go to your library's catalogue on the Web. List the Dewey Decimal location of the three AICPA reference books. If your library does not subscribe to all of these books, suggest where you could go to view these research tools.

Government Accounting Databases

23. What is the title of GASB Concept Statement No. 5? What is the purpose of the reporting discussed in the Concept? When was this Concept Statement last modified?

24. What does the Statement of Federal Accounting Standard No. 33 discuss? When was Standard No. 33 promulgated? What was the purpose of the Standard?

Financial Research Databases

25. Find the industry ranking in the music business. Who are the largest three companies in the music industry? What database did you use? Provide a financial comparison of these three companies.

26. Find the NAICS code for the property and casualty insurance business.

General Business Databases

27. Access a database overview of Real Networks, Inc. Then explain the significance of its RealPlayer line of Web products. Can you determine how many registered users exist for the RealPlayer line of products?

28. Go to the GlobalEDGE resource desk and identify three international business resources recommended for statistical sources.

Legal Databases

29. Find the titles of the two most recent articles from the *Journal of Accountancy* that discuss the term "money laundering."

30. Locate and identify two Accounting and Auditing Enforcement Releases by the SEC that address fraud. Explain how you conducted the research.

APPENDIX

FIGURE 6A-1 | WEB SITE ADDRESSES

Topic	Web site
ABI/Inform Global (article index)	www.proquest.com/en-US/catalogs/databases/detail/abi_inform.shtml
Accounting Research Manager	www.accountingresearchmanager.com
AICPA (accounting research tools)	www.aicpa.org
AICPA ReSOURCE (database)	www.aicpastore.com (search for ReSOURCE)
American Accounting Association	www.aaahq.org
American Psychological Association (APA)	www.apastyle.org
Associations Online	www.asaecenter.org/Directories/AssociationSearch.cfm
Audit Analytics (database)	www.auditanalytics.com
BNA Intellectual Property Library	www.bna.com/products/ip/iplw.htm
Business and Company Resource Center	www.gale.cengage.com/BusinessRC
Business Source Premier (database)	http://search.ebscohost.com
China Data Online (financial database)	http://chinadataonline.org
Compustat (academic financial database)	https://wrds.wharton.upenn.edu/demo/comp/inademo.shtml
CRSP (academic financial database)	www.crsp.com/products/stocks.htm
Dialog (financial database)	www.dialog.com
EBESCO Host (article index database)	http://search.ebscohost.com
Factiva (financial press database)	www.factiva.com

FIGURE 6A-1 | WEB SITE ADDRESSES (CONTINUED)

Topic	Web site
Federal Accounting Standards Advisory Board (FASAB)	www.fasab.gov
Federal Reserve Bulletin	www.federalreserve.gov/pubs/bulletin
Foundation Center (not-for-profit)	http://foundationcenter.org
Government Accounting Standards Board (GASAB)	www.gasb.org
GlobalEDGE (international business Web site)	http://globaledge.msu.edu/
Government documents	www.gpoaccess.gov
Guidestar (not-for-profit database)	www.guidestar.org
HeinOnline (article index database)	http://heinonline.org
Hoovers (financial database)	www.hoovers.com
International Monetary Fund	www.imf.org
Kompass (foreign business database)	www.compass-usa.com
LexisNexis (legal database)	www.lexis.com
LexisNexis Academic (legal database)	http://academic.lexisnexis.com/online-services/academic-overview.aspx
LexisNexis Directory of Sources	http://w3.nexis.com/sources
Mergent Online (financial database)	www.mergentonline.com
Morningstar Investment Resource Center	www.morningstar.com
NAICS (industry code)	www.census.gov/naics
Nikkei Telecom21 (article index)	www.nikkeieu.com/e/telecom/index.asp
New York Times	www.nytimes.com
Ohio State (academic finance Web sites)	http://fisher.osu.edu/fin/journal/jofsites.htm
ORBIS	www.bvdep.com/en/ORBIS.html
PCAOB (auditing standard setter)	www.pcaobus.org
Proquest Asian and Business Reference (article index database)	www.proquest.com/en-US/catalogs/databases/detail/pq_asian_business.shtml
RIA Checkpoint (tax database)	http://checkpoint.riag.com
Risk Metrics (academic database)	https://wrds.wharton.upenn.edu/demo/riskmetrics/index.shtml
Skyminder (credit info. Web site)	www.skyminder.com
Social Science Research Network	www.srrn.com
Stat-USA (statistical database)	www.stat-usa.gov
Thomson Research (financial database)	http://Research.thomsonib.com
U.S. Central Intelligence Agency	www.cia.gov
U.S. Department of State	www.state.gov
U.S. Import Export Bank	www.exim.gov
U.S. International Trade Administration	http://trade.gov/index.asp
U.S. Patent and Trademark Office	www.uspto.gov
Value Line (financial database)	www.valueline.com
Westlaw (legal database)	www.westlaw.com
Wilson Web	www.hwwilson.com
World Bank	www.worldbank.org
Worldscope (financial information)	http://thomsonreuters.com/products_services/financial/worldscope_fundamentals
WRDS (academic financial database)	https://wrds.wharton.upenn.edu

Tax Research for Compliance and Tax Planning

LEARNING OBJECTIVES

After completing this chapter, you should understand the following:

- Tax research goals.
- Tax research challenges.
- Tax research databases, such as RIA Checkpoint.
- Primary tax authorities, particularly the Code, treasury regulations, and cases.
- The tax research process.
- Professional standards affecting U.S. taxation.

Many taxpayers acquire professional assistance in completing their tax returns. Complexity in tax law and its application make strong tax research skills even more important. The purpose of this chapter is to present information and guidance in conducting tax research for both tax compliance and tax planning. The tax research methodology is actually very similar to accounting and auditing research.

TAX RESEARCH GOALS

The objective of tax research is to maximize the taxpayer's after-tax return or benefits. The objective is not necessarily to produce the lowest possible tax liability. Clients may value certainty of tax results or seek to minimize potential disputes with the IRS. This difference in viewpoint—maximizing after-tax benefits as opposed to minimizing tax—is especially important when one realizes that many tax-planning strategies involve some trade-off with pretax income, either in the form of incurring additional expenses, receiving less revenue, or both.

Tax researchers must distinguish between tax evasion, tax avoidance, and abusive tax avoidance. Tax evasion consists of illegal acts, such as making false statements of fact, to lower one's taxes. Tax advisors have professional responsibilities and must not condone any tax evasion. Tax avoidance seeks to minimize taxes legally, such as avoiding the creation of facts that would result in higher taxes. Tax avoidance is often the objective of tax research. The IRS now targets abusive tax avoidance by promoters of tax shelters and taxpayers investing in transactions that the IRS believes are intentionally being used to misapply the tax laws.

Tax research is an examination of all relevant tax laws given the facts of a client's situation in order to determine the appropriate tax consequences. The term *tax research* may vary depending on the context. Academic tax research is sometimes theoretical or policy-oriented research with the objective of providing new information that might describe the behavioral consequences of a change in the tax law or that will help shape decisions on how to change the tax law. Applied tax research addresses existing tax law, with the objective of determining its application to a given situation. In this book, the

> **QUICK FACTS**
>
> Tax avoidance legally seeks to minimize taxes.

term *tax research* is used solely in the professional sense, to relate to the tax problems of specific taxpayers rather than to society at large.

TAX RESEARCH CHALLENGES

Begin tax research by determining the relevant facts. Many tax disputes involve questions of fact rather than questions of law. Two common factual disputes include determining fair market value of property and the amount of deductible business expenses incurred, especially while traveling away from home on business. Presentation of the facts may include the arguments made by both the taxpayer and the IRS as well as the decision by any prior court.

> **EXAMPLE:** Does receipt of a diamond necklace constitute an excludable gift under Section 102 or taxable compensation for services?
>
> **Discussion:** The result depends upon all facts and circumstances relevant to the case. True love suggests the necklace is an excludable gift under Section 102; a one-evening relationship might suggest the payment of the diamond necklace is gross income under Section 61 as a return for companionship services. Any dispute with the IRS in such a situation is a question of fact, not law.

The researcher must also identify the precise legal issues for a given set of facts. Too often, there is a tendency among novice tax researchers to rush into a search for legal authority without an adequate understanding of the problem. The following example can help illustrate the benefit of spending time in the initial steps to determine the relevant facts and legal issues.

> **EXAMPLE:** The taxpayer operated refuse dumps. Land was acquired for business use. Land is not depreciable. What should the taxpayer argue to obtain a depreciation deduction?
>
> **Discussion:** Argue that the purchase price was primarily for the holes in the land for refuse, not the land itself. As the holes were filled in, the taxpayer depreciated the assigned cost of the holes. By characterizing part of the purchase as acquiring refuse holes, the taxpayer in *John J. Sexton*[1] was successful in taking a tax deduction. Less imaginative taxpayers and advisors had overlooked this idea.

After determining the facts and issues, the researcher must search for relevant legal authorities from among the massive array of tax authorities. Tax research is a process by which relevant tax law is applied to a given set of facts. To find the authority, it helps to have knowledge of how the tax law is organized and to develop skills in careful reading and analysis of the law. The law always controls, even if it contradicts accounting, economic, social, or moral theory.

The challenge is to select the correct legal authorities. In some situations, more than one answer may exist in law. The tax researcher may then inform the client on the relative merits and tax benefits of each defensibly correct option. Usually, however, only one tax result has an appropriate weight of legal authority. Determining the cutoff between a defensible tax treatment and one that is not defensible depends on whether the legal authorities backing the position provide substantial authority. Although applying this

---

RESEARCH TOOLS
ACL
AICPA reSOURCE
Codification
eIFRS
i2
Internet
LexisNexis Academic
RIA Checkpoint

QUICK FACTS

In tax research, more than one correct solution may exist.

---

[1] *John J. Sexton*, 42 T.C. 1094 (1964); Acq. 1970-1 C.B. 16.

standard is learned more through experience and professional judgment, the evidence should support winning one's case in the majority of instances.

Three types of activities involve tax research: tax compliance, tax planning, and tax litigation. For tax compliance, tax returns are typically prepared. Tax accountants generally perform both tax compliance and tax planning work. Lawyers also engage in tax planning and handle tax litigation work to take a tax case to court.

Tax compliance is sometimes referred to as *closed-fact engagements*. All the facts have already occurred when the work is being performed. For tax compliance, the researcher's job is limited to discovery of relevant facts and law because the factual burden of proof generally rests with the taxpayer in the event of an audit.

Tax-planning engagements are sometimes referred to as *open-fact engagements* because not all of the relevant facts have transpired. Tax planning considers how to carefully execute tax avoidance, that is, controlling the facts that actually occur in order to produce an optimal after-tax result for the taxpayer. The rendering of well-researched tax planning advice is generally regarded as the hallmark of a true professional.

Tax litigation arises after the taxpayer is audited and intensifies if settlement with the IRS is not reached. The work may begin by double-checking prior tax research and researching the more rarely used tax sources that are beyond the practical scope of this text for accountants. If significant litigation potential becomes apparent, the tax accountant or client should consult with an experienced tax attorney.

TAX RESEARCH DATABASES

Tax research databases include both primary and secondary authorities. The two most used primary authorities by accountants are the Code and Regulations. Secondary sources are useful for acquiring a basic understanding of topics. A popular secondary source is the *Masters of Tax Guide*, which summarizes the tax law. Today's tax professionals generally use tax research databases through a publisher's Web site, or use a DVD to ensure access when the Internet is not available.

Several publishers produce databases that are useful for tax research. Some researchers use the massive online legal databases, such as LexisNexis and Westlaw, discussed in the prior chapter. Other researchers use specialized tax research databases, such as those provided by the Research Institute of America (RIA) and Commerce Clearing House (CCH).

Both RIA and CCH tax databases include primary tax authorities and helpful secondary sources, such as tax services, citators, news updates, and journal articles. RIA's tax database RIA Checkpoint includes RIA's tax services: Federal Tax Coordinator and United States Tax Reporter. CCH's tax database Intelli Connect includes CCH's tax services: Standard Federal Income Tax Reporter and Tax Research Consultant. An important difference between the RIA and CCH tax databases is how each displays the results. While RIA Checkpoint shows the number of results by source category, CCH's Tax Research Network mixes the results but displays them by what the CCH software believes is most relevant.

Popular Web sites for the tax researcher are presented in Figure 7-1. The Web has enabled Congress, the IRS, the courts, and others to make their sources more available. The IRS Web site provides downloadable tax forms and instructions as well as plain English, unofficial versions of the Treasury Regulations and daily news updates.

QUICK FACTS

Tax services in a tax research database help find relevant cases.

RIA Checkpoint

RIA Checkpoint contains various tax research libraries, such as international, federal, state, and local, and estate planning. The opening research screen should appear as in

FIGURE 7-1 | INTERNET TAX SITES

Commerce Clearing House	www.cch.com
Enrolled Agents	www.irs.gov/taxpros/agents
Internal Revenue Service	www.irs.gov
Research Institute of America (RIA)	http://ria.thomsonreuters.com
Tax Analysts	www.taxanalysts.com
Tax and Accounting Sites Directory	www.taxsites.com
Tax Court Opinions	www.ustaxcourt.gov
Tax Planning	www.smartmoney.com
Tax Software	www.intuit.com
Tax World	www.taxworld.org

Figure 7-2. One tab on top of the opening screen is "Training and Tips." Use this tab to access "Getting Started" and the "Demo," which are listed on the left side of the screen. Various choices for practice areas in tax are provided in the drop-down box in the upper left side of the RIA Checkpoint screen. The researcher usually wants to limit the research to the relevant parts of the federal practice area of taxation.

FIGURE 7-2 | RIA CHECKPOINT OPENING SCREEN

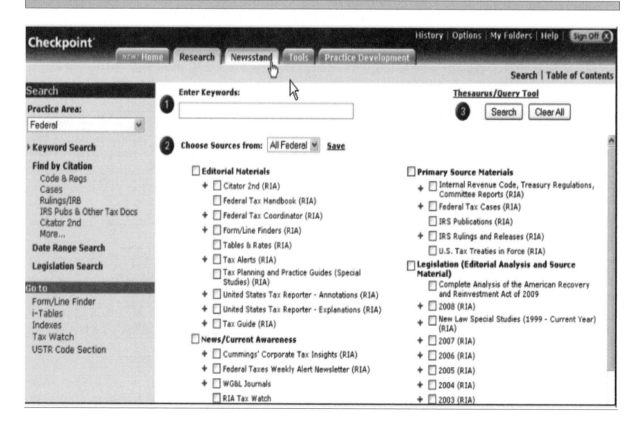

PRIMARY TAX AUTHORITIES

An understanding of the primary sources of tax authority and how to utilize RIA Checkpoint database and its tax services will help the researcher locate the relevant law. Primary authority generally comes from the following sources:

- **Statutory sources:** The Internal Revenue Code, the U.S. Constitution, and tax treaties
- **Administrative sources:** Treasury Regulations, Revenue Rulings, and revenue procedures
- **Judicial sources:** Case decisions from the various courts

This section overviews the most widely primary sources of tax law. Constitutional concerns are not discussed because they rarely arise for federal tax, although they may arise for state taxes.

Tax treaties usually attempt to eliminate double taxation from income subject to tax in two countries. If the tax transaction at issue involves a foreign national or arose in a foreign country, tax researchers should begin their research determining if there is any applicable tax treaty. The United States has tax treaties with many countries. Some tax treaty information is available on the IRS Web site, as well as in tax research databases. Using an index on the Web, such as www.taxsites.com (international page), can also help lead to finding relevant tax treaty information.

The Code

The Code or IRC is the popular name for U.S. statutory law on federal taxation. The official name is the Internal Revenue Code of 1986 as Amended, located in Title 26 of the United States Code. The Code is the statutory foundation of all federal tax authority. When new tax legislation is passed, such as the American Recovery and Reinvestment Act of 2009, the provisions in the law are codified, that is, rearranged logically in the Code.

To cite a specific tax provision, tax researchers use the Code section number and the specific provisions within that Code section. For example, cite "Code § 11(a)," instead of the more cumbersome "Subtitle A, Chapter 1, Subchapter A, Part II, Section 11, Subsection (a) of the Internal Revenue Code of 1986 as Amended." If a Code section refers to one of the organizational divisions of the Code, the researcher should use the table of contents to clarify what code sections are included.

A Find by Citation approach in a tax research database is an easy and efficient method to view a specific Code section. For RIA Checkpoint, the link to the citation is on the left side of the screen. The citation approach often provides a template box to assist the researcher in accessing the desired Code section or other authority.

Always cite a provision within a Code section with as much precision as possible. Thus, it is essential to know that each section is divided into subsections, paragraphs, subparagraphs, and clauses. Within parentheses following the Code section number, subsections use lowercase letters, paragraphs use numbers, subparagraphs use capital letters, and clauses use lowercase roman numerals. Only if a Code section existed back under the 1939 codification does the current Code not include a small letter before a paragraph number, such as section 212(3) for the deduction of tax services.

The general rule of a Code section is usually provided in subsection (a). Read subsection (a) carefully and scan the remaining subsection headings to search for other relevant provisions in the Code section. Reading the Code requires moving around within the section and even into other sections in order to understand the meaning of a phrase used with the Code section. A Code section will sometimes explicitly reference another

> **RESEARCH TIPS**
>
> Always cite as precisely as possible within a Code section.

FIGURE 7-3	ANALYSIS OF A CODE OF A SECTION

Sec. 132. Certain Fringe Benefits

(a) Exclusion from gross income. Gross income shall not include any fringe benefit which qualifies as a:

    1. no-additional-cost service.

    2. qualified employee discount.

    3. working condition fringe.

    . . .

(c) Qualified employee discount defined. For purposes of this section:

    1. Qualified employee discount. The term "qualified employee discount" means any employee discount with respect to qualified property or services to the extent such discount does not exceed:

        A. in the case of property, the gross profit percentage of the price at which the property is being offered by the employer to customers, or

        B. in the case of services, 20 percent of the price at which the services are being offered by the employer to customers.

    2. Gross profit percentage.

Code provision. More often, however, make an effort to connect different sections that effect the meaning of a phrase within a Code section. The Code requires careful reading skills. Little words such as "or" between paragraphs can create big differences in meaning. Thus, the reader should consider highlighting significant words so as to place the reading into proper perspective.

RESEARCH TIPS

To understand the general rule of a Code section, read subsection (a) carefully.

EXAMPLE: How does one read the example of Section 132 on fringe benefits related to employee discounts?

Discussion: First read subsection (a) carefully to understand the general rule that among the excludable fringe benefits is a qualified employee discount. Then scan the subsections to search for other relevant provisions. Subsection (c) defines qualified employee discount. Section 132(c)(1)(A) states that, for property, the discount cannot exceed "the gross profit percentage." Look to see if this term is defined within subsection (c) or elsewhere in the Code section. Indeed, Section 132(c)(2) defines the gross profit percentage. Note that the paragraphs (1) and (2) are more indented than the subsections (a) and (c) and the subparagraph (A) is even further indented.

The Code may seem confusing at first. For example, the Code sometimes defines concepts differently for various sections.

EXAMPLE: Do related parties for tax purposes include brothers and sisters?

Discussion: Related parties for purposes of Code Section 267, disallowance of losses between related parties, are defined in subsection (b) to include brothers and sisters as part of the family relationship for purposes of constructive ownership of stock. In contrast, Section 318, on the constructive ownership of stock for purposes of defining related parties for subchapter C corporations, does not consider brothers and sisters as related.

Many tax researchers now rely extensively on online access to read the Code and other relevant tax law. Historically, accountants acquired a new paperbound edition of the Code after each major tax law change. They also bought a useful secondary source book, such as CCH's *Master Tax Guide*.

Tax services are secondary sources that are especially helpful in finding relevant cases. The online version of a tax service reproduces multivolume, comprehensive sets of books that are organized either topically or by Code section number. Topical tax services, such as RIA's *Federal Tax Coordinator*, are generally easier to read and provide footnote support to the primary authorities. Tax services organized by Code section number are commonly called annotated tax services and provide short annotations on cases and sometimes Revenue Rulings that interpret that Code section. Annotated tax services, such as CCH's *Standard Federal Income Tax Reporter*, usually provide a greater depth of research than a topical tax service. Both RIA and CCH provide both topical and annotated tax services.

For recently enacted changes to the Code, one should examine the Report by the Staff of the Joint Committee on Taxation ("the Blue Book"). The Joint Committee produced compromises to reconcile differences in proposed legislation passed by both the House of Representatives and the Senate. The Blue Book explains those changes and often provides the basis for future Treasury Regulations interpreting the modified Code sections. Tax services will often include the most relevant parts of the Blue Book. Less reliable congressional sources include the House Ways and Means Committee Reports, the Senate Finance Committee Reports, congressional hearings, and individual speeches inserted into the Congressional Record.

Administrative Authorities (Particularly Treasury Regulations)

Once Congress has enacted a tax law, the federal government's executive branch implements it by interpreting and enforcing the law. Thus, the Treasury Department creates Treasury Regulations. The IRS, the largest division of the Treasury Department, issues lesser administrative authorities and enforces the tax law through audits and making adjustments in a taxpayer's self-reported tax liability.

Treasury Regulations Treasury Regulations provide general guidance that interpret and clarify the statutory law. The number of Treasury Regulations interpreting a code section varies widely. While some Code sections have many treasury regulations, other sections have no regulations.

Three major types of Treasury Regulations are proposed, temporary, and final regulations. Treasury Regulations first appear in proposed form in the *Federal Register*. The IRS has sometimes subsequently modified or withdrawn a proposed regulation. After major changes in the Code, temporary regulations are eventually issued, which are legally binding, but expire after three years. Final regulations are issued only after going through the official process for notice and comment at public hearings. The regulation is then published as a Treasury Decision in the *Federal Register* and later codified into Title 26 of the *Code of Federal Regulations*.

Two types of final Treasury Regulations are legislative and interpretive. Legislative regulations arise when a Code section directs the Secretary of the Treasury to create regulations to carry out the purposes of the section. Interpretive regulations arise under the authority of Code Section 7805(a), which expressly provides that the Treasury Department Secretary "shall prescribe all needful rules and regulations for the enforcement of this title." You must comply with both types of final Treasury Regulations.

To find a relevant regulation, scan the titles of the regulations that interpret the code section at issue. While most tax research databases attempt to link the regulations to the related Code section, some databases make an effort to link each regulation to a particular Code subsection or paragraph. If the title of the regulation appears to have potential application, look over the contents of that regulation. Then carefully read potentially relevant parts of the regulation. Some Treasury Regulations are helpful by providing clarifying examples on a topic. Other Treasury Regulations may directly address topics that the relevant Code section did not mention.

EXAMPLE: Does the deduction for travel away from home on business include a business associate?

Discussion: Section 162(a)(2) allows a deduction for ordinary and necessary business expenses for traveling while away from home on business. Travel expenses are disallowed for the spouse, dependent, or other individual accompanying the taxpayer under Section 274(m)(3). The other individual does not include a business associate. Treas. Reg. § 1.274-2(g).

Notice that the citation for a Treasury Regulation references the Code section that the regulation interprets. The Code section that the regulation interprets is evident after the decimal point and before the hyphen that precedes the subdivisions of the regulation. Although Treasury Regulations are found in Title 26 of the Code of Federal Regulations (CFR), they are more commonly referenced merely by Treasury Regulation section. The citation for a Treasury Regulation begins with the part number that identifies the general area of taxation to which the regulation is related, such as "1" for an income tax regulation:

Part 1	Income Taxes
Part 20	Estate Taxes
Part 25	Gift Taxes
Part 31	Employment Taxes
Parts 48, 49	Excise Taxes
Part 301	Procedural Rules

In the following example citation of a regulation, one can tell at a glance that the regulation cited applies to Code Section 274. However, the subdivisions of the regulation have no relationship with the subdivisions within the Code section. The "2" in the citation following the hyphen and "274" indicate that this is the second regulation issued interpreting Code Section 274. Two appropriate forms of a citation of the same regulation are as follows:

$$26 \text{ CFR } \S \quad 1.274\text{-}2(g)$$
$$\text{Treas. Reg. Sec.} \quad 1.274\text{-}2(g)$$

Identification as Regulation _____

Part Number _____

Applicable Code Section _____

Subdivisions within the Regulation _____

Carefully check that any Treasury Regulations relied upon remains applicable to the current Code section of interest. Parts of a regulation may become obsolete because of a recent change in the Code language. The Treasury Department is frequently slow to amend or remove regulations. Commercial tax services are often helpful in pointing out concerns with particular regulations.

Revenue Rulings and Revenue Procedures Revenue Rulings apply the law to a specific set of completed facts. Revenue Rulings are often based on further IRS review of previous private letter rulings issued upon taxpayers' requests concerning the tax outcomes of specific proposed transactions. In contrast to the general guidance provided in Treasury Regulations, Revenue Rulings provide issues, facts, and law and analysis on applying the law to a particular set of facts. They do not carry the same level of authority as Treasury Regulations do. Revenue Rulings are issued by the IRS and represent the position that IRS revenue agents must follow in auditing tax returns.

The citation to a Revenue Ruling does not reference the Code section that it addresses. However, for the researcher's convenience, a tax service, such as RIA Checkpoint, will sometimes follow the Revenue Ruling citation with the relevant Code section. The researcher should remove that Code section reference when citing the Revenue Ruling. Always check the status of a Revenue Ruling before relying on it. For example, the IRS may modify, revoke, or supersede a Revenue Ruling. For convenience, the major tax services provide update links or warnings to determine the current status of a Revenue Ruling. Revenue Rulings are first published in the Internal Revenue Bulletin (IRB) and later in the Cumulative Bulletin (CB). A researcher might encounter either of the following citations for the same Revenue Ruling:

CITATION: **Rev. Rul. 2001-34, IRB No. 28, 31**
                       Rev. Rul. 2001-34, 2001-2 C.B. 31

Year of Issue _____
34th Ruling of Year _____
Reporter _____
   Internal Revenue Bulletin or Cumulative Bulletin _____
   Number of Weekly Issue for IRB, then Initial page _____

Revenue Procedures are created by the IRS to announce administrative procedures that taxpayers must follow. Revenue Procedures are similar in weight of authority to Revenue Rulings. They are both found in the same sources. They are also cited in the same manner except that the prefix "Rev. Proc." is used instead of "Rev. Rul."

Examples of lesser administrative authorities by the IRS that lack precedential value in court include IRS Notices and Private Letter Rulings (PLRs). IRS Notices are useful when they outline expected future Treasury Regulations that the IRS might take years to create. PLRs are issued on a proposed transaction but are binding on the IRS only with respect to the particular taxpayer requesting the ruling, assuming all material facts were disclosed.

IRS publications explain how to complete various tax forms and topics. For example, IRS Publication 901 discusses U.S. tax treaties. While the IRS publications are useful for tax compliance purposes, they merely interpret the law and are actually secondary authority. IRS publications are often used by taxpayers completing their own tax returns and by non-accountant tax preparers.

Caution: Many government sources are often miscategorized as primary sources because the government created the source. This miscategorization is evident in RIA Checkpoint's list of primary sources. Within this text, secondary authority exists when the source lacks precedential value for various taxpayers to rely on the source.

Judicial Sources of Tax Authority Judicial decisions in common law countries, such as the United States, are considered part of the law. Judicial law is created by consistently treating similar cases in the same fashion under the applicable statute and regulations. While Congress sets forth the words of law and the administrative branch interprets and enforces those words, it is the judiciary that has the final say as to what the words really mean when applied in a particular case.

Examining prior judicial decisions to determine the meaning of a given phrase in the Code is sometimes necessary. To conduct the research on case law effectively, the tax researcher needs a working knowledge of judicial concepts, the various federal courts, and the hierarchy. Knowledge of the judicial system is necessary to appraise the authoritative weight of decisions rendered by the various federal courts.

U.S. Tax Court This specialized court considers only tax cases. Its nineteen judges are usually highly knowledgeable tax lawyers. Although the Tax Court is located in Washington, DC, judicial hearings are held in several major cities during the year. Most Tax Court cases involve only a single judge, who submits an opinion to the chief judge. The Tax Court's Web site reprints its recent decisions, provides its rules of practice, and gives other information.

Two types of Tax Court cases are processed: regular and memorandum. A regular decision is when the Tax Court's chief judge decides a case is announcing a new principle in the law. On rare occasions, en banc decision occurs, which involves a review by all of the Tax Court judges for an important tax issue. A memorandum decision is made if the Tax Court is just applying already announced principles to a different set of facts. Prior to 1943, both regular and memorandum decisions were published by the government under the title United States Board of Tax Appeals (BTA).

Many taxpayers use the Tax Court to litigate the IRS audit adjustment to avoid prepaying the amount of taxes in dispute. The Tax Court may rule differently on identical fact patterns for two taxpayers residing in different circuit court of appeals jurisdictions in case of inconsistent holdings by the circuit courts. This is because, within each circuit, the Tax Court will follow precedents of that court of appeals (known as the Golsen rule).[2] Besides not having jury trials, the Tax Court has unique rules to expedite the court's process, such as requiring the taxpayer and IRS to work together to establish the facts.

The IRS will issue either an acquiescence or nonacquiescence for most Tax Court regular decisions that the IRS has lost. Acquiescence means the IRS expects to follow the decision of the Tax Court when dealing with cases of similar facts and circumstances. A nonacquiescence indicates the IRS will not follow the Tax Court's decision when handling similar cases. This IRS issuance does not apply to either memorandum decisions or decisions by any other courts. Announcements of either acquiescence (Acq.) or nonacquiescence (Nonacq.), are published in the IRB and CB.

The Small Claims division of the Tax Court considers tax disputes of $50,000 or less. The expedited process and less costly procedures are the advantages for a taxpayer to elect having the Small Claims division of the Tax Court decide the case. The disadvantage of using the Small Claims division is that appeals are not allowed. The Small Claims division decisions are not published by the government because they do not have precedential value. However, tax research databases will sometimes publish such nonprecedential authority.

Other Courts If a taxpayer prepays the amount in dispute with the IRS and then sues for a refund, the taxpayer must first use either a U.S. District Court or the U.S. Court of Federal Claims. Only in a district court can one obtain a jury trial. However, a jury can decide only questions of fact, not questions of law. Each state has at least one federal district court. About 25 percent of the U.S. Court of Federal Claims' cases are

QUICK FACTS

Taxpayers in Tax Court do not prepay the taxes in dispute.

RESEARCH TIPS

Tax Court's Small Claims division considers disputes of $50,000 or less.

---

[2] *Jack E. Golsen*, 54 T.C. 742 (1970).

tax cases. This court was previously known as the U.S. Claims Court and the U.S. Court of Claims.

In the U.S. Court of Appeals, either taxpayers or the IRS may appeal decisions of the Tax Court and the district courts. The appeal is made to the circuit in which the taxpayer resides. Because there are thirteen courts of appeals (eleven regional ones, the DC Circuit, and the Court of Appeals for the Federal Circuit), the Federal Circuit appellate court will hear appeals on tax issues only if they arise from decisions of the U.S. Court of Federal Claims. Normally, a review by a court of appeals consists of a panel of three judges and is limited to the application of law, not the redetermination of facts. Courts of appeal are obligated to follow the decisions of the Supreme Court but not those from other circuit courts of appeal.

The U.S. Supreme Court is the ultimate forum for appeal. However, it considers only a handful of tax cases each year, usually those in which courts of appeal have reached different conclusions on the same issue. Either the taxpayer or the IRS can request the Supreme Court to review a court of appeals decision. The Supreme Court hears the case only if it grants the "writ of certiorari" (reported as "Cert. Granted"). If the Supreme Court refuses a case, certiorari is denied (reported as "Cert. Den."). The Supreme Court simply will not review the case, and the decision of the court of appeals will stand.

Precedent is the principle that governs the use of prior decisions as law. The courts use precedents to build stability and order into the judicial system. Decisions concerning similar prior cases are used as guides when deciding new cases. The process of finding analogous cases from the past and convincing the tax authorities of the precedential value of those cases is the essence of judicial tax research.

The hierarchy of court decisions determines whether a case is precedent. A Supreme Court decision on an issue is precedent for all courts as long as the statute remains unchanged. A taxpayer sometimes tries to argue a narrow application of the court's holding or interpretation of the law so as to distinguish the unfavorable precedent. Court of appeals decisions provide precedent for all cases in their respective circuits. The decisions of other circuit courts of appeals are merely influential, not precedent. The Tax Court follows precedent set by the appellate court of the circuit in which the taxpayer resides. Thus, consistency in the application of law is maintained within a jurisdiction even though an inconsistency may exist in the law's application to taxpayers residing in other circuits.

> **QUICK FACTS**
> Court of appeals decisions provide precedent within each circuit.

> **QUICK FACTS**
> U.S. Supreme Court cases are precedent for all taxpayers.

FIGURE 7-4 | SOURCES OF TAX AUTHORITY

Legislative:	Internal Revenue Code
	Joint Committee Report on new legislation
Administrative:	Treasury Regulations (Final, Temporary, and Proposed)
	Revenue Rulings and Revenue Procedures
Judicial:	U.S. Supreme Court
	Courts of Appeal
	Tax Court (Regular Decisions and Memorandum Decisions)
	District Court
	U.S. Court of Federal Claims

STEPS IN CONDUCTING TAX RESEARCH

Tax research consists of five basic steps, as explained in Chapter 1. Those steps, as applied in the tax research context are:

1. Investigate the facts and identify the issues.
2. Collect the appropriate authorities.
3. Analyze the research.
4. Develop the reasoning and conclusion.
5. Communicate the results.

Step One: Investigate the Facts and Identify the Issues

Often, tax problems have a way of appearing deceptively simple to taxpayers. The taxpayer is often interested only in the final outcome and tax-planning advice. The tax adviser must always exercise due professional care in acquiring the facts and identifying the relevant legal issues regardless of the amount of money at stake.

> **EXAMPLE:** Determine how much is deductible under Code Section 170 for making a charitable contribution of land costing $100,000 when it has a $250,000 fair market value.
>
> **Discussion:** Depending on additional facts, the deduction can range from $0 to $250,000. Even the most cursory review of Section 170 reveals that the researcher needs to know more facts just to identify the real tax issues that impact the amount of any charitable deduction.

Preliminary research often causes the tax researcher to understand what additional facts are needed from the client. The new information might trigger new or more refined issues for research. The purpose of the following example is merely to illustrate the continually unfolding interrelationships between primary tax authorities and relevant facts in identifying and refining the real legal issues to research.

> **EXAMPLE:** In researching the character of the contributed land as ordinary income or capital gain property, assume the tax advisor discovers that the taxpayer claimed all real estate holdings as investments, despite a history of many prior real estate transactions. What issues and conclusions should the tax adviser identify?
>
> **Discussion:** The legal issue is whether the taxpayer's real estate activities constitute a trade or business under Section 162(a). If so, was the donated land held for sale in the normal course of the business? If the taxpayer was in the business of selling real estate, the land was held for sale in the normal course of that business, resulting in ordinary income, rather than capital gains which might benefit from lower tax rates.

Step Two: Collect the Appropriate Authorities

Search techniques needed to collect the appropriate tax authorities can include the keyword, table of contents drill-down, index, and citation approaches. The most difficult part of the search is to find relevant cases. While not every Code section and regulation has judicial cases interpreting their language, most sections have cases that apply the statutory and administrative law to a particular set of facts.

FIGURE 7-5 | SEARCH BY TABLE OF CONTENTS APPROACH IN RIA CHECKPOINT

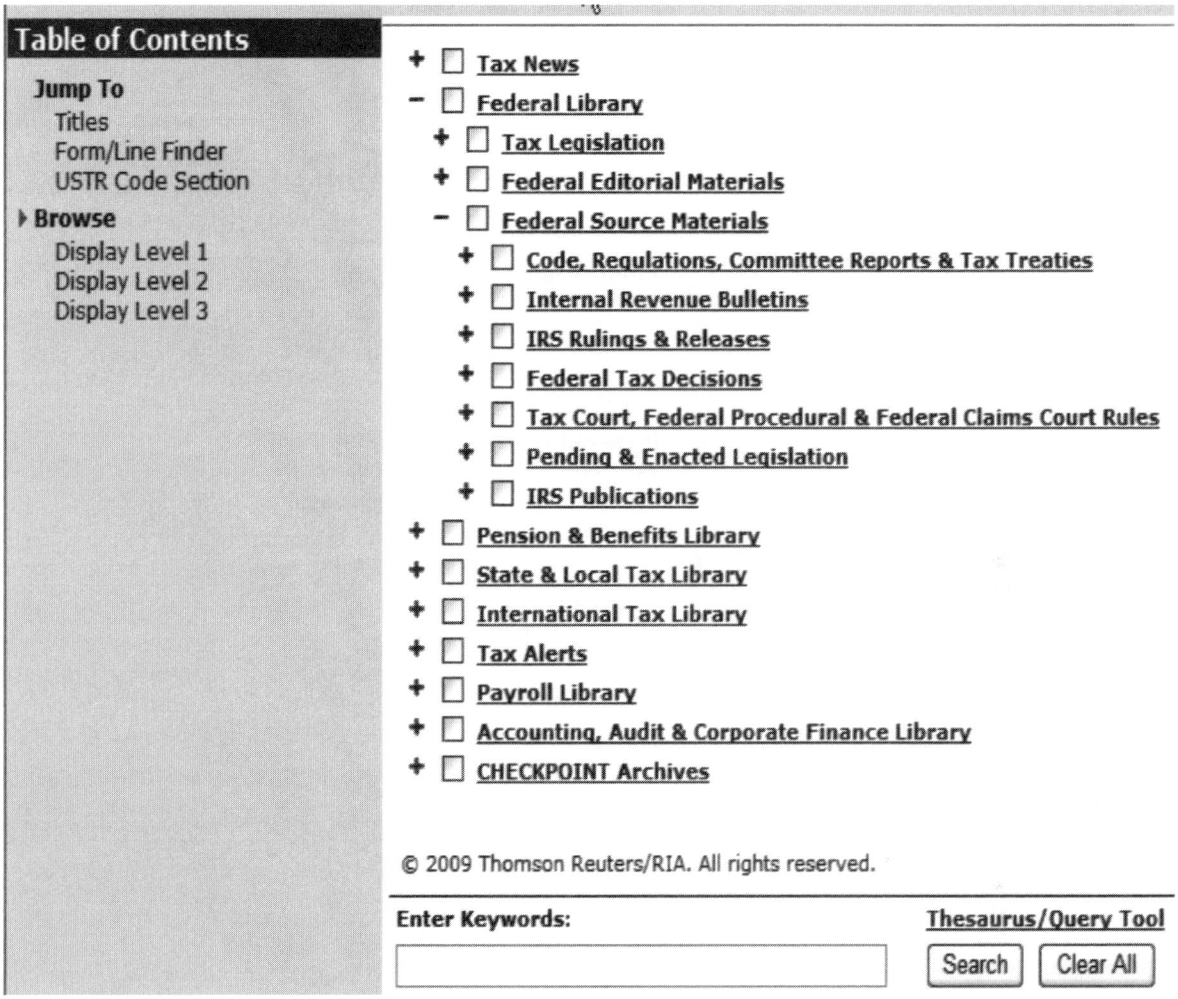

Table of Contents

Jump To
Titles
Form/Line Finder
USTR Code Section
▸ Browse
Display Level 1
Display Level 2
Display Level 3

+ ☐ **Tax News**
− ☐ **Federal Library**
  + ☐ **Tax Legislation**
  + ☐ **Federal Editorial Materials**
  − ☐ **Federal Source Materials**
    + ☐ **Code, Regulations, Committee Reports & Tax Treaties**
    + ☐ **Internal Revenue Bulletins**
    + ☐ **IRS Rulings & Releases**
    + ☐ **Federal Tax Decisions**
    + ☐ **Tax Court, Federal Procedural & Federal Claims Court Rules**
    + ☐ **Pending & Enacted Legislation**
    + ☐ **IRS Publications**
+ ☐ **Pension & Benefits Library**
+ ☐ **State & Local Tax Library**
+ ☐ **International Tax Library**
+ ☐ **Tax Alerts**
+ ☐ **Payroll Library**
+ ☐ **Accounting, Audit & Corporate Finance Library**
+ ☐ **CHECKPOINT Archives**

© 2009 Thomson Reuters/RIA. All rights reserved.

Enter Keywords: **Thesaurus/Query Tool**

[   ]   [Search]   [Clear All]

A keyword search is often used to find relevant cases interpreting the Code or regulations. However, note that the search engines for different databases do not always search the entire database. A keyword search is sometimes likely to overwhelm the researcher with many documents that are not on point. Also, tax research databases differ in presenting the search results.

A table of contents drill-down search approach in a tax database enables one to proceed from the relevant Code section to tax services to find relevant annotations of cases that interpret that Code section. Annotations provide a one- or two-sentence explanation of the case. For example, when one finds the relevant Code section and provision within it, most online tax services will provide hyperlinks to the authorities discussed. If the case appears potentially relevant, the researcher should then read the entire case to ensure its relevance, extract sufficient information to understand the case, and generally write a paragraph on that case.

FIGURE 7-6 SEARCH BY CITATION: RIA TEMPLATES FOR CODE AND REGULATIONS

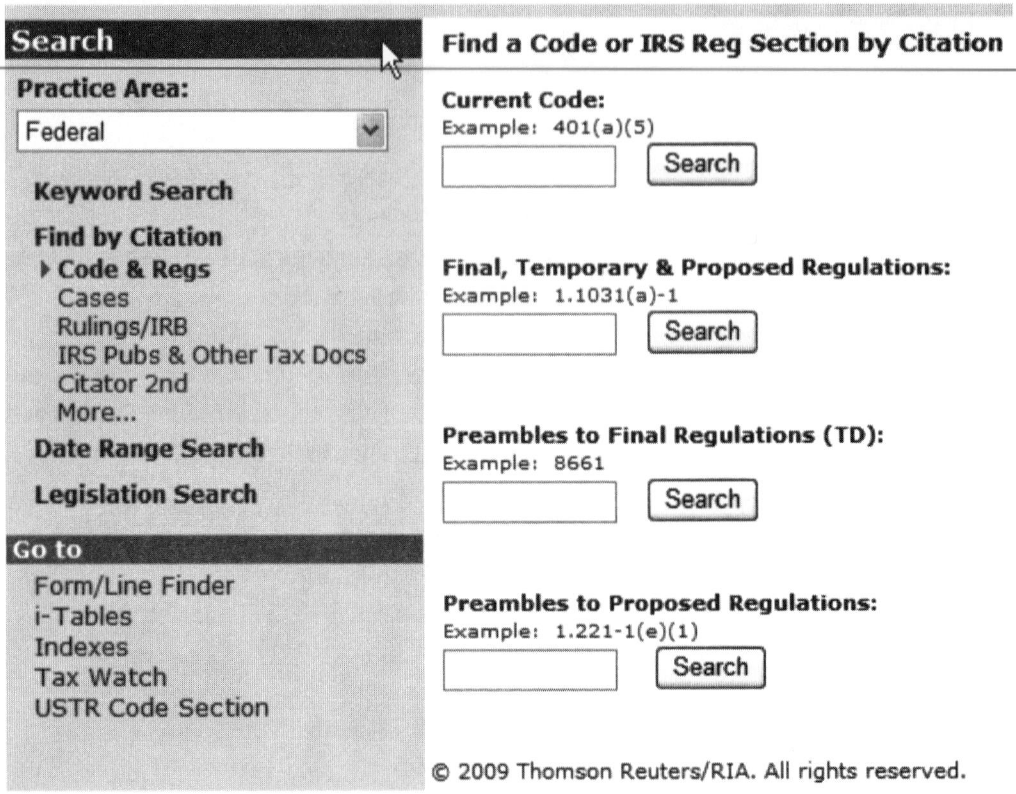

Checkpoint screen shot, published online at http://checkpoint.riag.com.

The index approach is similar to viewing an index in the back of the book. Indices exist for the Code, tax services, and selected other sources. Access to the indices in RIA Checkpoint is near the bottom left side of the opening research screen.

Citations enable the researcher to collect the authorities quickly. Whether one uses online tax databases or hardbound books to find the case is irrelevant; the citation is the same. Case citations generally use the following format: *case name*,volume number, reporter, initial page number where the case begins, the court if not evident from the reporter, and year of the court's decision. When one uses a tax research database, note that the database's style of case citation may differ slightly from the official style that the tax researcher should use.

Tax publishers RIA and CCH provide useful court reporters that include all federal court decisions concerning taxation, except for those from the Tax Court. Thus, included in the reporters are tax cases from U.S. district courts, Court of Federal Claims, court of appeals, and the Supreme Court. The RIA court reporter is called *American Federal Tax Reports* (AFTR, AFTR2d, AFTR3d) while the CCH product is *United States Tax Cases* (USTC). AFTR and USTC are found in the publisher's tax research database: RIA Checkpoint or CCH Tax Research Network. Accountants usually cite non–Tax Court cases in either AFTR or USTC. *Caution:* USTC neither refers to Tax Court cases nor includes them.

Supreme Court decisions are published by the U.S. Government Printing Office in *U.S. Supreme Court Reports* (U.S.). They are also unofficially published by such reporters as AFTR and USTC. A parallel citation exists to show multiple locations for finding a case. A citation to a case need not include any nonofficial sources for accessing the case; however, it's often helpful to include such information. The following example provides a parallel citation to a tax decision by the Supreme Court: *Ballard v. Commissioner*, 544 U.S. 40; 95 AFTR2d 1302 (2005).

Courts of appeal decisions are officially published in the *Federal Reporter* (F., F.2d, F.3d), and the tax decisions are unofficially reprinted in RIA's AFTR series and CCH's USTC. The first name in a case citation indicates the party appealing the prior court's decision. The following citation refers to a 2008 decision by the court of appeals for the Federal Circuit: *National Westminster Bank v. United States*, 512 F.3d 1347; 2008-1 USTC 50,140 (Fed. Cir. 2008).

U.S. District Court decisions are officially published in the *Federal Supplement* (F. Supp., F. Supp. 2d). Finding the decisions of the U.S. Court of Federal Claims and its predecessor courts is more complicated. Decisions rendered between 1929 and 1932 and after 1959 appear in the *Federal Reporter—2d or 3d Series* (F.2d or F.3d), while those issued between 1932 and 1960 are in the *Federal Supplement* (F. Supp.). A sample citation is *United States v. Textron Inc.*, 507 F. Supp. 2d 138, 2007 (D.R.I. 2007).

Tax Court case citations distinguish regular and memorandum decisions because they are in different reporters. Tax Court regular decisions are published by the government in *United States Tax Court Reports* (TC). Tax Court memorandum decisions are published by RIA and CCH reporters called *TC Memorandum Decisions* (T.C. Memo) and *Tax Court Memorandum Decisions* (T.C.M.). The following illustrates the citation to different Tax Court decisions.

Nelson v. Comm'r, 130 T.C. 70 (2008).

Case Name
Volume Number
Reporter
  United States Tax Court Reporter
  CCH Tax Court Memorandum Decisions
Initial Page Number
Year

Gomez v. Comm'r, 95 T.C.M. 1304 (2008).

Case Name
Volume Number
Reporter
  United States Tax Court Reporter
  CCH Tax Court Memorandum Decisions
Initial Page Number
Year

Step Three: Analyze the Research

A working knowledge of primary tax authorities is needed because of the enormous volume and the many sources of tax authorities. Such knowledge should include both understanding the nature of the sources and where to locate them. By understanding the legal hierarchy of tax authorities, the researcher can assess their relative weight. For cases and Revenue Rulings, the strength of authorities varies depending on the court, the age of the decision as a proxy for a greater likelihood that the law has changed, and the client's set of facts.

The analysis of the tax research is often the most difficult part of tax research. General guidelines for analysis are listed below:

1. The Code is the strongest authority. However, the Code does not always answer many questions arising from a given factual situation.

2. Treasury Regulations are the next strongest authority.

3. Court decisions interpret the Code and regulations. A court can overturn a Code section only if it is unconstitutional. A court will overturn a Treasury Regulation only if the regulation is totally unreasonable.

4. Supreme Court cases apply to all taxpayers. Circuit court of appeals decisions apply only to taxpayers residing in that circuit. However, circuit court cases are often influential elsewhere.

5. IRS Revenue Rulings and Revenue Procedures are binding only on IRS revenue agents, not on the courts. Thus, weight of authority for Revenue Rulings exists only if the taxpayer is arguing before the IRS.

A citator is used to check whether a case continues to have validity. A citator presents the judicial history of a case. Courts may affirm or reverse a prior court's decision or any part of the case. The higher court may sometimes issue the appropriate legal standard and then remand the case back to the prior court for a decision that applies that law. A citator also traces subsequent judicial references to the case, which helps to indicate the influence of a court's reasoning on other courts. Figure 7-7 displays the citator in RIA Checkpoint.

EXAMPLE: A link to the citator in RIA Checkpoint appears on the search screen on the left side. In using the citator, the researcher enters the citation for the case to evaluate.

An ability to research effectively both primary and secondary tax authorities is a necessary skill for the tax advisor. Secondary authorities on taxation are often helpful in locating and assessing relevant primary tax authority. They may provide valuable analyses, research already performed by leading tax professionals and scholars, and unique insights on a wide variety of tax issues. Secondary authority does not carry precedential weight. Secondary sources that are more commonly used in tax are provided in Figure 7-8. Secondary authority generally comes from the following types of sources:

• Lesser IRS administrative pronouncements, such as private letter rulings (PLRs), IRS publications, and IRS notices.

• Tax service explanations, such as in RIA's *Federal Tax Coordinator*.

• Treatises and textbooks.

• Articles from professional tax journals and law reviews.

• Tax newsletters and Web sites.

Step Four: Develop the Reasoning and Conclusion

In reaching a solution to a tax issue, the tax researcher will apply relevant tax authorities related to the issues and facts. As in accounting and auditing research, professional judgment in tax also plays an important role in reasoning. Always consider the weight of authority so as to start with the strongest, most logical source, such as a Code section or subsection. For cases, try to use the strongest cases possible, which depends on the level of the court, whether the judge's remark was the holding of the case or merely influential passing remarks (dicta), and the similarity of the facts. The reasoning includes a discussion of how each potentially relevant legal authority is applied to the set of facts or is distinguishable from them.

FIGURE 7-7 | RIA CITATOR 2ND FOR UPDATING CASES

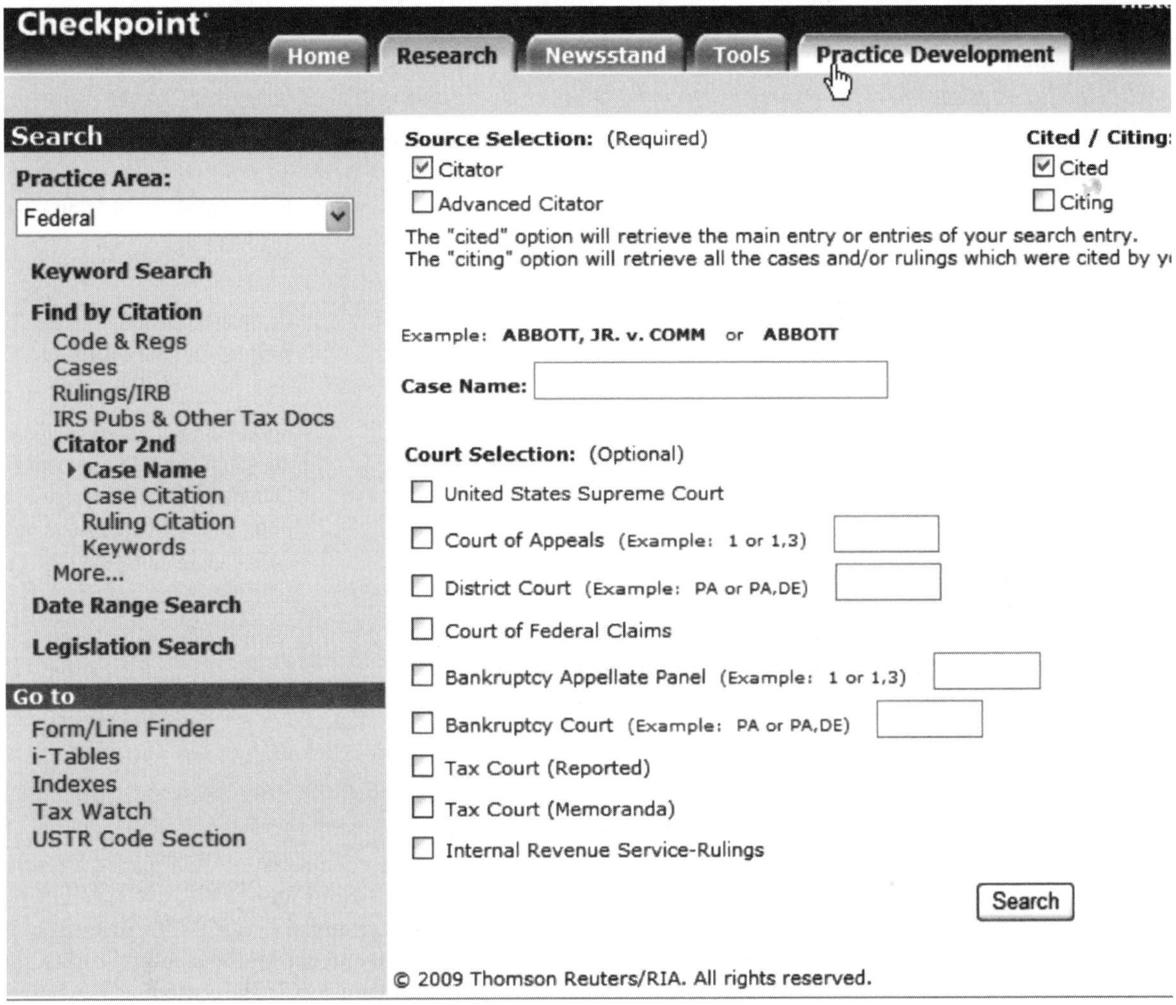

Checkpoint screen shot, published online at http://checkpoint.riag.com.
© 2009. Thomson Reuters RIA. Reprinted with permission. All rights reserved.

Document the relevant law and apply each source discussed in the reasoning before reaching a conclusion. In certain situations, no clear solution is apparent due to unresolved issues of law or perhaps incomplete facts from the client. Written documentation is important for communicating the research findings to others or constructing tax planning advice. Documentation of the research process is especially important if the client is audited on this tax issue. When the tax return is under audit, the person who completed the tax return two years ago may have departed. Carefully document the research to avoid both IRS penalties and litigation from an unhappy client.

As part of tax planning, the tax professional will determine how to structure the facts and possible legal alternatives for the client's problem. The professional should present likely consequences for each alternative. The client, in discussion with the tax professional, will then select the best alternative given the facts.

RESEARCH TIPS

Document your tax research in a memo for the client file.

FIGURE 7-8 | POPULAR SECONDARY SOURCES IN TAX

TAX JOURNALS

Journal of Taxation	Warren, Gorham & Lamont
TAXES—The Tax Magazine	Commerce Clearing House
The Tax Adviser	American Institute of CPAs

TAX NEWSLETTERS

Daily Tax Report	Bureau of National Affairs, Inc.
Tax Notes	Tax Analysts

TAX REFERENCE BOOKS

Master Tax Guide	Commerce Clearing House
IRS Practice and Procedure	Warren, Gorham & Lamont

TAX SERVICES

United States Tax Reporter	Research Institute of America
Federal Tax Coordinator 2d	Research Institute of America
Standard Federal Tax Reporter	Commerce Clearing House
Tax Management Portfolios	Bureau of National Affairs, Inc.
Mertens Law of Federal Income Taxation	Callaghan & Company

TAX TREATISES

Bittker and Eustice: *Federal Income Taxation of Corporations and Shareholders*	Warren, Gorham & Lamont
McKee, Nelson, and Whitmire: *Federal Taxation of Partnerships and Partners*	Warren, Gorham & Lamont

Step Five: Communicate the Results

A structured tax research memo format for the completed tax research is usually used. Subheadings typically exist to assist the reader. The conclusion is often placed after the issues. An example of a very brief memo is provided in Figure 7-9.

In the reasoning, check that all relevant sources of authority are briefly discussed. A case is often presented in a separate paragraph with a sentence for the facts of the case, the court's holding, and the reasoning behind the court's decision. In the reasoning, it is best to explain how each authority discussed applies to the client's set of facts rather than assume that the reader will see the same connection of relevant law to the client's set of facts.

FIGURE 7-9 | BRIEF RESEARCH MEMO ILLUSTRATED

FACTS: Tim gave Mary a diamond engagement ring worth $2,000 when Mary was a travel companion for Tim's month-long business trip to Europe.

ISSUE: Whether a taxpayer who receives an engagement ring while serving as a travel companion can exclude the value of the ring as a gift under Section 102(a).

CONCLUSION: A taxpayer can exclude the fair market value of an engagement ring as a gift.

REASONING: Gross income under Section 61(a) includes all income, including compensation for services, unless otherwise excluded. The value of a gift is excluded under Section 102(a). The U.S. Supreme Court defined a gift as coming from real love and affection and not from a business relationship in *Comm'r v. Duberstein*, 363 U.S. 278 (1960). Tim's engagement to Mary suggests true love for transferring the ring so as to qualify as gift under the analysis of *Comm'r v. Duberstein*, 363 U.S. 278 (1960). The value of the engagement ring is excludable under Section 102(a) and not part of Mary's gross income under Section 61(a) because it is not compensation for services.

A letter to the client about the research should focus on what the client wants to know, the bottom line results, and tax planning advice. The letter should clearly and briefly express the major points in a less technical format than a research memo. The client cannot often judge the quality of the research and may use the quality of the communications as a proxy to judge your abilities. The tax professional should follow up significant oral communications with a letter or e-mail.

Effective communication often requires a presentation tailored to the intended audience. Professional judgment is required in determining how much detail to express when preparing any given client letter, tax research memo, or other written document. The goal is to make sure that clients completely understand both the potential benefits and risks of any recommended actions. Whatever the level of technical sophistication of the client for whom the research is performed, a client letter should set forth at least a statement of the relevant facts, the tax issues involved, the researcher's conclusions, and the legal authorities and reasoning upon which the conclusions are based. Guidelines for preparing each section of the research report include the following.

QUICK FACTS

Develop strong writing skills for effective client communications.

Relevant Facts

1. Include all the facts necessary for answering the tax question(s) at issue.
2. Usually state the events in chronological order and provide a date for each event.
3. Provide references to any available documentation of the facts.
4. Let the client review the written description of the facts for accuracy and completeness.

Issues Identified

1. State each issue as precisely as possible, referencing where in the Code the issue arises.
2. Incorporate in each issue the critical facts for determining the applicable law.
3. Describe each issue in a separate sentence.
4. Arrange the tax issues in a logical order.

Conclusions

1. State a brief separate conclusion for each tax issue presented.
2. Review the quality of the written memo or client letter communications.
3. Sign and date the client letter that communicates the results and tax planning advice.

Authorities and Reasoning

1. Provide a detailed, logical analysis to support each of the research conclusions.
2. Separately present the authorities and the reasoning underlying each issue.
3. Always begin discussing a relevant Code section before going to a regulation or case.
4. For court decisions, concisely summarize the facts, holding, and reasoning.
5. Provide a proper citation for each authority mentioned.
6. Apply the precise findings of each legal authority cited to the facts.
7. Consider providing possible alternatives having a reasonable possibility of success on the merits of the issue. Assess the legal support underlying each alternative.

QUICK FACTS

A tax research memo provides facts, issues, conclusions, authorities, and reasoning.

PROFESSIONAL STANDARDS FOR TAX SERVICES

Various professional standards affect tax practice. Foremost is the IRS Circular 230, which governs who can practice before the IRS and provides enforceable rules of conduct and strict standards on written advice related to potential legally questionable tax shelters. Under Circular 230, a CPA, lawyer, and those passing an IRS exam to qualify as enrolled agents can practice before the IRS. Rules of conduct in Circular 230 include using due diligence and not working for a contingent or unconscionable fee in preparing any original tax return.

Circular 230 provides strict standards on any written tax advice, including e-mails regarding covered opinions on tax avoidance transactions, as identified in Treas. Reg. § 1.6011-4(b)(2). This standard has led most tax professionals to provide a disclaimer on every e-mail. Even more importantly, as a result of recent Circular 230 reforms, tax accountants have refocused on offering professional services rather than sales of questionable tax planning packages.

The AICPA Statements on Standards for Tax Services (SSTSs) supplement the AICPA Code of Professional Conduct for CPAs in tax practice. The SSTS address such topics as the use of estimates on the taxpayer's returns, making a departure from a position previously decided by the court or IRS administrative proceedings, and responsibilities after learning about an error on the taxpayer's previously filed tax return. The AICPA has also issued a few interpretations of these standards, such as one on tax planning. The SSTS are available on the AICPA Web site under its materials on taxation. Future tax professionals are encouraged to read these professional standards and apply them in practice.

> **EXAMPLE:** When preparing or signing a tax return, when must a CPA in good faith not rely, without verification, on information that the taxpayer or third party prepares?
>
> **Discussion:** If the information appears incorrect, incomplete, or inconsistent on its face or on the basis of other facts, the CPA has a duty to make further inquiry (SSTS No. 3).

The CPA exam often tests tax research skills in the simulation part of the exam's regulation section. For the simulation, the CPA exam provides a database with a tab for research, providing the Code and the Treasury Regulations. The CPA exam now has several short simulation problems. The AICPA's simulation problem example shown in Chapter 1 is reproduced and answered in this chapter's appendix. One looks under the research tab to find the relevant Code or Treasury Regulations.

SUMMARY

Accountants perform tax research for both tax compliance and tax planning. For any tax issue, the researcher must find and understand the major primary authorities: the Code, Treasury Regulations, and cases. Using a tax research database such as RIA Checkpoint is a necessity in practice. Tax researchers must carefully cite to their authorities and apply them to the client's facts. Professional standards apply to accountants and tax professionals. In the process of understanding tax research, one develops an appreciation for the complexity, excitement, and skills required for a tax professional.

DISCUSSION QUESTIONS

1. Explain the difference between tax evasion, tax avoidance, and abusive tax avoidance.

2. Identify tax research goals.

3. Identify and explain the basic steps of the tax research process.

4. Discuss the challenges in tax research.

5. Distinguish between tax compliance and tax planning.

6. Identify the differences between a Treasury Regulation and a Revenue Ruling.

7. Explain the meaning of the term *precedent* for tax research.

8. What does it mean when the IRS announces a nonacquiescence?

9. Identify the sources that are published in the IRB.

10. Besides Revenue Rulings and Revenue Procedures, identify three other types of sources that the IRS generates.

11. Explain when one would encourage a client to go to district court rather than Tax Court.

12. Discuss how to use RIA Checkpoint to find relevant cases.

13. Identify what cases are provided in AFTR and USTC.

14. Compare and contrast Tax Court regular decisions with Tax Court memorandum decisions.

15. Diagram the court hierarchy, showing the three courts of original jurisdiction on the bottom, two courts in the middle, and the U.S. Supreme Court on top.

16. Discuss the structure of a tax research memo.

17. Locate three different tax Web sites, and identify three different items available on each Web site.

18. Describe the analysis and reasoning in a tax research memo.

EXERCISES

1. Find each of the following on the Web:
   a. A copy of your state's 1040 tax form.
   b. A copy of Publication 597, "Information on the United States–Canada Income Tax Treaty."
   c. Two proposed taxation bills, and briefly summarize each.

2. Which of the following tax sources are primary authorities?
   a. Tax services
   b. Tax Court memorandum decisions
   c. Revenue Procedures
   d. IRS publications
   e. Temporary Treasury Regulations

3. Use a tax research database to answer the following:
   a. Paraphrase Code Section 61(a)(4).
   b. What is the general content of Code Section 166(d)?
   c. Find the precise authority within the Code that defines *net long-term capital gains*.
   d. Find the precise authority within the Code that determines when the gain on the sale of a home is taxable.

4. Use a tax research database and answer the following questions. Then repeat the problem using a different tax research database and compare their ease of use.
   a. Conduct a search of the U.S. Treasury Regulations using the keyword "moving expenses." List three documents from your search and their dates.

b. Conduct a search of the IRB/CB using the keyword "tuition credit." List the three most recent documents produced from your search. Use proper citation format.

5. After getting selected in Disney's training program, Minsu became a rock star. His family paid $22,000 to get Minsu trained. How much of these expenses paid by his family are deductible? Reference the specific authority in the Code and regulations.

6. Find the Code section that explains the amount of the penalty for failure to include reportable transaction information with the return. How much is that penalty?

7. Under Treas. Reg. § 1.6011-4, how is a reportable transaction described?

8. Central Michigan Medical Association (CMMA) is planning on hiring a new cardiologist who currently lives in Dallas, Texas. The cardiologist owns a home in Dallas. Due to the depressed housing market, he would incur a loss of $80,000 if it were sold. In order for the new doctor to relocate to Michigan, he requests that CMMA reimburse him for the loss to be incurred on the sale of his Dallas home. In conducting tax research, what are some tax issues to consider in regards to the tax treatment for the loss reimbursement? Identify the key issues as precisely as possible.

9. Use a tax research database and identify the general content of each of the following Internal Revenue Code sections:

a. § 62(a)(2)

b. § 162(e)(4)

c. § 262(b)

d. § 6702(a)

10. Use a tax research database and list the major Code sections for the following topics:

a. Gift tax

b. Capital gains

c. Stock dividends

d. Business energy credits

11. Identify the general contents of each of the following subchapters and parts of the Code:

a. Subchapter A

b. Subchapter C

c. Subchapter K, part 1

d. Subchapter S

12. You loaned your roommate $4,500 for next semester's tuition. Your roommate promised to pay you back next summer from his summer employment. However, next summer, you realized that your roommate never found a job, but vacationed all summer in Europe. He e-mails you and informs you of his inability to pay off his debt. Can you claim any tax deduction? Focus primarily on the Internal Revenue Code for your research.

13. Use a tax service to find the definition of a *material adviser* in the Code. What type of list must the material advisor maintain? Give the authorities for your answers, using proper citation format.

14. Which Treasury Regulation provides rules for foreign-owned U.S. corporations and foreign corporations engaged in a trade or business within the United States (reporting corporations)? What IRS form is a reporting corporation required to file that relates to reportable transactions with a related party?

15. Determine the number of Treasury Regulations issued for each of the following Code sections 101, 183 and 385. Provide a citation to the last Regulation for each Code Section.

Using the Code

16. What deduction does § 162(a)(2) specifically authorize? What Code provision in another section disallows some of those deductions? Explain.

17. What is the penalty provided under Code Section 6662(b)(2)? Where in that Code section is that penalty defined? Explain the definition in your own words.

18. Determine whether employer contributions to employees' health and accident plans create gross income for the employee. Give the answer and describe the process used to find the answer, including the tax research database used, the successful method of search, and the relevant provision within the applicable code sections.

Using Treasury Regulations

19. Examine Treas. Reg. § 1.183-2. What Code section and language within that Code section does the Treasury Regulation interpret? What does the Treasury Regulation state are the nine relevant factors?

20. Find the Treasury Regulation that determines whether educational expenses can qualify as deductible business expenses. Give the citation for the general rule within that regulation.

21. Assume Sally is a professor who has a PhD in accounting and teaches tax courses. She decides that it would help her teaching to earn a law degree with a heavy emphasis on tax classes. Can she deduct the cost of the tax courses offered as part of her law degree? Explain and cite to specific provisions in the Code and Treasury Regulations.

Locating Cases

22. Locate *Ballard v. Commissioner*, 544 U.S. 40; 95 AFTR 2d 2005-1302 (2005). What was the main issue before the Supreme Court? What did the Supreme Court do with the appellate court's decision?

23. Find and read a Tax Court regular decision that discusses whether hair transplants are deductible medical expenses. Give the official citation to the case. What did the Tax Court hold? If a case with similar facts were decided today, would the Tax Court reach a similar conclusion? Explain.

Locating Revenue Rulings

24. Locate Revenue Ruling 2003-25, identify the topic, and find the date of the Revenue Ruling. What is the applicable Code section?

25. Locate Revenue Procedure 2008-20, identify the topic, and find the date of the Revenue Procedure. What is the applicable Code section? What IRS tax form addresses the same topic?

Evaluating Different Sources

26. Assume that the taxpayer has a tax issue in which the only authority on point is the following: (a) an unfavorable circuit court of appeals case from the same circuit as the taxpayer's residence and (b) a favorable decision from a district court in another circuit. What does one advise the taxpayer?

27. Assume that the taxpayer has a tax issue in which the only authority on point is the following: (a) an article written by a famous tax lawyer that supports taxpayer's position and (b) a Revenue Ruling that does not support taxpayer's position. What does the researcher advise the taxpayer?

28. Assume that the taxpayer has a tax issue in which the only authority on point is as follows: (a) a private letter ruling that favors the taxpayer's position and (b) a Tax Court regular decision that opposes taxpayer's position. What does the researcher advise the taxpayer?

Conducting Tax Research and Documentation

29. Assume that your best friend has a full scholarship offer for playing football at the University of Colorado at Boulder. The scholarship covers tuition, dorm room, and meal costs at the university. Write a brief memo explaining the tax consequences of the scholarship, documenting the relevant authorities.

30. Assume that your older sister agrees to tutor you for a month in math. She normally charges clients $500 for similar services. In return, you agree to write a brief memo explaining the tax consequences to both you and your sister. You would normally charge $100 for your services. Write the issue.

31. What were the issue(s) involved in *National Westminster Bank v. United States*, 512 F.3d 1347; 101 AFTR2d 2008-490, 2008-1 USTC ¶50,14 (Fed. Cir. 2008)? What is the proper citation for the prior decision in this case?

32. Use a tax service, such as United States Tax Reporter, to answer the following questions:

    a. If your school provides an athletic scholarship to an athlete, does the athlete have gross income?

    b. Can the athlete deduct his or her expenses for such items as clothing, meals, and fitness camp?

33. Use the citator to update the decision in *United States v. Textron Inc.*, 507 F. Supp. 2d 138 (D.R.I. 2007). Determine if any case has cited this decision or any subsequent decisions in this case. What topic does this important case address that impacts accountants?

34. Myrtle loaned Sven $150,000 for his gardening supplies company. A drought occurred during the year. Because Sven was unable to repay the loan, Myrtle accepted the following plan to extinguish Sven's debt. Sven is to pay cash of $3,000 and transfer ownership of the gardening property having a value of $80,000 and a basis of $60,000. Sven must also transfer stock with a value of $30,000 and a basis of $45,000. Find a relevant Treasury Regulation. Read Code Section 108 and *James J. Gehl*, 102 T.C. 74 (1994). Determine how much gross income Sven should report from the extinguishment of his debt.

APPENDIX

FIGURE 7A-1 CPA EXAM, REGULATION SECTION, TAX SIMULATION PROBLEM

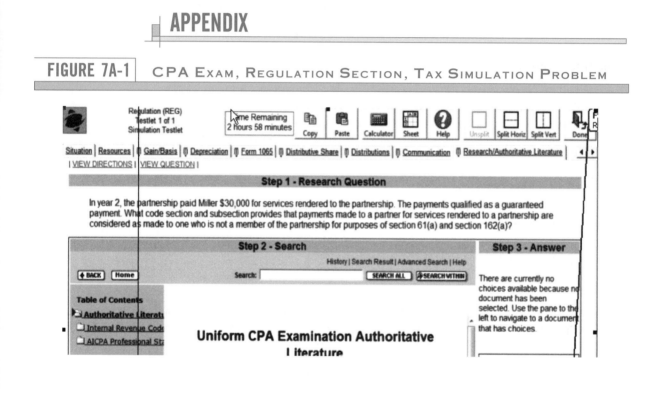

EXAMPLE: In year two, the partnership paid Miller $30,000 for services rendered to the partnership. The payments qualified as a guaranteed payment. What Code section and subsection provide that payments made to a partner for services rendered to a partnership are considered as made to one who is not a member of the partnership for purposes of Section 61(a) under the Research/Authoritative Section 162(a)?

Discussion: Search for "guaranteed payment" in the Code and discover § 707(c). Literature tab and "Sec. 707. Transactions between partner and partnership (c) Guaranteed payments

> To the extent determined without regard to the income of the partnership, payments to a partner for services or the use of capital shall be considered as made to one who is not a member of the partnership, but only for the purposes of Section 61(a) (relating to gross income) and, subject to Section 263, for purposes of Section 162(a) (relating to trade or business expenses)."

Assurance Services and Auditing Research

LEARNING OBJECTIVES

After completing this chapter, you should understand:

- The types of assurance and consulting services and the applicable standards.
- The environment for the assurance services standard-setting process.
- Authoritative auditing support.
- The Public Company Accounting Oversight Board (PCAOB).
- How to utilize the AICPA's professional standards in research.
- The role of auditing in the public sector.
- The hierarchy of the AICPA Code of Professional Conduct.
- The role of professional judgment in the research process.
- International dimensions of auditing.

Because information technology has had a significant impact on the accounting profession and society in general, the public accounting profession has focused on its willingness and ability to design and offer additional value-added services, in addition to such traditional services as tax preparation and auditing. Technological changes have encouraged accounting professionals to transform from number crunchers and certifiers of information to decision support specialists and enhancers of information. Many professionals who keep abreast of the major changes in the profession and technology have adapted their practices and market orientation to these new value-added assurance services. Some practitioners are also expanding the area of consulting services offered to clients. As a result, the practitioner/researcher must become aware of these new assurance services and the related authoritative standards and restrictions that apply in offering these services.

ASSURANCE SERVICES

In order to focus on the needs of users of decision-making information and improve the related services that accountants provide, an AICPA committee conducted research that consisted of assessing customer needs, external factors, information technology, and needed competencies to offer these new value-added services. These services are referred to as *assurance services*, defined as follows:

> Assurance Services are independent professional services that improve the quality of information, or its context, for decision makers.

Notice that this definition of assurance services implies that the service itself will add value to the user, not necessarily just the report. Additionally, an independent professional must offer the assurance services in order to improve the quality of the information or its context. Current examples of such assurance services proposed by the AICPA include CPA WebTrust, CPA ElderCare/Prime Plus, and CPA Performance View services.

Therefore, assurance services are considered three-party contracts—involving the client, the assurer (that is, accountant), and the third party to whom the accountant is providing assurance. An example of an assurance service engagement is where Consumers Union tests a product and reports the results or ratings in *Consumer Reports*.

An overview of assurance services versus consulting services is presented in Figure 8-1. Specific details are provided in the following sections of this chapter. As depicted, the traditional audit service is an attestation function that falls under the broader term of assurance services. As a professional conducting research, one must recognize the professional standards for attestation and consulting engagements.

Consulting Services and Standards

Attestation and audit services are considered special types of assurance services. Consulting services do not fall under the umbrella of assurance services. Historically,

FIGURE 8-1 | ASSURANCE AND CONSULTING SERVICES UMBRELLAS

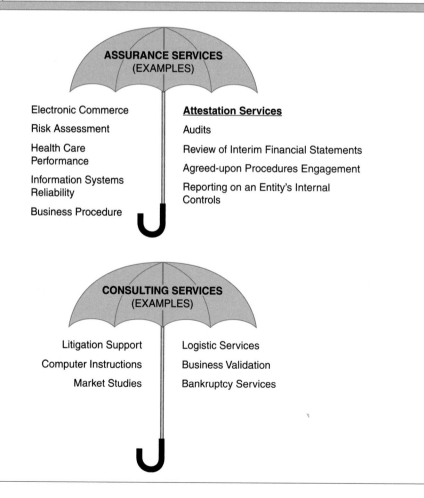

consulting services offered to clients (two-party contracts) by CPAs were referred to as *management consulting services* or *management advisory services*. These services have generally evolved from accounting-related matters in connection with audits or tax engagements. In a consulting engagement, the CPA develops findings and conclusions, which are followed with recommendations for the benefit of the client. This is in contrast to an attest engagement (a three-party contract) whereby the CPA reports on the reliability of a written assertion that is the responsibility of a third party. Examples of consulting engagements include litigation support services, computer installation engagements, and various market studies for clients.

The typical consulting engagement is quite similar to the research process presented in this text. The consulting engagement would normally include:

- Determination of the client's objectives
- Fact-finding
- Definition of the problem
- Evaluation of the alternatives
- Formulation of a proposed action
- Communication of the results
- Implementation and follow-up[1]

Professional standards for consulting services include general standards and specific consulting standards. In rendering professional services (including consulting), general standards of the profession are located in Rule 201 of the AICPA Code of Professional Conduct, as discussed later in this chapter. Additionally, the AICPA has issued Statements on Standards for Consulting Services (SSCS), which provide standards for the practitioner rendering consulting services. These standards are located in the AICPA's Professional Standards database, also discussed later in this chapter.

AUDITING STANDARD-SETTING ENVIRONMENT

Auditing is indispensable in a society where credit is extended widely and business failures regularly occur and where investors wish to study the financial statements of many enterprises. The purpose of the audit report is to add credibility to the financial information. The general environment for auditing is very dynamic and constantly evolving as various factors impact the audit process.

The independent auditor's role serves a secondary communication function; the audit opinion is expressed on the financial information reported by management. The auditor's primary concern is whether the client's financial statements are presented in accordance with GAAP. The auditor must conduct the audit in a manner that conforms to auditing standards and take actions that are guided by professional ethical standards. Additionally, in nonaudit engagements, the accountant must use relevant attestation standards and statements for compilation and review services, as well as standards for accountants' services on prospective financial information (that is, forecasts and projections).

Attestation Services and Standards

Society increasingly seeks attestation services (a subset of assurance services) from the accounting profession. In the past, attestation services were normally limited to audit

---

[1] *AICPA Professional Standards*, vol. 2, Section CS-100.05.

opinions on historical financial statements based upon audits that followed generally accepted auditing standards (GAAS).

More recently, professional accountants render opinions on other representations, such as reporting on management's report as to the effectiveness of the entity's internal controls, as now required by the Sarbanes-Oxley Act of 2002. Accountants were concerned that existing standards or guidelines did not meet the demands of society. As a result, the AICPA developed attestation standards and related interpretations to provide a general framework for attest engagements.[2]

The term *attest* means to provide assurance as to the reliability of information. The AICPA has defined an attest engagement as follows:

> An attest engagement is one in which a practitioner is engaged to issue or does issue a written communication that expresses a conclusion about the reliability of a written assertion that is the responsibility of another party.[3]

QUICK FACTS

Attestation services provide assurance as to the reliability of information.

Whether the attestation service is for the traditional audit of financial statements or reporting on an entity's internal control or prospective financial information, the professional accountant must follow certain guidelines and standards in rendering these attestation services. In conducting an attest engagement, the professional accountant reviews and conducts tests of the accounting records deemed necessary to obtain sufficient evidence to render an opinion. Choosing the accounting records and other information to review and deciding the extent to examine them are strictly matters of professional judgment, as many authoritative pronouncements emphasize.

Figure 8-2 presents the major elements of the attestation environment that face accountants in conducting the research for an attest engagement. Figure 8-3 presents

FIGURE 8-2 | ATTEST RESEARCH ENVIRONMENT

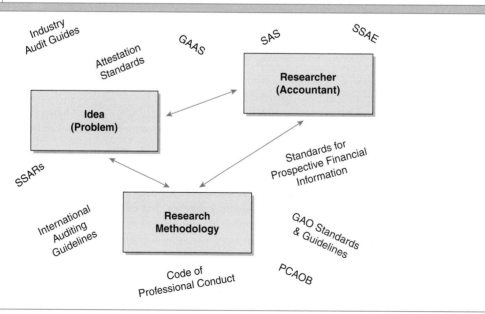

FIGURE 8-3 | ATTEST ENGAGEMENTS AND GUIDELINES

Attest Engagement	Guidelines	Issued by
Audit and attest services for nonpublic companies	Generally Accepted Audit Standards (GAAS) Statements on Auditing Standards (SASs)	Auditing Standards Board (ASB)
Accounting and Review Review Services	Statements on Standards for Accounting and Review (SSARs)	Accounting and Review Services Committee (ARSC)
Accountant's Services on Prospective Financial Information	Statements on Standards for Accountant's Services on Prospective Financial Information	Auditing Standards Board
Other Attest Services	Statements on Standards for Attestation Engagement	ASB, ARSC, and the Management Consulting Services Executive Committee
Audit and attest services for public companies	Auditing and Related Professional Practice Standards	Public Company Accounting Oversight Board (PCAOB)

an overview of attest engagements and relevant guidelines. The following sections of this chapter provide an overview of the standard-setting environment for attestation services, the auditing standard-setting process, authoritative auditing pronouncements, and the role of professional judgment in the research process. The chapter also includes a discussion of how the researcher utilizes the AICPA's reSOURCE database in research, a summary of the attestation standards and compilation and review standards, as well as an overview of auditing in the public sector and the international dimensions of auditing. The appendix to this chapter presents examples of opening screen shots to the CPA exam that requires one to conduct auditing/attestation research utilizing the AICPA's Professional Standards.

During the past decade, as the range of attestation services has expanded, many CPAs have found it difficult to apply the basic concepts underlying GAAS or the standards of the Public Company Accounting Oversight Board (PCAOB) to various attestation services. Attestation services have also included the following examples: reporting to the client on which computer system is the cheapest or has the most capabilities, reporting on insurance claims data, and reporting on compliance with regulatory requirements. (In one instance, Wilson Sporting Goods requested an accounting firm to attest to the statement that Wilson's Ultra golf ball outdistance its competitors!)

Consequently, the AICPA has issued Statements on Standards for Attestation Engagements, Statements on Standards for Accounting and Review Services, and Statements on Standards for Accountants' Services on Prospective Financial Information to provide a general framework and set reasonable guidelines for an attest function. The desire is to respond to the changing environment and demands of society.

The broad guidelines for an attest engagement were issued by the AICPA's Auditing Standards Board (ASB) in conjunction with the Accounting and Review Services Committee and the Management Consulting Services Executive Committee. As listed in Figure 8-4, these attestation standards do not supersede any existing standards, but are considered a natural extension of the ten GAAS. The design of these attestation standards provides guidance to the professional to enhance both consistency and quality in the performance of attest services.

> **QUICK FACTS**
> AICPA has issued various authorities for different services.

FIGURE 8-4 | ATTESTATION STANDARDS

General Standards

1. The practitioner must have adequate technical training and proficiency to perform the attestation engagement.
2. The practitioner must have adequate knowledge of the subject matter.
3. The practitioner must have reason to believe that the subject matter is capable of evaluation against criteria that are suitable and available to users.
4. The practitioner must maintain independence in mental attitude in all matters relating to the engagement.
5. The practitioner must exercise due professional care in the planning and performance of the engagement and the preparation of the report.

Standards of Fieldwork

1. The practitioner must adequately plan the work and must properly supervise any assistants.
2. The practitioner must obtain sufficient evidence to provide a reasonable basis for the conclusion that is expressed in the report.

Standards of Reporting

1. The practitioner must identify the subject matter or the assertion being reported on and state the character of the engagement in the report.
2. The practitioner must state the practitioner's conclusion about the subject matter or the assertion in relation to the criteria against which the subject matter was evaluated.
3. The practitioner must state all of the practitioner's significant reservations about the engagement, the subject matter, and, if applicable, the assertion related thereto in the report.
4. The practitioner must state in the report that the report is intended solely for the information and use of the specified parties under the following circumstances:
   - When the criteria used to evaluate the subject matter are determined by the practitioner to be appropriate only for a limited number of parties who either participated in their establishment or can be presumed to have an adequate understanding of the criteria.
   - When the criteria used to evaluate the subject matter are available only to specified parties.
   - When reporting on subject matter and a written assertion have not been provided by the responsible party.
   - When the report is on an attest engagement to apply agreed-upon procedures to the subject matter.

Source: *AICPA Professional Standards*, vol. 1, AT Section 101.

Auditing Standards

Auditing standards differ from audit procedures in that auditing standards provide measures of the quality of performance, whereas audit procedures refer to the specific acts or steps to perform in an audit engagement. Auditing standards do not vary; they remain identical for all audits. Audit procedures often change, depending on the nature and type of entity under audit and the complexity of the audit.

In contrast to GAAP, which is not identified with exactness, the AICPA has formally adopted ten broad requirements for auditors to follow in examining financial statements, classified as general standards, fieldwork standards, and reporting standards. These ten requirements, GAAS, are listed in Figure 8-5. In addition to the issuance of GAAS, the AICPA published a series of Statements on Auditing Standards (SASs).

FIGURE 8-5	GENERALLY ACCEPTED AUDITING STANDARDS

General Standards

1. The auditor must have adequate technical training and proficiency to perform the audit.

2. The auditor must maintain independence in mental attitude in all matters relating to the audit.

3. The auditor must exercise due professional care in the performance of the audit and the preparation of the report.

Standards of Fieldwork

1. The auditor must adequately plan the work and must properly supervise any assistants.

2. The auditor must obtain a sufficient understanding of the entity and its environment, including its internal control, to assess the risk of material misstatement of the financial statements whether due to error or fraud.

3. The auditor must obtain sufficient appropriate audit evidence by performing audit procedures to afford a reasonable basis for an opinion regarding the financial statements under audit.

Standards of Reporting

1. The auditor must state in the auditor's report whether the financial statements are presented in accordance with generally accepted accounting principles (GAAP).

2. The auditor must identify in the auditor's report those circumstances in which such principles have not been consistently observed in the current period in relation to the preceding period.

3. When the auditor determines that informative disclosures are not reasonably adequate, the auditor must so state in the auditor's report.

4. The auditor must either express an opinion regarding the financial statements, taken as a whole, or state that an opinion cannot be expressed, in the auditor's report. When the auditor cannot express an overall opinion, the auditor should state the reasons therefore in the auditor's report. In all cases where an auditor's name is associated with financial statements, the auditor should clearly indicate the character of the auditor's work, if any, and the degree of responsibility the auditor is taking, in the auditor's report.

Source: *AICPA Professional Standards*, vol. 1, AU Section 150.

SASs supplement and interpret the ten GAAS by clarifying the audit procedures or prescribing the auditor's report in both form and content. SASs serve as the primary authoritative support in conducting an audit and are a major source of authoritative information when conducting auditing research. These SASs are incorporated into the AICPA's loose-leaf service and online *Professional Standards*, which provided a continuous codification of SASs.

Thus, the codification of auditing standards organizes logically the essence of the auditing standards. The prefix AU is used to refer to the codified auditing topic. If AU is followed by 2, this section interprets general standards on auditing. Thus, AU 210 addresses standards relating to training, AU 220 summarizes the standards relating to independence, and AU 230 addresses due professional care. If AU is followed by a 3, this section interprets fieldwork standards. Reporting standards are located in AU followed by a 4, 5, or 6. The PCAOB is currently using the codified version of the auditing standards as interim standards. The PCAOB is reviewing and updating audit standards for public companies, as discussed later in this chapter.

Various forms of GAAS are also recognized by governmental and internal auditors. The General Accountability Office (GAO), through the comptroller general of the United States, has issued Governmental Auditing Standards, often referred to as the Yellow

Book. The Institute of Internal Auditors has also issued auditing standards, called the Standards for the Professional Practice of Internal Auditing, under which internal auditors operate. The comptroller general has established the U.S. Auditing Standards Coordinating Forum composed of members from the PCAOB, GAO, and the ASB, which meets several times during the year to facilitate coordination and constructive working relationships between the groups. The main focus of discussion is the convergence of auditing standards among the forum members.

AUDITING STANDARD-SETTING PROCESS

Concern has always existed as to who should set auditing standards for the independent auditor. Prior to establishment of the SEC, Congress debated having audits conducted by governmental auditors. However, the auditing standard-setting process remained in the private sector. SASs were created by the ASB as the AICPA's senior technical committee on auditing standards.

Auditing interpretations on the application of SASs are created by the staff of the Auditing Standards division of the AICPA. The interpretations are not considered as authoritative as SASs. However, auditors must justify any departure from an auditing interpretation issued by the Auditing Standards division of the AICPA. Other publications of the Auditing Standards division include a number of Industry Audit Guides (Figure 8-6) and SOPs.

The Sarbanes-Oxley Act of 2002 transferred the responsibility for auditing and attestation standard setting for public companies to the PCAOB, as explained in the next section. An overview of the current hierarchy of authoritative auditing support is presented in Figure 8-7. The auditor needs to understand each of the sources listed, particularly the PCAOB's auditing standards and the predecessor SASs by the AICPA.

Unlike an audit that expresses whether the financial statements are in conformity with GAAP, the accountant's examination of prospective financial statements provides assurance only as to whether (1) the prospective financial statements conform to the AICPA's guidelines and (2) the assumptions used in the projections provide a reasonable basis for a forecast or projection. The accountant must provide a report on any attestation service provided, as described in the various attestation and auditing standards. (See Figures 8-4 and 8-5.)

Public Company Accounting Oversight Board (PCAOB)

RESEARCH TIPS

Use the Public Company Accounting Oversight Board (PCAOB) authorities for auditing public companies.

The PCAOB has the legal responsibility under the Sarbanes-Oxley Act to establish GAAS, attestation, ethics, and quality control standards for those accounting firms auditing public companies. PCAOB has adopted a rule that requires all registered public accounting firms to adhere to the board's auditing and related practice standards in connection with the preparation or issuance of any audit report for an issuer and in their auditing and related attestation practices. Going forward, the board's new standards are called Auditing and Related Professional Practice Standards.

Standards for auditors of nonpublic companies are currently within the domain of the AICPA. The reconstituted mission of the AICPA's ASB includes the following three main issues:

1. To develop auditing, attestation, and quality control standards for non-issuer engagements, such as privately held commercial entities, nonprofit organizations, and governmental entities.

FIGURE 8-6 | AICPA AUDIT AND ACCOUNTING GUIDES

Agriculture Producers and Agriculture Cooperatives

Airlines

Analytical Procedures

Assessing and Responding to Audit Risk in a Financial Statement Audit

Audit Sampling

Auditing Revenue in Certain Industries

Auditing Derivative Instruments, Hedging Activities, and Investments in Securities

Brokers and Dealers in Securities

Casinos

Common Interest Realty Associations

Construction Contractors

Employee Benefit Plans

Entities with Oil- and Gas-Producing Activities

Federal Government Contractors

Government Auditing Standards and Circular A-133 Audits

Health Care Organizations

Life and Health Insurance Entities

Investment Companies

Not-for-Profit Organizations

Personal Financial Statements

Property and Liability Insurance Companies

Prospective Financial Statements

Service Organizations: Applying SAS No. 70, as amended

State and Local Governmental Units

---

2. To contribute to the development and issuance of high-quality national and international auditing and assurance standards.

3. To respond to the needs for practical guidance in implementing professional standards.

The PCAOB initially adopted as interim standards the AICPA's auditing, attestation, and quality control standards, as well as the AICPA's ethics and independence standards. Thus, the PCAOB uses the AICPA standards, as of April 2003, as the authoritative standards for public company audits until superseded or amended by the PCAOB.

AICPA reSOURCE Database

The AICPA reSOURCE database includes a comprehensive compendium of the AICPA literature consisting of Professional Standards, Accounting Trends and Techniques, Technical Practice Aids, Auditing and Accounting Guides, and Audit Alerts. The Professional Standards segment of this database is also utilized on the CPA exam in conducting auditing research.

RESEARCH TOOLS
ACL
AICPA reSOURCE
Codification
eIFRS
i2
Internet
LexisNexis Academic
RIA Checkpoint

FIGURE 8-7 | AUDITING AUTHORITATIVE SUPPORT

Primary Authoritative Support

1. General Application
   a. Generally Accepted Auditing Standards (ASB)
   b. Statements on Auditing Standards (ASB)
   c. Auditing and Related Professional Practice Standards (PCAOB)
   d. Auditing Interpretations
   e. AICPA Code of Conduct
   f. Internal Auditing Guidelines
2. Special Application to Certain Entities
   a. Industry Audit Guides
   b. Statements of Position of the Auditing Standards Division
   c. Government Auditing Standards (GAO)

Secondary Authoritative Support

1. Audit Research Monographs
2. AICPA Audit and Accounting Manual
3. Journal articles and textbooks

RESEARCH TIPS

Access auditing standards in the AICPA reSOURCE database.

To conduct auditing research utilizing the AICPA's online reSOURCE database would consist of the following steps. The opening screen of the online version of the database appears in Figure 8-8. Clicking on the AICPA Professional Standards link provides the opening screen to the Professional Standards as depicted in Figure 8-9. The table of contents (TOC) appears on the left side of the screen. Clicking on the plus (+) box next to a phrase will expand the TOC section. Note the tabs across the top right of the screen.

To conduct a specific search, click on the research tab, and the search screen appears, as in Figure 8-10. If one was searching for the guidance in using a specialist, the keywords would be inserted on this screen, resulting in the display of Figure 8-11.

RESEARCH TIPS

Keep track of the location of relevant literature on the AICPA reSOURCE database.

AICPA CODE OF PROFESSIONAL CONDUCT

A distinguishing mark of any profession is the establishment and acceptance of a code of professional conduct. Such a code outlines a minimum level of conduct that is mandatory and enforceable upon its membership. A code of ethics emphasizes both the profession's responsibility to the public as well as to colleagues. Every CPA in the practice of public accounting has the responsibility to follow the AICPA Code of Professional Conduct and its applicability to audit, tax, and consulting services.

QUICK FACTS

The AICPA Code of Professional Conduct includes enforceable rules.

The AICPA Code of Professional Conduct consists of principles, rules, interpretations, and ethics rulings. The principles serve as the basic framework for the rules. The rules are mandatory and enforceable. Periodically, the Professional Ethics division of the AICPA issues ethics rulings and interpretations for the purpose of clarifying the Code. The interpretations render guidance to the accountant as to the scope and applicability of the rules. Ethics rulings help to clarify specific situations confronted by the accountant.

FIGURE 8-8 | AICPA ONLINE PUBLICATIONS SCREEN

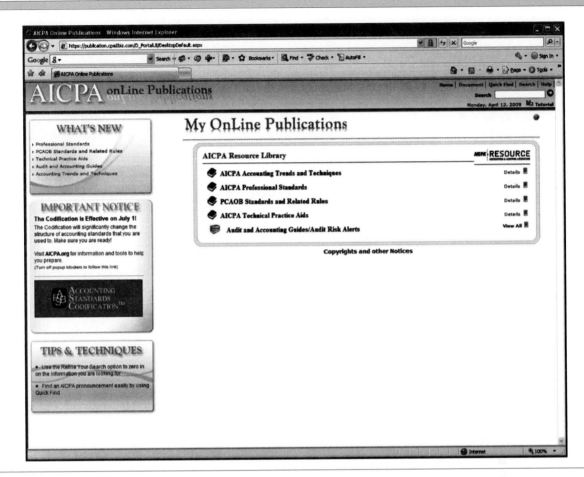

The hierarchy of AICPA principles, rules, interpretations, and ethics rulings are depicted in Figure 8-12.

Departure from the rules may result in disciplinary action, unless the accountant can justify the departure under the circumstances. Disciplinary action may lead to suspension or termination of AICPA membership. Furthermore, a violation of professional conduct may result in revocation of a CPA certificate or license to practice by a state board of accountancy. In many cases, the revocation is also sanctioned by the SEC for auditors of public companies.

Although the AICPA Code of Professional Conduct applies to all members, certain rules are specifically applicable to the independent auditor. Rule 202 requires compliance with professional standards and is stated as follows:

> **Rule 202—Compliance with standards**. A member who performs auditing, review, compilation, management consulting, tax, or other professional services shall comply with standards promulgated by bodies designated by Council.[4]

---

[4] *AICPA Professional Standards*, vol. 2, Section ET-202.

FIGURE 8-9 | AICPA PROFESSIONAL STANDARDS SCREEN

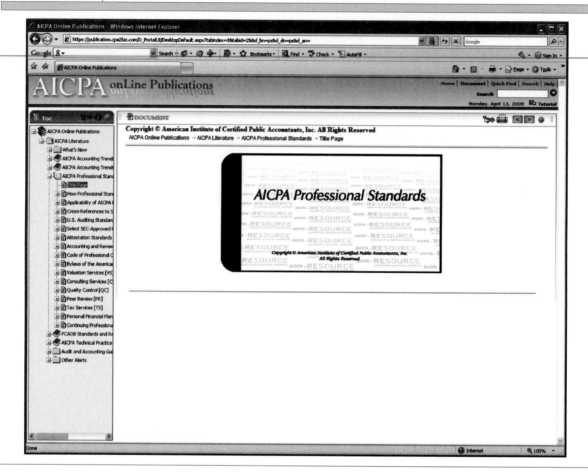

Rule 203 generally prohibits the auditor from expressing an opinion that financial statements are in conformity with GAAP if the statements contain any departure from the official pronouncements of the FASB, its predecessors, the GASB, and the IASB for international accounting standards. Rule 203 is stated as follows:

> **Rule 203—Accounting principles**. A member shall not (1) express an opinion or state affirmatively that the financial statements or other financial data of any entity are presented in conformity with generally accepted accounting principles or (2) state that he or she is not aware of any material modifications that should be made to such statements or data in order for them to be in conformity with generally accepted accounting principles, if such statements contain any departure from an accounting principle promulgated by bodies designated by Council to establish such principles that has a material effect on the statements taken as a whole. If, however, the statements or data contain such a departure and the member can demonstrate that due to unusual circumstances the financial statements would otherwise have been misleading, the member can comply with the rule by describing the departure, its approximate effects, if practicable, and the reasons why compliance with the principle would result in a misleading statement.[5]

---

[5] *AICPA Professional Standards*, vol. 2, Section ET-203.

FIGURE 8-10 | SEARCH TAB

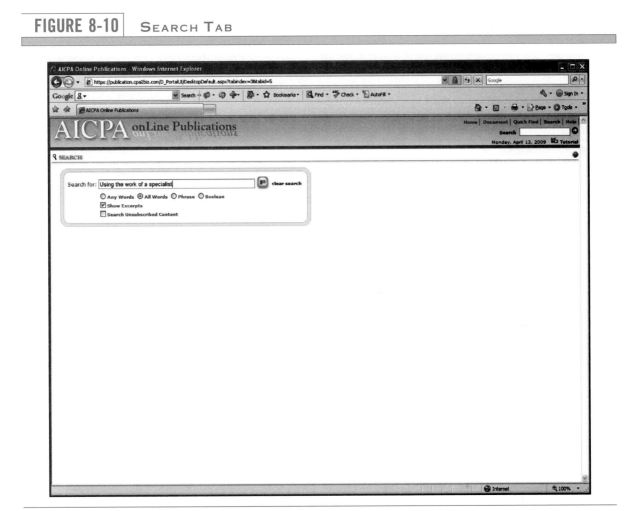

As noted in the previous two rules, it is important to emphasize that the CPA must comply with GAAS or PCAOB standards and have familiarity with GAAP when expressing an audit opinion. Therefore, the practitioner should master the research methodology in order to determine if the audit is in compliance with GAAS and the entity is following GAAP.

Rule 203 was clarified with the issuance of the following interpretations:

Interpretations under Rule 203—Accounting principles: 203-1—Departures from established accounting principles. Rule 203 was adopted to require compliance with accounting principles promulgated by the body designated by Council to establish such principles. There is a strong presumption that adherence to officially established accounting principles would in nearly all instances result in financial statements that are not misleading.

However, in the establishment of accounting principles, it is difficult to anticipate all of the circumstances to which such principles might be applied. This rule therefore recognizes that, upon occasion, there may be unusual circumstances where the literal application of pronouncements on accounting principles would have the effect of rendering financial statements misleading. In such cases, the proper accounting treatment is that which will render the financial statements not misleading.

QUICK FACTS

An audit opinion requires the CPA to comply with GAAS or PCAOB standards and review GAAP.

QUICK FACTS

Interpretation of the AICPA Rules of Conduct provides guidelines as to the scope and application of the rules.

FIGURE 8-11 | AICPA AUDITING STANDARDS SEARCH REQUEST

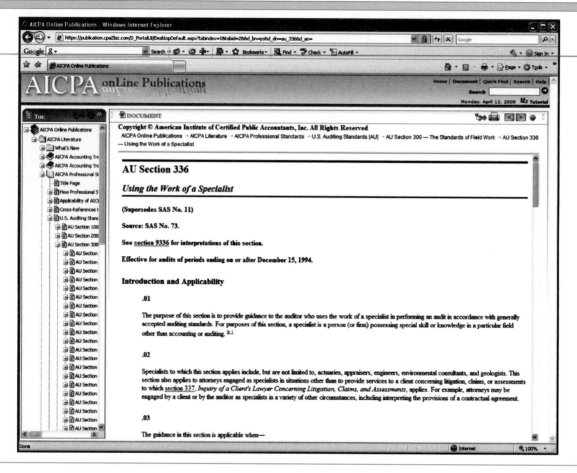

FIGURE 8-12 | HIERARCHY OF THE AICPA CODE OF PROFESSIONAL CONDUCT

Level 1	**Principles**—The Principles provide the framework for the development of the Rules.	Official Section of the Code
Level 2	**Rules**—The Rules serve as the enforceable part of the Code that governs the professional services of the AICPA members.	
Level 3	**Interpretations of the Rules of Conduct**—Interpretations are those that have been adopted by the professional ethics division's executive committee to provide guidelines as to the scope and application of the Rules.	Members who depart from interpretation of rulings must justify such departures.
Level 4	**Ethics Rulings**—The Ethics Rulings consist of formal rulings made by the professional ethics division's executive committee. Their Rulings summarize the application of the Rules and Interpretations to particular factual circumstances.	

The question of what constitutes unusual circumstances as referred to in Rule 203 is a matter of professional judgment involving the ability to support the position that adherence to a promulgated principle would be regarded generally by reasonable men as producing a misleading result.

Examples of events that may justify departures from a principle are new legislation or the evolution of a new form of business transaction. An unusual degree of materiality or the existence of conflicting industry practices are examples of circumstances that do not ordinarily qualify as unusual in the context of Rule 203.

AUDITING STANDARDS IN THE PUBLIC SECTOR

Government officials and the general public are concerned about how the public's money was spent and whether government is achieving its goals funded by taxpayer dollars. Thus, to a large degree, the standards and guidelines used in a governmental audit are similar to auditing requirements in the corporate sector. Federal, state, and local governments have historically placed substantial reliance on the auditing requirements of the AICPA's Auditing Standards division. However, various governmental regulatory bodies have addressed specific governmental audit concerns.

The GAO's Government Auditing Standards (Yellow Book) are applicable to all governmental organizations, programs, activities, and functions. Government auditing standards have the objective of improving the quality of governmental audits at the federal, state, and local levels. These governmental standards were founded on the premise that governmental accountability should go beyond identifying the amount of funds spent in order to measure the manner and effectiveness of the expenditures. Therefore, these standards provide for an audit scope to include financial and compliance auditing as well as auditing for economy, efficiency, and effectiveness of program results. Under federal legislation, federal inspector generals must follow these GAO auditing standards. Also, these standards are audit criteria for federal executive departments and agencies.

Currently, three audit levels affect governments. The first level consists of the GAAS issued by the AICPA. Building upon the AICPA standards are the Government Auditing Standards and federal audit requirements. The Government Auditing Standards, considered add-ons to GAAS, are also known as generally accepted government auditing standards (GAGAS), promulgated under the auspices of the GAO by the GASAB. The federal requirements are found in the OMB Circular A-133, Audits of States, Local Governments, and Nonprofit Organizations.

The GAO recognizes other sets of professional auditing standards under GAGAS § 1.15. AICPA fieldwork and reporting standards are incorporated by reference for financial statement audits. PCAOB and IAASB auditing standards are used in conjunction with GAGAS for financial statement audits. The Institute of Internal Auditors' standards are used in conjunction with GAGAS for performance audits.

Other major audit guidelines for nonprofit organizations are listed in Figure 8-13. The issuance of the Single Audit Act of 1984 (Public Law 98–502) was particularly important because it incorporated the concept of an entity-wide financial and compliance single audit. This act requires an annual audit of any state or local government unit that receives federal financial assistance. The single audit concept eliminated the need for separate financial and compliance audits conducted by the various federal agencies from whom the entity has received funding. By congressional directive, the director of the Office of Management and Budget (OMB) has the authority to establish policy, guidelines, and mechanisms to implement single, coordinated financial and compliance audits of government grant recipients.

FIGURE 8-13	MAJOR GUIDELINES FOR PUBLIC SECTOR AUDITING

GAO	General Accountability Office
	Government Auditing Standards ("the Yellow Book")
OMB	Office of Management and Budget
	"Single Audit Act"
AICPA	American Institute of CPAs
	Attestation Standards
	Generally Accepted Auditing Standards (GAAS)
	Audit Guides: Audits of Not-for-Profit Organizations
	Audits of Federal Government Contractors
	Audits of State and Local Governmental Units
	Audits of Health Care Organizations
	Statements of Position

INTERNATIONAL AUDITING STANDARDS

The International Federation of Accountants (IFAC) has had a broad objective to develop a worldwide accounting profession with harmonized standards. To meet the objective relating to auditing standards, the IFAC initially established the International Auditing Practices Committee to develop and issue International Standards on Auditing (ISA) on the form and content of audit reports.

The purpose of the ISA is to improve the uniformity of auditing practices throughout the world. Additionally, the IAPC issues International Auditing Practice Statements (IAPSs) that provide practical assistance in implementing the international standards, but do not have the authority of the international standards. In 2002, IFAC created a new International Auditing and Assurance Standards Board (IAASB) that now has the responsibility of developing international auditing standards. More recently, a Public Interest Oversight Board was created to review the IAASB.

The ISAs apply to every independent audit of financial information, regardless of the type or size of the entity under audit. However, within each country, local regulations govern. To the extent that the ISAs conform to the specific country's regulations, the audit will be considered in accordance with the standards. In the event that the regulations differ, the members of the IAASB will work toward the implementation of the ISAs, if practicable, within the specific country. These standards and other publications of the IAASB are available at www.ifac.org.

Moving forward with auditing standard setting, there exists a movement for standards convergence similar to the convergence to IFRS. The GAO's position on auditing standards convergence is that standard setters should work together to achieve core auditing standards that are universally accepted. Where there is a clear and compelling reason, the individual standard-setting bodies should develop additional standards necessary to meet the needs of their respective constituencies. The nature of any differences from core auditing standards and the basis for the differences also should be communicated. The GAO is working with the International Organization of Supreme Audit Institutions (INTOSAI) to advance government auditing standards in the international arena.

The official position of the ASB on convergence is that it will develop standards (SAS) using the ISAs as the base standard and modify the base standard only where modifications are deemed necessary to better serve the needs of U.S. users of audited financial statements of nonissuers. Currently, the ASB has a process to converge its standards with those of the IAASB and redraft them using a clarity convention.

COMPILATION AND REVIEW SERVICES

In response to the needs of nonpublic clients,[6] regulatory agencies, and the investing public, the public accounting profession offers compilation or review services to clients rather than conducting a more expensive audit examination in accordance with GAAS. Compilation and review of financial statements are defined as follows:

Compilation: a service presenting, in the form of financial statements, information that is the representation of management without undertaking to express any assurance on the statements.

Review: a service performing inquiry and analytical procedures that provide the accountant with a reasonable basis for expressing limited assurance that there are no material modifications that should be made to the statements in order for them to be in conformity with GAAP or, if applicable, with another comprehensive basis of accounting.[7]

Therefore, the basic distinction between these two services is that a review service provides limited assurance about the reliability of unaudited financial data presented by management, whereas a compilation engagement provides no assurance as to the reliability of the data. In a compilation, the CPA prepares financial statements only from information supplied by management. The CPA in a compilation need not verify this information furnished by the client and therefore provides no assurance regarding the validity of this information.

The AICPA established guidance for the public accountant for compilation and review services with the issuance of Statements on Standards for Accounting and Review Services (SSARS). To date, the committee has issued seventeen statements.

QUICK FACTS
For reviews, use AICPA Statements on Standards for Accounting and Review Services.

ROLE OF JUDGMENT IN ACCOUNTING AND AUDITING

Accountants and auditors exercise professional judgment in considering whether the substance of business transactions differs from its form, in evaluating the adequacy of disclosure, in assessing the probable impact of future events, and in determining mate-riality limits. This informed judgment on the part of the practitioner is the foundation of the accounting profession. In providing an attest engagement, the result is often the rendering of a considered opinion or principled judgment. In effect, the auditor gathers relevant and reliable information, evaluates and judges its contents, and then formalizes an opinion on the financial information or statements.

A review of current authoritative literature reveals that certain pronouncements require disclosure on the applicable accounting principle for a given business transaction. Other pronouncements provide only general guidelines and, in some cases, suggest acceptable alternative principles. The process of applying professional judgment in choosing among alternatives is not carried out in isolation, but through consultation with

QUICK FACTS
Disclosure of accountancy principles varies depending on the authority and accounting judgment.

---

[6] The distinction between a public versus nonpublic client is based on whether the entity's securities are traded publicly on a stock exchange or in the over-the-counter market.

[7] AICPA, Accounting and Review Services Committee, Statement on Standards for Accounting and Review Services, No. 1, "Compilation and Review of Financial Statements" (1978).

other professionals knowledgeable in the area. In rendering professional judgment, the accountant/auditor must exercise critical thinking skills in the development of a solution or opinion.

Statement on Auditing Standards No. 5 makes the following point on the use of professional judgment in determining conformity with GAAP:

> The auditor's opinion that financial statements present fairly an entity's financial position, results of operations, and changes in financial position in conformity with generally accepted accounting principles should be based on his judgment as to whether
>
> (a) the accounting principles selected and applied have general acceptance;
>
> (b) the accounting principles are appropriate in the circumstances;
>
> (c) the financial statements, including the related notes, are informative of matters that may affect their use, understanding, and interpretation;
>
> (d) the information presented in the financial statements is classified and summarized in a reasonable manner; that is, neither too detailed nor too condensed; and
>
> (e) the financial statements reflect the underlying events and transactions in a manner that presents the financial position, results of operations, and changes in financial position stated within a range of acceptable limits; that is, limits that are reasonable and practicable to attain in financial statements.[8]

In order to render an opinion based upon professional judgment, the auditor often considers the opinions of other professionals. In such cases, the practitioner can use several published sources to determine how others have dealt with specific accounting and reporting applications of GAAP. The AICPA publishes Technical Practice Aids, which contains the Technical Information Service. This service consists of inquiries and replies that describe an actual problem that was encountered in practice and the interpretation and recommendations that were provided along with relevant standards and other authoritative sources.

ECONOMIC CONSEQUENCES

Because time is a scarce commodity, the auditor should weigh the cost-benefit trade-offs in extending the audit research process. The researcher should address the problem until eliminating all reasonable doubt relating to the issue, recognizing the hidden costs of making an improper audit decision.

Enforcement of professional audit work occurs at many levels. Quality control reviews are expected within a CPA firm. Peer reviews are conducted by other firms. The PCAOB conducts inspections of CPA firms. The inspections are generally used for the enhancement of the audit process, but also used for PCAOB enforcement sanctions. Audit quality has increased because of PCAOB inspection reports. The SEC can still issue an Accounting and Auditing Enforcement Release on a CPA firm. Litigation results in a review of audit quality. Besides the legal damages from an association with a negligent audit, the

---

[8] *AICPA Professional Standards*, vol. 1, Section AU-411-04.

auditor can face criminal penalties; SEC, FTC, and other government sanctions; loss of reputation among the auditor's peers; and a significant loss of existing clients in a competitive environment.

If sloppy audit work is revealed to the public through failures of major corporations or investment vehicles, pressure is placed on Congress to change the audit environment, as happened under Sarbanes-Oxley. As congressional and other investigations continue in financial reform, only time will reveal the effects upon the audit environment.

SUMMARY

This chapter has presented an overview of assurance services, the auditing standard-setting environment, standards for international audits, compilation and review services, and professional ethics. Familiarity with this information, in particular the types of authoritative pronouncements that exist, will aid the practitioner in the research process.

In researching an accounting or assurance services issue, the practitioner must use professional judgment in the decision-making process. Experience is undoubtedly the primary factor in developing good professional judgment. However, this text presents a research methodology that should aid in the development and application of professional judgment.

DISCUSSION QUESTIONS

1. What is an assurance service engagement?

2. Define an attest engagement. Is an audit engagement an attest service?

3. Identify three other attest services in addition to the normal financial statement audit.

4. Differentiate between auditing standards and attestation standards.

5. What guidelines exist for the performance of accounting and review services?

6. Differentiate between auditing standards and auditing procedures.

7. Discuss the relationship between GAAS and Statements on Auditing Standards (SAS).

8. Discuss the applicability of the first and third general standards of GAAS to accounting and auditing research.

9. What is the PCAOB? What standards does it issue?

10. State the objective of the Single Audit Act. When is this act applicable?

11. List the primary auditing guidelines for public sector auditing.

12. Explain the importance of the Code of Professional Conduct in the performance of an audit.

13. Explain the significance of Rules 202 and 203 of the AICPA Code of Professional Conduct.

14. How may accounting or auditing research aid the practitioner in complying with Rules 202 and 203 of the Code of Professional Conduct?

15. What role does professional judgment play in the daily activities of the accountant or auditor?

16. What authoritative auditing literature that has general applicability in practice is considered primary authoritative support?

17. What guidelines are available for the accountant in serving the needs of the nonpublic client?

18. What authoritative body exists as to the development of international auditing standards?

EXERCISES

1. Access the International Federation of Accountants Web site (www.ifac.org) and briefly describe the following two International Auditing Standards: ISA 500 and ISA 505.

2. Utilizing Figure 2-3 (Universal Elements of Reasoning), identify the eight elements for the following: A prospective client has requested a report as to the reliability of its electronic commerce activities on the Internet. You are trying to decide the type of assurance service engagement this would involve.

3. Access the AICPA Professionals Standards and determine the AU section number that discusses the forms of confirmations.

4. Access the AICPA Professional Standards. In the By-laws section, determine the requirements for becoming a member of the AICPA.

5. Utilizing the AICPA Professional Standards database, conduct research to answer the following questions:

   a. In addition to completing the audit of Jack's Manufacturing, Inc., for the coming year, your firm has been requested to review the interim financial statements for the first three quarters of the year. The engagement partner has requested your assistance in preparing a draft of the appropriate report for the review. Locate and print out an example of an appropriate review report.

   b. You are the staff auditor for a large client that has two subsidiaries located in foreign countries. Because your firm does not have offices near these subsidiaries, your firm will be using other auditors to aid you in the audit of the parent company. The audit partner on the engagement has requested your assistance as to the type of audit report necessary in order to share responsibility with these other auditors. Identify the authoritative literature paragraph citation for a shared audit report and print out an example of the report for the partner.

6. Access the AICPA Web site (www.aicpa.org) and locate the ASB under auditing and attestation standards. Examine the approved highlights of the ASB. What were the last three auditing standards issued by the ASB?

7. Access the PCAOB Web site (www.pcaobus.org) and list two new or proposed auditing standards issued by the PCAOB.

AICPA reSOURCE Database

If you have access to the AICPA reSOURCE database, attempt to complete the following practice exercises. (*Note:* You can also complete these exercises with a hard copy of the AICPA Professional Standards.)

8. You have been requested by a potential client to conduct an agreed upon procedures engagement related to the client's pension plan. Access the AICPA database and determine what type of service this is: audit, attestation, or consulting engagement. Also identify the specific standard governing this type of service.

9. When is it appropriate to issue an adverse audit opinion? Cite the specific Professional Standard section used for your answer.

10. Utilize the AICPA database to answer the following issue brought to you by a co-worker. The co-worker believes that only the general standards of the AICPA Code of Professional Conduct apply to consulting engagements. Are there any other general standards that apply to a consulting engagement in addition to the general standards of the Code?

APPENDIX

CPA Exam Audit Simulation

As previously stated, the CPA exam has simulations in the auditing section of the exam. In conducting research in these simulations, one will be utilizing the AICPA Professional Standards, as depicted in Figure 8-9. A CPA candidate needs to be proficient in using this database. Figure 8-1A provides an example of a question in the opening screen of a sample simulation. Clicking on the research/authoritative literature tab will open up the Professional Standards to conduct your research.

FIGURE A8-1 | SIMULATION RESEARCH SCREEN FOR AUDITING AND ATTESTATION

(NOTE THE RESEARCH QUESTION UNDER STEP 1)

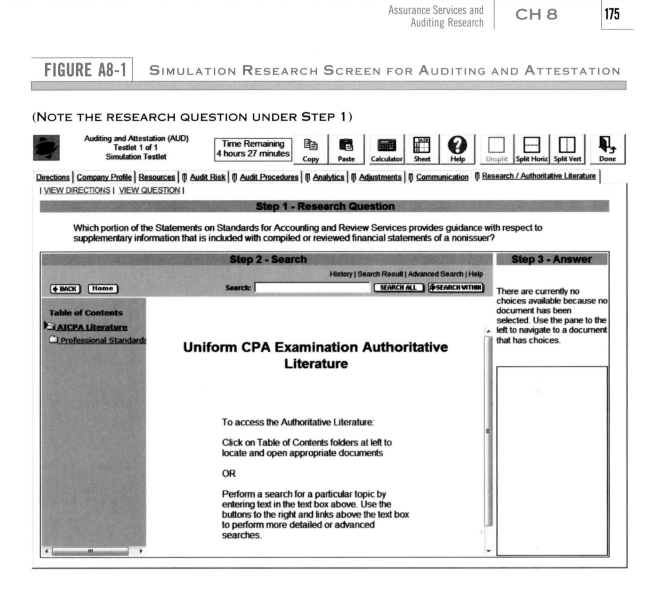

Refining the Research Process

LEARNING OBJECTIVES

After completing this chapter, you should understand:

- How to execute the five basic steps in the research process.
- The process of identifying the issues or problems to research.
- How to collect evidence from data, authorities, and other sources.
- The skill of evaluating the research results and various alternatives.
- Develop and communicate a well-reasoned, documented memo and conclusion.
- How to remain current with the expanding body of authorities and data.
- International complexities in practice.
- Skills for the CPA exam.

METHOD OF CONDUCTING RESEARCH

Accountants are confronted with problems related to the proper accounting treatment for given transactions or the proper financial presentation of accounting data and disclosures. The focus of the research will determine what appropriate alternative principles exist and what potential administrative support exists for those alternatives. Apply professional judgment in selecting one accounting principle from the list of alternatives. Always use a systematic method for conducting research.

The following example problem demonstrates the application of the research methodology, as depicted in Figure 9-1. Think through each part of the problem and the research steps in order to comprehend the complete research process.

> **EXAMPLE FACTS:** Sony is a multinational company headquartered in Tokyo, Japan, with over one thousand subsidiaries worldwide. Sony decided to expand its entertainment business in the United States, overseen by its subsidiary Sony-USA. Therefore, Sony-USA purchased two companies to form Sony Music and Sony Pictures. Because of these acquisitions, Sony assumed debt of $1.2 billion and allocated $3.8 billion to goodwill. On Sony's annual report filed with the SEC, Sony reported only two industry segments: electronics and entertainment. While Sony Music was profitable, however, Sony Pictures had produced continued losses of approximately $1 billion. Sony's founder, Akio Morita has asked your firm, XYZ, CPAs, to identify and explain any major potential accounting or tax concerns from these facts, but does not want you to worry about consolidations.

> ### QUICK FACTS
> Research identifies the relevant facts and issues, collects the applicable authorities, analyzes the results and identifies alternatives, develops conclusions, and communicates the results.

FIGURE 9-1 | OVERVIEW OF THE RESEARCH PROCESS

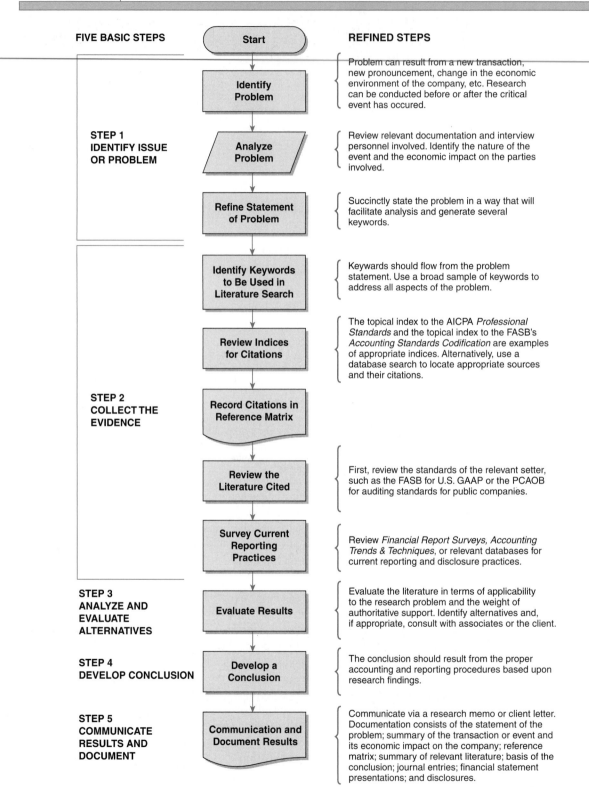

FIVE BASIC STEPS

REFINED STEPS

Start

Identify Problem

Problem can result from a new transaction, new pronouncement, change in the economic environment of the company, etc. Research can be conducted before or after the critical event has occured.

STEP 1
IDENTIFY ISSUE
OR PROBLEM

Analyze Problem

Review relevant documentation and interview personnel involved. Identify the nature of the event and the economic impact on the parties involved.

Refine Statement of Problem

Succinctly state the problem in a way that will facilitate analysis and generate several keywords.

Identify Keywords to Be Used in Literature Search

Keywords should flow from the problem statement. Use a broad sample of keywords to address all aspects of the problem.

Review Indices for Citations

The topical index to the AICPA *Professional Standards* and the topical index to the FASB's *Accounting Standards Codification* are examples of appropriate indices. Alternatively, use a database search to locate appropriate sources and their citations.

STEP 2
COLLECT THE
EVIDENCE

Record Citations in Reference Matrix

Review the Literature Cited

First, review the standards of the relevant setter, such as the FASB for U.S. GAAP or the PCAOB for auditing standards for public companies.

Survey Current Reporting Practices

Review *Financial Report Surveys, Accounting Trends & Techniques*, or relevant databases for current reporting and disclosure practices.

STEP 3
ANALYZE AND
EVALUATE
ALTERNATIVES

Evaluate Results

Evaluate the literature in terms of applicability to the research problem and the weight of authoritative support. Identify alternatives and, if appropriate, consult with associates or the client.

STEP 4
DEVELOP CONCLUSION

Develop a Conclusion

The conclusion should result from the proper accounting and reporting procedures based upon research findings.

STEP 5
COMMUNICATE
RESULTS AND
DOCUMENT

Communication and Document Results

Communicate via a research memo or client letter. Documentation consists of the statement of the problem; summary of the transaction or event and its economic impact on the company; reference matrix; summary of relevant literature; basis of the conclusion; journal entries; financial statement presentations; and disclosures.

Step One: Identify the Issues or Problems

To start the research, reread the problem provided to establish the facts and identify the issues or problems in clear and concise statements. Handle this task systematically by using the following three-part approach:

1. Identify the preliminary problem.
2. Analyze the problem.
3. Refine the problem statements.

Identify the Preliminary Problem   First, recognize potential problems in accounting, auditing, and tax. Company management, such as the controller or tax director, often initiates this problem identification process. Companies sometimes hire outside assistance from CPA firms. Because the initial statements of potential problems are usually very general and vague, one must develop the skill in analyzing the problem and then refining the statement of the problem or issues.

> **EXAMPLE of preliminary issue 1:**   Can Sony amortize the goodwill, or must the company write down the goodwill?
>
> **EXAMPLE of preliminary issue 2:**   Did Sony's financial statement presentation of two industries comply with relevant authorities?

Analyze the Problem   Additional facts are often needed in research. Thus, the problem sometimes requires one to go back and acquire more from one's manager or even the client. Certain types of facts, such as related party situations and dates, are almost always relevant. Sometimes, an important fact to clarify is exactly which entity or person is the client.

Analyzing the problem is similar to an auditor conducting planning for an audit. The auditor will acquire more information about the business and potential risks. One might begin by going to a financial research database, such as S&P NetAdvantage, to acquire additional information about the company. Also, one might begin some problems by examining the relevant corporate Web sites. Usually, corporate Web sites offer an About the Company link, which explains more about the history and current structure of a company.

> **EXAMPLE of analysis:**   Corporate Web sites might help to reveal corporate structures for Sony, such as its subsidiary, Sony-USA, which has its own subsidiaries, such as Sony Entertainment, Sony Music, and Sony Pictures.

Examine historic SEC filings, such as the 10-K annual report for a public company or the Form 20-F, annual report for a foreign-owned public company. Prior to 2009, foreign companies had to reconcile their accounting from international accounting standards to U.S. GAAP. Included in annual report with the SEC are various nonfinancial items, such as the company's management, the board of directors, and qualitative and quantitative disclosures about the market risk. Key financial information in the SEC filing includes the company's financial data, operating and financial revenue prospects, major shareholders, and related party transactions. The Investor Relations part of the corporate Web site often provides easy access to annual reports filed with the SEC.

> **EXAMPLE of additional analysis:**   Prior to 2009, Sony has filed SEC Form 20-F for several years, which reconciled the accounting to U.S. GAAP. These filings are publically available through either the SEC database (EDGAR) or accessing

the company's financial information in various financial research databases or LexisNexis Academic. Assume the review of Sony's SEC filings finds the following information:

1. When Sony purchased the motion pictures business, it projected a loss for only ~~five years. Sony assumed that Sony Pictures would become profitable.~~

2. Sony suffered a significant loss after amortization and financing costs from the acquisition for the past four years. Moreover, in the current year, Sony Pictures sustained a loss of nearly $450 million, double the amount that Sony had planned. Sony Pictures had accumulated total net losses of nearly $ 1 billion.

3. Goodwill of $2.7 billion associated with the acquisition of Sony Pictures was written down by Sony early in the year.

4. Sony combined the results of Sony Music and Sony Pictures and reported them as Sony Entertainment. Sony Entertainment showed little profit. Sony's consolidated financial statements did not disclose the losses from Sony Pictures.

Refine the Problem Statement   Refine the problem statement with more sophistication by incorporating the critical facts and the main authority for resolving the problem, after having identified the preliminary problem and engaged in initial problem analysis. Basic knowledge of relevant professional authorities helps the professional accountant to determine what additional facts are needed in refining the problem. Thus, a professional often conducts some initial research, as discussed in step two, and then returns to step one to refine the problem statement. The initial research may prompt the need for requesting additional facts.

EXAMPLE for more facts: The treatment for goodwill changed in 2001 for accounting purposes, the year for Sony's acquisitions is critical. Assume the desired analysis is for the current year. (One could actually determine the real year by examining corporate histories of Sony, such as presented in the chapter on databases and other tools.)

EXAMPLE of refined issue 1:   Determine whether an annual write-down of goodwill and its impairment is necessary for an acquisition of a company with continued losses.

EXAMPLE of refined issue 2:   Determine whether financial statement disclosures of two segments are needed when one industry has two businesses with different financial trends. The concern is to avoid misleading financial statement users in violation of Securities Exchange Act § 13(a).

Step Two: Collect the Evidence

The collection of evidence generally involves searching for all relevant authorities, whether in accounting, auditing, or tax. Often, one should also review insightful nonauthoritative sources, such as a survey of present industry practices, information about the industry, or relevant articles about the client company or problem.

Identify Keywords for Research   Keywords are needed in some cases to locate the relevant authorities. The statement of the problem should enable one to generate the initial keywords necessary to access the appropriate sections of the authorities and professional literature. Additional keywords are sometimes identified after the search has begun, as one acquires more knowledge about various terms of art.

EXAMPLE: Identify keywords for research after the initial analysis and refined statement of the problem. Keywords are often used in a database search.

FIGURE 9-2 | POTENTIAL KEYWORDS FOR THE SONY PROBLEM

Accounting Authorities Search

Goodwill	Write-down
Impairment	Financial statements disclosure
Segment disclosure	Business combination

Business Knowledge Search

Sony	Sony Entertainment
Sony Music	Sony Pictures

EXAMPLE: Potential keywords for the Sony problem are shown in Figure 9-2.

To find relevant legal and professional authorities, the researcher may encounter cross-references that circle back to original starting point. Some identified keywords may prove useless in the search. Don't get discouraged. Continue to conduct the search for authorities and helpful nonauthoritative literature carefully and systematically. This approach will help make the process less frustrating and more efficient.

If applying U.S. accounting standards, then search the FASB Accounting Standards Codification. Figure 9-3 demonstrates the keyword citation diagram under old U.S. GAAP authorities.

A diagram sometimes aids the researcher in conducting and documenting an efficient literature search. Start by listing the keywords identified from the statement of the problem. Review these terms for relevant cross-references to other terms, whether broader, narrower, or related terms. Examine these additional terms for potential citations. List the citations in logical order, such as by the hierarchy of relevant authorities when one exists, such as for legal authorities, government accounting, or auditing authorities. Always start with the highest level of primary authority. Use authoritative support to explain or further interpret part of the stronger authority.

Locate and Examine the Relevant Authorities Determine the appropriate financial accounting framework and database to use to check for current standards. Use FASB

FIGURE 9-3 | ACCOUNTING KEYWORD/CITATION DIAGRAM FOR THE EXAMPLE USING OLD U.S. GAAP

Keyword	Reference Descriptions	Citation
Goodwill	Goodwill	ASC 805-740-55-9 ASC 350-30-25-3
Write-down		No relevant citation
Impairment	Goodwill and relevant impairment test	ASC 350-20-35-49
	Recognition and measurement of an impairment loss	ASC 350-20-35-31
Financial statement disclosures	Recognition and measurement	CON 5, par 7
Segment disclosure	Disclosure of segments	ASC 280-10-50-23 to 24
Business combination	Business combination	ASC 805-10-15-3 to 4

Accounting Standards Codification to find relevant, authoritative citations to solve research issues involving U.S. GAAP. Use IFRS/IAS to resolve international GAAP that a foreign multinational company is likely to use even for SEC filings. If using IFRS/IAS, determine whether to use the less complicated IFRS for small to medium sized entities. If one does not have subscription access to the sources, remember that an accounting database may help locate relevant accounting information. Ideally, reference the primary authorities as precisely as possible, such as where in the FASB Accounting Standards Codification or the IAS/IFRS the authorities arises. However, some firms are satisfied with a reference to the general standard at issue.

A hierarchical structure of authorities often exists for the relevant accounting, auditing, or tax authorities. Recall that some official accounting standard-setting bodies continue to maintain a hierarchy of authorities, such as the IASB, GASB, or FASAB. If a hierarchy does exist, begin the review of authorities by examining the highest-level authorities. Note the scope of any authorities reviewed. Save time by scanning potential authorities for their relevance. Avoid making detailed reviews of authorities and pronouncements that are not applicable to the specific facts and issues for the transaction under investigation.

RESEARCH TIPS

If a hierarchy of authorities exist, begin by examining its highest level.

EXAMPLE on goodwill: A summary of the relevant authorities on goodwill is as follows:

Goodwill is an intangible asset that often arises from a business combination. It is a separate line item in the statement of financial position. Goodwill is not amortizable because it has an indefinite useful life. Potential impairment of goodwill in each reporting unit requires annual testing. ASC 350-20-35-1 and 28 (IAS 36.10). A reporting unit includes segments of an operating unit for which disclosure is needed. The impairment is generally measured by comparing the fair value to the reported carrying value of goodwill. ASC 350-20-35-4 (IAS 36.105). Impairment losses are recognized in the income statement. The notes to the financial statements must disclose each goodwill impairment loss if the loss is probable and can be reasonably estimated. The segment from which the business arose must disclose the loss. ASC 350-20-50-1 and 2 (IAS 36.129). Caution: Previously, goodwill was presumed to have a finite life and amortized over forty years. Also, the tax treatment of goodwill differs from financial accounting. Goodwill is a qualifying intangible for amortization over fifteen years under IRC § 197(a) and (d)(1)(A).

EXAMPLE on segment disclosure: The following is a summary of the relevant portions of accounting and SEC accounting literature on segment disclosure:

Segment disclosure reporting is required for public companies in their annual financial statements. ASC 280-10-50-10 (IFRS 8.2). The objective of segment disclosure is to provide users of financial statements with information about the business' different types of business activities and various economic environments. ASC 280-10-50-6 (IFRS 8.1). Operating segments earn revenues and expenses, have results regularly reviewed by management, and have discrete financial information. ASC 280-10-50-1 (IFRS 8.5). Operating segments should exist if the revenue is 10 percent or more of the combined revenues, or assets are 10 percent or more of the combined assets. ASC 280-10-50-12 (IFRS 8.13).

Disclosure of segment information must include nonfinancial general information, such as how the entity identified its operating segments and the types of products and services from which each reportable segment derives its revenues. ASC 280-10-50-40 (IFRS 8.22). Required financial information includes the reported segment profit or loss, segment assets, the basis of measurement. ASC 280-10-50-29 (IFRS 8.21). Reconciliation is required of the totals of segment revenues, reported segment profit or loss, segment assets, and other significant items to corresponding business enterprise amounts. ASC 280-10-50-30 and 31 (IFRS 8.28).

Filing reports periodically with the SEC is required for every issuer of a security under the Exchange Act of 1934. The reports must include any information to ensure the required financial statements were not misleading in light of the circumstances. Prior to 2009, foreign-owned companies with registered securities had to reconcile the accounting in the annual financial statement to U.S. GAAP under SEC Form 20-F.

Sometimes obtain additional non-authoritative insight into the background and rationale underlying these key authorities. For example, one could examine old U.S. GAAP by looking at FASB Statements (FAS) No. 141 on goodwill and FAS 131 on segment disclosure. Abbreviations are regularly used for the research and its documentation, such as shown in Appendix A.

Do not ignore colorable authorities, pronouncements that other researchers might believe address the research problem, but you believe are irrelevant. Review colorable authorities for potential application and possible references to other appropriate sources. Discussions within these authorities may add insights into the problem at hand.

Review Insightful Nonauthoritative Sources   Sometimes extend the search to insightful nonauthoritative literature or relevant standards within a profession. Nonauthoritative materials may help one understand the authorities. Nonauthoritative sources may include looking at guidance issued by AICPA; industry practices; published research studies; credible, relevant Web sites; databases for secondary source literature; and other respected sources. Reviewing nonauthoritative materials supplements the primary task to examine the real authorities for any accounting and auditing research.

Determining how other companies with similar circumstances or transactions have handled the accounting and reporting procedures could involve a review of *Accounting Trends and Techniques*, issued by the AICPA. Sometimes, a discussion of the issue is appropriate. One normally does not discuss any specifics with professionals outside of one's accounting firm. If one does engage a discussion of the issue with outside peers, such as colleagues on the Internet, one must always exercise due professional care in completely protecting client confidentiality.

Use databases to find secondary sources. For example, investigate significant businesses competitors or hot issues within the relevant industry. Search within an article index database for insightful articles on a business or its operations. Access standards issued by a professional organization, such as the standards to help determine valuation for fair market value purposes.

> **EXAMPLE of insightful nonauthoritative sources:**   Use financial research databases to better understand the music industry, Sony Music, or the issues. One might discover that Sony Music is the second-largest music company in the United States, which suggests that separate segmental reporting is needed. Relevant Web sites may provide one with valuable information, such as the studies provided by government agencies, financial organizations and markets (for example, the New Yok Stock Exchange, operated by NYSE Euronext), professional organizations (for example, the Institute of Internal Auditors), and search engines and their tools (for example, Google's advanced search page). Reviewing these Web sites sometimes helps the researcher find the latest information on the topic in question.

Step Three: Analyze the Results and Identify Alternatives

Exercise professional judgment in carefully reviewing the results and identifying potential alternative solutions. Evaluate the quality and amount of authoritative support for the research problem. Given a more principled approach to accounting standards, alternative solutions may have justification. Review the evidence and alternatives with other accountants knowledgeable in the field. One might check industry practices to verify any different possibilities for alternative reporting.

EXAMPLE problem: Recall the refined statement of the problem for Sony. The first issue was whether an annual write-down of goodwill was necessary for an acquisition of Sony Pictures after continued losses. The second issue was whether financial statement disclosures of Sony and Sony Entertainment were adequate under Securities Exchange Act Section 13(a) when Sony Entertainment had two businesses (music and pictures) with different financial trends.

EXAMPLE analysis: Through an examination of documents, discussions with persons involved, and application of accounting authorities, assume the following analysis is made:

1. The carrying value of Sony Pictures exceeded its fair value. Similarly, the carrying amount of Sony Pictures' goodwill exceeded the implied fair value of Sony Pictures' goodwill. The impairment of goodwill loss was probable and can be reasonably estimated.
2. Sony should report separately information about each operating segment that met any of the 10 percent quantitative thresholds.
3. Sony may *not* combine Sony Music and Sony Picture as one reportable segment for many reasons—for example, they do not have similar economic character-istics. Other reasons include the fact thatthe businesses are not similar in either the nature of the products, the nature of the production processes, the type or class of customer for their products and services, or the methods used to distribute their products.
4. Disclosure of Sony Music and Sony Pictures segmental information should fundamentally provide information about their reported segment profit or loss. Other information to disclose includes the types of products from which each reportable segment derives its revenues, any reconciliations needed from the total segment revenues, and interim period information.
5. The amount assigned to goodwill acquired was significant in relation to the total cost of purchasing Sony Pictures. Therefore, Sony must disclose the following information for goodwill in the notes to Sony Entertainment's financial state-ments: (1) the total amount of goodwill and the expected amount deductible for tax purposes and (2) the amount of goodwill by reportable segment.
6. The authoritative accounting standards provide principled support for recog-nizing writing down goodwill of an acquired entity with continuous losses. Write down goodwill when a loss is probable and can be reasonably estimated. Sony must provide separate financial reporting for Sony Pictures because Sony Music and Sony Pictures do not share similar economic characteristics.

RESEARCH TIPS

Support the conclusion with logical, well-reasoned analysis.

Step Four: Develop a Conclusion

A conclusion is generally a very short statement answering the issue. The conclusion should logically arise from well-reasoned analysis. The conclusion is often placed after the statement of the problem. If more than one issue exists, have the conclusion address each issue.

EXAMPLE of conclusion on Issue 1:   The write-down of goodwill of an acquired entity with continuous losses is required.

EXAMPLE of conclusion on Issue 2:   The financial statement disclosure of only two industries when one industry has two businesses with different financial trends is misleading.

EXAMPLE of combined conclusion: The authoritative literature supports the write-down of the goodwill of an acquired entity with continuous loss. The amount of the write-down is equal to the difference between the carrying value of goodwill and the fair value. The financial statement disclosure of only two industries when one industry has two businesses with different financial trends is misleading.

Step Five: Communicate the Results

Communicate the results of the research using the writing and oral skills discussed in a previous chapter. Communication of research results are often sent to clients in a brief, formal letter. Recall that e-mail is more generally reserved for more informal communications.

Document any research results. An example of a documentation worksheet that an accounting firm might use to organize the pertinent research information for its records using U.S. GAAP is shown in Figure 9-4. Given the time pressures within the profession, sometimes, the relevant portions of the authorities are simply copied and pasted into a document and attached to the document worksheet. While the authors advocate as much precision as possible, given current practices in accounting research, the example document worksheet provides the authors' view of the appropriate documentation needed for references to the accounting authorities.

A research memo includes detailed documentation. Such a memo is often appropriate for more sophisticated clients or problems. Slightly different structures for research memos and documentation exist among accounting firms. A brief research memo using both ASC and IAS/IFRS is shown in the appendix. In general, a research memo should include the following documentation:

1. A statement of the relevant facts and the issues or problems

2. A summary of the conclusions

3. References to legal and authoritative literature used, along with a brief explanation of the relevant parts of the authority

4. The application of authorities, including a description of the authoritative support for each alternative; Explain why the alternatives were discarded and the recommended procedure or principle was selected.

The precision expected for documentation should increase in future years due to the increased documentation requirements under PCAOB audit standards, the easier research capabilities from FASB accounting standards codification, and increased legal penalties during the last decade. A well-documented memo is more likely to assure any reviewer that the researcher has an understanding of the authorities and the research problem.

RESEARCH TIPS

Document the relevant research and communicate appropriately.

QUICK FACTS

Summary of the Research Steps
1. Step One: Identify the Issues or Problems
2. Step Two: Collect the Evidence
3. Step Three: Analyze the Results and Identify the Alternatives
4. Step Four: Develop the Conclusions
5. Step Five: Communicate the Results

LESSONS LEARNED FOR PROFESSIONAL PRACTICE

Many challenges confront researching effectively and efficiently. By using the suggested five-step process, one is more likely to solve the problem accurately and in a time-efficient manner. While research is both an art and a science, as one develops more experience in research, one will find the research easier and exciting. Make sure the research work is well documented. One never knows when one's work will get tested within the firm's quality review program, reviewed by an auditor (perhaps in a peer review process), inspected by the PCAOB if one is part of a registered firm, or even defended in court.

FIGURE 9-4 | EXAMPLE DOCUMENTATION WORKSHEET OF RESEARCH UNDER U.S. GAAP

Client information
Name: Sony Corporation of America

Address: 550 Madison Ave, 33rd Floor
         New York, NY 10022-3211
Client code #118

I. Problem Identification or Statement of the Problems

Whether an annual write-down of goodwill under FASB ASC (IFRS/IAS) was necessary for an acquisition of a company with continued losses

Whether financial statement disclosures of only two industries when one industry had two businesses with different financial trends violated FASB ASC (IAS/IFRS) and was misleading under Securities Exchange Act § 13(a)

Contact person (Client):
Akio Morita—Chairman
Kimiko Tanaka—Administrative Assistant

II. Research Evidence (Keywords Utilized):

Disclosure
Goodwill
Impairment
Segment disclosure
Business combination

References (citations):

ASC 280-10-50-various
ASC 805-30-30-1
ASC 350-20-35-4 and 28
ASC 350-20-50-1 and 2
IAS 36 and IFRS 8
IRC § 197
1934 Exchange Act § 13(a)

Database (library resources) Utilized:

FASB Accounting Standards Codification
FASB CCH Accounting Research Manager
eIFRS for IFRS/IAS
RIA Checkpoint for tax
Web sites for the entities involved

III. Alternatives Available
No other alternatives are permissible.

IV. Conclusions

The write-down of goodwill of an acquired entity with continuous losses is required. ASC 805-30-30-1 and 350-20-35-1 (IFRS 3.B12 and IAS 36.10). The financial statement disclosure of only two industries when one industry has two businesses with different financial trends is misleading under Securities Exchange Act § 13(a) and needs revising under ASC 280-10-50-various.

Professional accounting research of accounting authorities based on codified principles is much easier than the old system in the United States of various rules-based pronouncements in the GAAP hierarchy. Recall that the FASB's accounting standards now use the more conceptual approach, similar to the IAS/IFRS, which the SEC is considering as a replacement for GAAP in 2014. Then use professional judgment in the application of the standards, particularly in a litigious society.

SEC accounting research is important not only for its direct application to public companies, but also for those learning to comprehend the potential regulatory environment that all accountants could face if additional crises arise in the profession.

Absorb the examples in this chapter by locating and reading each authority cited. The process of finding and reading the authorities will give you a better feel for the real research process. The inspiration for this example arose from SEC Accounting and Auditing Enforcement Release No. 1061. While the case over-simplifies those facts, it lays a foundation from which to more easily tackle the entire case.

REMAIN CURRENT IN KNOWLEDGE AND SKILLS

Remain current in knowledge by studying new updates of authorities or new pronouncements. A systematic plan to remain current usually achieves the best results. Regularly read accounting and business periodicals, newsletters, and other sources. Currency is essential with the typical expansion of accounting, auditing, and tax authorities. Consider adopting some of the following techniques in your plan to remain current in knowledge:

1. **Use checklists:** Maintain a checklist of new developments to assist in remaining current. Accountants prepare listings of updates to the FASB Accounting Standards Codification or new pronouncements and indicate which clients the change may affect. Pronouncements having no direct immediate impact on any client are often placed in a "rainy day" reading file.

2. **Summarize new authorities:** Acquire or prepare summaries of new authorities at regular intervals. Such summaries identify and describe new legal, accounting, auditing, and tax authorities. Distribute the information to staff members through e-mail, presentations within the firm, attendance at continuing education seminars, or other means.

3. **Read periodicals:** Read several accounting and business periodicals that summarize and explain new authorities. For example, read the *Wall Street Journal*, the AICPA's *Journal of Accountancy*, and leading professional publications in one's area of expertise, such as *Internal Auditor* or the *Tax Adviser*. Successful accountants regularly engage spend time reading about new professional standards, technological enhancements for practice, management concerns, and many other accounting and business topics.

4. **Check database updates:** Check for news on a company of interest or specialized industry news of interest.

5. **Browse Web sites:** Browse Web sites that capture relevant information on a timely basis, which is then reviewed by the practitioner. Use the newsgroups on the Internet to discuss topics of interest to you and your clients.

6. **Read accounting newsletters:** Take advantage of sophisticated newsletters that update practitioners on current events. Newsletters are distributed by standard setters, publishers, large accounting firms, and others. They are increasingly being distributed via e-mail. Major newsletters by standard setters include the following:

    *   **Action Alert.** FASB summarizes board actions and future meetings in this weekly publication, available through e-mail.

    *   **GASB Report.** GASB summarizes new statements, exposure drafts, interpretations, or technical bulletins in a quarterly publication.

    *   **CPA Letter.** AICPA produces this online newsletter to address such topics as AICPA board business, new pronouncements on auditing, disciplinary actions against members, upcoming events, and more. This newsletter is one of almost twenty newsletters created by the AICPA. Other newsletters are often targeted toward specialty areas in accounting.

Remaining knowledgeable on every detail of all new authorities is not possible. However, every practitioner must develop and consistently use various techniques to acquire current professional knowledge. Currency is especially important with authorities and pronouncements that directly affect one's clients. Participate in continuing professional education to help learn about new developments in a formal, structured setting.

Remain current in skills, whether by continued research practice or training. Accountants will need even more skills in the future for new research opportunities, analysis, communication, or other needs. Today's professional world is much different from what the accountant experienced a generation ago, with the advances in technology, increased complexities in business, expanded sources of authority, increased regulation, and other developments.

The professional accounting world will undoubtedly continue to evolve as new business practices develop, changes in the economy occur, and financial scandals are uncovered. Failure to remain current in either knowledge or skills is likely to violate one's professional responsibilities and increase the chances of losing one's job, professional sanctions, costly malpractice lawsuits, or government action.

INTERNATIONAL COMPLEXITIES IN PRACTICE

In a global economy, one may desire to research the data, professional authorities, or legal environment in other jurisdictions. For example, researching authorities enables one to have a more sophisticated discussion with accounting professionals in a foreign country and best represent their multinational clients who conduct business in multiple countries. However, due diligence in understanding, researching, analyzing authorities and data, and communicating solutions is essential.

Increasingly, accountants are accessing foreign authorities or data to engage in collaborative work or ask foreign professionals sophisticated questions. Yet, differences around the world, both cultural and societal, may lead to various interpretations or actions based on the same data or professional authorities. Foreign regulators sometimes provide formal or informal interpretations or guidance on IFRS. One should not assume that all parts of the world have the same degree of professional commitment in reporting or high enforcement standards. Reporting incentives are influenced by such factors as a country's legal system, strength of the auditors, and a company's financial compensation scheme.

Outsourcing of accounting work to low-cost jurisdictions is likely to continue to increase, especially as more countries adopt IFRS/IAS. The accountants overseeing any outsourced work need to exercise extra due care to ensure that the foreign professionals meet the professional standards interpretations that are expected in the United States or other highly developed country.

SKILLS FOR THE CPA EXAM

Skills in practice identified for the CPA are classified in three categories: knowledge and understanding, application skills that include research and analysis, and communication skills. Knowledge is acquired through education or experience and familiarity with information. Understanding is the process of using concepts to address the facts or situation. Knowledge and understanding skills represent almost half of the skills tested on the CPA exam.

Application skills of judgment, research, analysis, and synthesis are required to transform knowledge. Judgment includes devising a plan of action for any problem, identifying potential problems, and applying professional skepticism. Research skills include recognizing keywords, searching through large volumes of electronic data, and organizing data from multiple sources. Analysis includes determining compliance with standards, noticing trends and variances, and performing appropriate calculations. Synthesis includes solving unstructured problems, examining alternative solutions, developing logical conclusions, and integrating information to make decisions. Application skills require technological competencies in using spreadsheets, databases, and computer software. Application skills represent between one-third and almost one-half of the skills tested on the CPA exam.

Communication skills include oral, written, graphical, and supervisory skills. Oral skills include attentively listening, presenting information, asking questions, and exchanging technical ideas within the firm. Written skills include organization, clarity, conciseness, proper English, and documentation skills. Graphical skills include organizing and processing symbols, graphs, and pictures. Supervisory skills include providing clear directions, mentoring staff, persuading others, negotiating solutions, and working well with others. Communication skills represent 10 to 20 percent of the skills tested on the CPA exam.

Using the five-step research process demonstrated in this chapter substantially helps to develop the necessary skills for the CPA exam. For any research problem, learn the facts and understand the problem or issues. Acquire knowledge about the client's needs and desires in order to understand the alternative and best solutions to the problem. Knowledge and understanding of accounting should also include the various standard setters and their authoritative sources and the nonauthoritative sources available in various databases, Web sites, hardbound books, newsletters, and other secondary sources.

Use application skills such as identifying keywords for research. Develop the skills of locating and reviewing the relevant authorities. Analyze how the authorities apply to the particular facts in the research problem. Synthesize information with the help of insightful, nonauthoritative sources. Use professional judgment as you refine the issues with greater specificity and develop well-reasoned conclusions.

Develop strong communication skills not only for the CPA exam and research memos, but in handling the day-to-day tasks and interactions that typify the work of accountants and business professionals. Communicate the results of the research, as appropriate.

Although the CPA exam tests knowledge, application, and communication skills in much shorter questions than in the professional world, the goals presented are the same in preparing one as the knowledgeable and skilled professional for the various work that accountants perform.

SUMMARY

One should follow the five-step research process to (1) identify the issues or problems, (2) collect the evidence, (3) analyze the results and identify the alternatives, (4) develop the conclusions, and (5) communicate the results. The professional accountant must remain knowledgeable about current professional standards and develop skills in researching accounting, auditing, and tax issues. These attributes increase management's confidence and respect in your work as a accountant, auditor, or tax professional. By following the advice in this text, you are more easily able to fulfill your future professional role and responsibilities.

DISCUSSION QUESTIONS

1. What is the focus of accounting, auditing, and tax research?
2. What is the three-part approach used to identify the problem or precise issue?
3. Explain two ways to collect evidence.
4. How are keywords used to evaluate and collect evidence?
5. How might one determine accounting alternatives?

6. What is the purpose of a research memorandum?

7. What documentation is needed in the research process?

8. How will you keep current on authoritative accounting standards?

9. What are some of the complexities in international practice?

10. What skills are needed for the CPA exam?

EXERCISES

1. Examine 17 CFR part 229.306 and explain the legal requirements for an audit committee. *Hint*: Use either a legal database, such as LexisNexis Academic, or search Title 17 of the Code of Federal Regulations.

2. Locate SEC Accounting and Auditing Enforcement Release No. 1062. What did that SEC release discuss? *Hint*: In the SEC Web site, while accountants refer to the source as AAER, the SEC will list the same release as FR-#. The release is issued by the Enforcement division of the SEC. It is often more productive to use a commercial service with a stronger index. LexisNexis and CCH's Accounting Research Manager are examples of two databases having many SEC releases.

3. Does a tax treaty exist between the United States and Japan? If so, when was it signed?

4. Compare the international treatment of segment reporting to the U.S. GAAP treatment.

5. Identify the competitor companies to Sony Music and how they rank. Identify your sources.

6. Major Research Problem 1: An audit partner of a CPA firm invested in a computer side business with a member of the board of directors of a public company that sells insurance and is an audit client of that CPA firm. Identify any potential problems. Conduct preliminary research to find the relevant source at issue. Refine the problem statement. Research and locate the relevant professional authorities and determine if there is any colorable authority in the law that prohibits such a relationship. If so, try to find the interpretation of the law that the SEC may have issued. Analyze, consider alternatives, and develop the conclusion. Write a research memo on the problem.

7. Major Research Problem 2: Midwest Realty, Inc., is a regional real estate firm. Andrea Midwest incorporated the firm eleven years ago. She is the founder, president, and the majority stockholder. Recently, Midwest decided to expand her successful local real estate firm into a regional operation. She established offices in major cities across the Midwest. Midwest Realty, Inc. leased the office space. The standard lease agreement included a ten-year, noncancelable term and a five-year option renewable at the discretion of the tenant. Two years ago, the residential home market was depressed in the Midwest due to movement of factory jobs abroad, a shaky economy, and tight credit policies. So Midwest decided to eliminate ten offices located in depressed economic areas that she believed would not recover in the housing market during the next five years. This year, Midwest Realty, Inc. closed the ten offices. Midwest Realty, Inc., however, was bound by the lease agreements on all these offices. The company subleased four of the ten offices, but continued to make lease payments on the six remaining vacated ones. Midwest Realty properly classified the lease commitments as operating leases. The controller for the company, Calvin Brain, expressed concern to Midwest about the proper accounting for the lease commitments on the six remaining offices available for subleasing. Brain believes they must recognize that the future lease commitments are a loss for the current period. However, the executives of Midwest disagree and believe that the rental payments are period costs to recognize as an expense in the year paid. Midwest is confident that the company can sublease the vacant offices within the next year and avoid booking a loss and corresponding liability in this accounting period. Midwest has, however, given Brain the job of researching this problem and making recommendations supported by current authoritative accounting pronouncements. Brain has asked your firm, XYZ, CPAs, to help in the development of the recommendations. Complete all five steps for this research problem, documenting each step.

APPENDIX A

Abbreviations Commonly Used in Citations

An alphabetized list of organizations creating professional or legal authorities shows the major accounting, auditing, or tax abbreviations for their sources. This list includes various FASB accounting authorities discontinued after the FASB Accounting Standards Codification and accounting authorities previously discontinued by the AICPA.

Issuance Abbreviation Title of Issuance (Division of the Standard Setter or Comment)

AICPA	American Institute of Certified Public Accountants
AAG	Audit and Accounting Guide (add hyphen and three-letter abbreviation for each)
APB	Accounting Principles Board Opinions (predecessor to FASB)
APBS	Accounting Principles Board Statements (predecessor to FASB)
ARB	Accounting Research Bulletins (AICPA's predecessor to APB)
AT	Attestation part of codified AICPA Professional Standards
AU	Auditing part of codified AICPA Professional Standards
AUG	Industry Audit Guide (add hyphen and three-letter abbreviation for each)
AUIJ	Auditing Interpretations (Auditing Standards Board)
ET-INT	Ethics Interpretations of Rules of Conduct (Professional Ethics division)
ET-RLNG	Ethics Rulings (Professional Ethics division)
ET-RULE	Code of Professional Conduct—Rules
PRP	Standards for Performing and Reporting on Peer Reviews (National PRC)
SAR	Statements on Standards for Accounting and Review Services
SARI	Accounting and Review Services Interpretations (ARS Comm.)
SAS	Statements on Auditing Standards (Auditing Standards Board—ASB)
SECPS	SEC Practice Section Statement on Standards
SOP	Statements of Position (Accounting Standards division, prior to ASB)
SSAE	Statement on Standards for Attestation Engagements (ASB)
SSAEI	Attestation Engagements Interpretations (Auditing Standards Board)
SSARS	Standards on Accounting and Review Services
SSCS	Statements on Standards for Consulting Services (Consulting Executive Committee)
SSTS	Statements on Standards for Tax Services (Tax Executive Committee)
SSVS	Statements on Standards for Valuation Services (Business Valuation Committee)
FASB	**Financial Accounting Standards Board**
CON (SFAC)	FASB Statements of Financial Accounting Concepts
EITF	FASB Emerging Issues Task Force Consensus (EITF Abstracts)
FAS (SFAS)	FASB Statements of Financial Accounting Standards
FIN	FASB Interpretations
FTB	FASB Technical Bulletins
FASAB	**Federal Accounting Standards Advisory Board**
SFFAS	Statement of Federal Financial Accounting Standards
SFFAC	Statement of Federal Financial Accounting Concepts

(*continued*)

Issuance Abbreviation Title of Issuance (Division of the Standard Setter or Comment) (continued)

GAO	**Government Accountability Office**
GAGAS	Generally Accepted Government Auditing Standards (Comptroller General)
GASB	**Government Accounting Standards Board**
GAC	Statements of Financial Accounting Concepts
GAS	Statements on Governmental Accounting Standards
GASI	Interpretations
GAST	Technical Bulletins
IASB	**International Accounting Standards Board**
IAS	International Accounting Standards
IFRIC	International Financial Reporting Interpretations Committee Interpretations
IFRS	International Financial Reporting Standards
SIC	Standing Interpretations Committee Interpretations
IFAC	**International Federation of Accountants**
IAU	International Statements on Auditing (IAASB—International Auditing and Assurance Standards Board)
IPSAS	International Public Sector Accounting Standards (IPSAB—International Public Sector Accounting Board)
ISAE	International Standards of Attestation Engagements (IAASB)
ISQC	International Standards of Quality Control (IAASB)
IIA	**Institute for Internal Auditors**
Standards	Standards for Professional Practice of Internal Auditing
OMB	**Office of Management and Budget**
CASB	Cost Accounting Standards Board Standards (Office of Federal Procurement Policy)
CASB-I	Cost Accounting Standards Board Interpretations (OFFP)
CIR	Circulars (includes audit standards for state and local government and nonprofit organizations)
PCAOB	**Public Company Accounting Oversight Board**
AS	PCAOB Auditing Standards (interim standards use AICPA's SAS)
AT	Attest Engagement Standards (interim standards use AICPA's SSAE)
AU	Codified Auditing Standards
QC	Quality Control Standards
REL	Releases (when approved by PCAOB)
Rules	Rules (when approved by both PCAOB and SEC)
U.S. Congress	
33 Act	Securities Act of 1933
34 Act	Securities Exchange Act of 1934
IRC	Internal Revenue Code of 1986, Title 26 of the United States Code
SOX	Sarbanes-Oxley Act of 2002
U.S. SEC	**Securities And Exchange Commission**
AAER (ER)	Accounting and Auditing Enforcement Releases (Enforcement division)
ASR	Accounting Series Releases (stopped in 1982)
FRP	Codification of Financial Reporting Policies

(continued)

Issuance Abbreviation Title of Issuance (Division of the Standard Setter or Comment) (continued)

FRR (FR-#)	Financial Reporting Releases (OCA—Office of Chief Accountant)
Reg. FD	Regulation Fair Disclosure (17 C.F.R. parts 240, 243, and 249)
Reg. S-K	Regulation S-K (Integrated Disclosure Rules, 17 C.F.R. part 229)
Reg. S-X	Regulation S-X (Requirements for Financial Statements, 17 C.F.R. part 210)
Rel.	Releases (various types including AAER, FRR, and the following)
	33-# Release interpreting Securities Act of 1933
	34-# Release interpreting Securities Exchange Act of 1934
SAB	Staff Accounting Bulletins (Corporate Finance division and Office of Chief Accountant)

U.S. Treasury Department

Rev. Proc.	Revenue Procedure (IRS)
Rev. Rul.	Revenue Ruling (IRS)
Treas. Reg.	Treasury Regulation (26 C.F.R.)

Various Common Non–Standard Setter Abbreviations

10K	Annual Report by a public company filed with the SEC
EPS	Earnings per Share
GAAP	Generally Accepted Accounting Principles
GAAS	Generally Accepted Auditing Standards
MD&A	Management Discussion and Analysis of Financial Condition and Results of Operation
XBRL	Extensible Business Reporting Language

APPENDIX B

Sample Brief Memorandum

RE: Sony's Goodwill and Segment Reporting

Facts:

Sony is a Japanese multinational company that decided to expand its entertainment business in the United States. Sony purchased CBS Records and Columbia Pictures to form Sony Music and Sony Pictures. Because of these acquisitions, Sony assumed debt of $1.2 billion and allocated $3.8 billion to goodwill. On Sony's Annual Report filed with the SEC, Sony reported only two industry segments: electronics and entertainment. While Sony Music was profitable, Sony Pictures produced continued losses of approximately $1 billion. When Sony purchased the motion pictures operations, it projected a loss for only five years because it assumed that the motion pictures entertainment would become profitable. However, Sony suffered a significant loss after amortization and the costs of financing the acquisition for the past four years. Moreover, in the current year, Sony Pictures sustained a loss of nearly $450 million, double the amount that Sony had planned. To date, Sony Pictures has had total net losses of nearly $1 billion. Early in the year, Sony declared that it had written down $2.7 billion in goodwill associated with the acquisition of Sony Pictures. Sony combined the results of Sony Music and Sony Pictures and reported them as Sony Entertainment. Little profit was shown in Sony Entertainment. Sony's consolidated financial statements did not disclose the losses from Sony Pictures.

Issues:

(1) Whether an annual write-down of goodwill and its impairment is necessary under FASB ASC for the acquisition of a company with continued losses.

(2) Whether financial statement disclosures of two segments are needed when one industry has two businesses with different financial trends in order to avoid misleading financial statement users under Securities Exchange Act Section 13(a).

Conclusions:

(1) A write-down of goodwill of an acquired entity with continuous losses is required.

(2) The financial statement disclosure of only two industries when one industry has two businesses with different financial trends is misleading and needs revising.

Authorities on goodwill:

A summary of the relevant authorities on goodwill is as follows:

Goodwill is an intangible asset that often arises from a business combination ASC 805-30-30-1 (IFRS 3.B12). It is a separate line item in the statement of financial position. Goodwill is not amortizable because it has an indefinite useful life. Potential impairment of goodwill in each reporting unit requires annual testing ASC 305-20-35-1 and 28 (IAS 36.10). A reporting unit includes segments of an operating unit for which disclosure is needed. The impairment is generally measured by comparing the fair value to the reported carrying value of goodwill. ASC 350-20-35-4 (IAS 36.105). Impairment losses are recognized in the income statement. The notes to the financial statements must disclose each goodwill impairment loss if the loss is probable and can be reasonably estimated. The segment from which the business arose must disclose the loss. ASC 350-20-50-1 and 2 (IAS 36.129).

Caution: Previously, goodwill was presumed to have a finite life and was amortized over forty years. Also, the tax treatment of goodwill differs from financial accounting. Goodwill is a qualifying intangible for amortization over fifteen years under IRC § 197 (a) and (d)(1)(A).

Authorities on segment disclosure:

The following is a summary of the relevant portions of accounting and SEC accounting literature on segment disclosure:

Segment disclosure reporting is required of public companies in their annual financial statements. ASC 280-10-50-10 (IFRS 8.2). The objective of segment disclosure is to provide users of financial statements with information about the business's different types of business activities and various economic environments. ASC 280-10-50-6 (IFRS 8.1). Operating segments earn revenues and expenses, have results regularly reviewed by management, and have discrete types of financial information. ASC 280-10-50-1 (IFRS 8.5). Operating segments should be recognized if the revenue is 10 percent or more of the combined revenues or assets are 10 percent or more of the combined assets. ASC 280-10-50-12 (IFRS 8.13). Disclosure of segment information must include nonfinancial general information such as how the entity identified its operating segments and the types of products and services from which each reportable segment derives its revenues. ASC 280-10-50-40 (IFRS 8.22). Required financial information includes the reported segment profit or loss, segment assets, the basis of measurement. ASC 280-10-50-29 (IFRS 8.21). Reconciliation is required of the totals of segment revenues, reported segment profit or loss, segment assets, and other significant items to corresponding business enterprise amounts. ASC 280-10-50-30 and 31 (IFRS 8.28).

Filing reports periodically with the SEC is required for every issuer of a security under the Exchange Act of 1934. The reports must include any information needed to ensure that the required financial statements were not misleading in light of the circumstances. Prior to 2008, foreign-owned companies with registered securities had to reconcile the accounting in the annual financial statement to U.S. GAAP under SEC Form 20-F.

Application of authorities:

1. The carrying value of Sony Pictures exceeded its fair value; the carrying amount of Sony Pictures' goodwill exceeded the implied fair value of Sony Pictures' goodwill. The impairment of goodwill loss was probable and can be reasonably estimated.

2. Sony should report separate information about each operating segment that met any of the 10 percent quantitative thresholds.

3. Sony may not combine Sony Music and Sony Pictures as one reportable segment for any of the following reasons. They do not have similar economic characteristics. These businesses are not similar in the nature of the products, the nature of the production processes, the type or class of customer for their products and services, and the methods used to distribute their products.

4. Sony should disclose segmental information for Sony Music and Sony Pictures, providing information about their reported segment profit or loss. Other information to report includes the types of products from which each reportable segment derives its revenues, any reconciliations needed of the total segment revenues, and interim period information.

5. The amount assigned to goodwill acquired was significant in relation to the total cost of the acquiring Sony Pictures. Thus, Sony must disclose the following information for goodwill in the notes to Sony Entertainment's financial statements: (1) the total amount of goodwill and the expected amount deductible for tax purposes and (2) the amount of goodwill by reportable segment.

6. The authoritative sources require recognizing writing down goodwill of an acquired entity with continuous losses. Write down goodwill when a loss is probable and can be reasonably estimated. On the other hand, Sony must provide separate financial reporting for Sony Pictures because Sony Music and Sony Pictures do not share similar economic characteristics.

Fraud Investigative Techniques

LEARNING OBJECTIVES

After completing this chapter, you should understand:

- The definition of fraud.
- Different types of fraud.
- The components of the fraud triangle.
- The utilization of ACL and i2 Analyst Notebook in fraud investigations.
- An overview of a fraud examination and business investigation.
- The use of computer technology in fraud examinations/investigations.

Perhaps a client requests your help to determine if evidence exists of vendor kickbacks to certain employees in the purchasing department. Possibly a company's legal counsel has hired you to determine whether an officer of the company has any hidden assets as a result of an embezzlement scheme he or she carried out. Maybe you need to conduct background checks (due diligence checks) on potential strategic partners of a proposed joint venture. Sound like interesting assignments? These are a few examples of value-added forensic accounting services offered by accounting firms to their clients. Other common fraud auditor/examiner engagements in relation to an audit client could include the following:

- Providing assistance to the audit team in assessing the risk of fraud and other illegal acts.
- Providing assistance to the audit team in investigating potential fraud or other illegal acts.
- Conducting fact-finding forensic accounting studies of alleged fraud that could include bribery, wire fraud, securities fraud, money laundering, retail fraud, or theft of intellectual property.
- Conducting due diligence studies that could include public record checks or background checks on individuals in a hiring situation or on entities in a potential acquisition.
- Consulting as to the implementation of fraud prevention, deterrence, and detection programs.

These examples of fraud engagements demand that the investigator possess unique research skills in addition to the traditional skills presented in the previous chapters of this book.

In addition to the typical accounting, auditing, and tax services rendered by accountants, the profession is rapidly moving into other value-added services known as *fraud investigation* (or *litigation support*) or the broader, more comprehensive term *forensic accounting*. The terms *forensic accounting* and *litigation support* generally imply the use of accounting in a court of law. Thus, the services of an accountant in a fraud investigation or court case are often referred to as forensic accounting or litigation support services.

Fraud is a major problem for most organizations. Stories about fraud often appear in newspapers and business periodicals. A review of such articles reveals that fraud is not

QUICK FACTS

Forensic accounting is the use of accounting in a court of law.

perpetrated only against large organizations. One report in a business magazine has estimated that 80 percent of all crimes involving businesses are associated with small businesses. Although the full impact of fraud within organizations is unknown, various national surveys have reported that annual fraud costs to U.S. organizations exceed $900 billion (or 7 percent of their revenues) and are increasing.

RESEARCH TIPS

Develop fraud examination skills through education and experience.

Fraud examinations and background (due diligence) checks are not easy tasks. One must have the proper training, skills, and experience to conduct a successful fraud investigation. Many fraud investigators currently working in CPA firms obtained their experience working with various federal and local agencies, such as the IRS, FBI, or various levels of police work. Others obtained their fraud examination skills by attending conferences or seminars conducted by organizations such as the Association of Certified Fraud Examiners.

This chapter presents a basic overview of fraud and common red flags that may indicate its occurrence. Additionally, the chapter explains the basic steps of a financial fraud examination and the investigative techniques a forensic accountant may use. Because no two fraud investigations are alike, this chapter will provide a heightened awareness of the environment of fraud and present basic techniques for a fraud investigation. Also, with advances in technology, fraud examination is increasingly becoming more high tech. Thus, the chapter will highlight the use of computer software and the Internet as tools in fraud investigations. Discussion will focus on two major software products (ACL and i2's Analyst Notebook) that are utilized in fraud investigations.

DEFINITION OF FRAUD

In simplest terms, fraud is commonly defined as intentional deception, or simply lying, cheating, or stealing. *Black's Law Dictionary* defines fraud as:

> A generic term, embracing all multifarious means which human ingenuity can devise, and which are resorted to by one individual to get advantage over another by false suggestions or by suppression of truth. It includes all surprise, trickery, cunning, dissembling, and any unfair way by which another is cheated.

Concern about fraud applies to investors, creditors, customers, government entities, and others. Major perpetrators of financial statement fraud such as Enron, Sunbeam, WorldCom, and others have raised the public's awareness of the importance of fraud prevention and detection.

Laws that relate to fraud are often complex. The fraud examiner must become aware of the different types of fraud and will often require the legal assistance of an attorney. However, the different fraud-related laws have a common legal definition. As defined by the U.S. Supreme Court, fraud includes the following elements:

- A misrepresentation of a material fact
- Known to be false
- Justifiably relied upon
- Resulting in a loss

QUICK FACTS

Fraud is the misrepresentation of a material fact, known to be false, justifiably relied upon, resulting in a loss.

Thus, a fraud examination involves various procedures of obtaining evidence relating to the allegations of fraud, conducting interviews of selected witnesses and related parties, writing reports as to the findings of the examination, and, in many cases, testifying in a court of law as to the findings. A sufficient reason or suspicion (predication) is the basis for beginning a fraud examination. Often, this predication is based upon circumstantial evidence that a fraud has likely occurred. An employee complaint or unusual or unexplained trends in financial ratios may raise a suspicion that something is wrong. The fraud examination is conducted to prove or disprove the allegations.

TYPES OF FRAUD

Statement on Auditing Standards No. 99, "Consideration of Fraud in a Financial Statement Audit," distinguishes two categories of financial statement fraud: fraudulent financial reporting and misappropriation of assets.

The first category of fraud, *fraudulent financial reporting*, is usually committed by management in order to deceive financial statement users. Thus, fraudulent financial reporting (management fraud) refers to actions whereby management attempts to inflate reported earnings or other assets in order to deceive outsiders. Examples of management fraud would include overstating assets/revenues, price fixing, contract bidding fraud, or understating expenses/liabilities in order to make the financial statements look better than they really are. Figure 10-1 presents details of two examples of enforcement actions by the SEC relating to management fraud. Fraudulent financial reporting is generally the most costly type of fraud.

The second category of fraud, *misappropriation of assets*, is more commonly known as *employee fraud*. Misappropriation of assets refers to actions of individuals whereby they misappropriate (steal) money or other property from their employers. Various employee fraud schemes could include embezzlement, theft of company property, kickbacks, and others as listed in Figure 10-2. Misappropriation of assets is generally the most common type of fraud.

FIGURE 10-1	EXAMPLES OF MANAGEMENT FRAUD

Case One: Stephanie S. Ruskey, CPA, served as corporate controller of American Italian Pasta Company, a Delaware corporation that produces dry pasta. The Commission alleged that Ruskey and others at AIPC engaged in a fraudulent scheme that hid the true financial state of the company from the investing public by filing materially false and misleading financial statements in the company's annual reports. The complaint alleged that, to meet aggressive external targets, Ruskey and others engaged in numerous accounting practices that departed from GAAP, including capitalizing improperly millions of dollars of normal operating costs, understating trade promotion expenses, overstating the company's spare parts inventory, recognizing current period revenue on sales of products that were not shipped until after the end of the current periods, and eliminating the company's vacation and paid off liability.

It was ordered by the Commission that Ruskey be suspended from appearing or practicing before the Commission as an accountant.

Source: Accounting and Auditing Enforcement Release No. 2890 (September 29, 2008).

Case Two: Angel Alvarez-Perez and Annie Astor-Carbonell were former officers and directors of First BanCorp, a NYSE-listed bank holding company based in Puerto Rico. The Commission alleged that First BanCorp's senior management concealed the true nature of more than $4 billion worth of mortgage-related transactions from the company's independent auditor and the investing public. They were alleged to have profited from the transactions by earning over $100 million in net interest income with minimal risk. They improperly recognized income, created and backdated certain documents, and affirmatively misrepresented the terms of certain mortgage-related transactions to the company's independent auditor in order to avoid a restatement of the financial statements. Alvarez consented to a five-year office and director bar and a $100,000 civil penalty. Astor consented to a five-year officer and director bar and $75,000 civil penalty and was suspended from appearing or practicing before the Commission as an accountant for five years.

Source: Accounting and Auditing Enforcement Release No. 2881 (September 17, 2008).

FIGURE 10-2 COMMON EXAMPLES OF FRAUD ACTIVITIES

Misappropriation of Assets

Account	*Schemes*
Cash	Skimming
	Forgery
	Kiting
	Phony refunds
	Larceny
	Fraudulent disbursements
Accounts/receivables	Lapping
	Fictitious write-offs
Purchases/inventory	Duplicate payments
	Nonexistent vendor
	Kickbacks
	Misdirected shipments
	Theft
Fixed assets	Unauthorized personal use of assets
	Fictitious burglary
Payroll	Phantom employees
	Falsified time cards

Fraudulent Financial Reporting

Fictitious revenues—recording of sales of goods or services that never occurred; timing differences and recognizing revenue in improper periods

Asset overstatement—recording certain assets as market values rather than the lower of cost or market

Unrecorded liabilities and expenses—not recording an environmental contingency that is probable and reasonably estimable

Improper disclosures—not disclosing related-party transactions or other significant events

Corruption

Conflict of interest

Bribery

Illegal gratuities

Economic extortion

RESEARCH TIPS

Approach each fraud investigation in a systematic manner.

One common categorization of fraud is by industry classification, such as financial institution fraud, health care fraud, or insurance fraud. Another classification of fraud uses six types:[1]

- **Employee embezzlement:** Fraud in which employees steal company assets either directly (stealing cash or inventory) or indirectly (taking bribes or kickbacks).
- **Management fraud:** Deception by top management of an entity primarily through the manipulation of the financial statements in order to mislead users of those statements.

[1] W. Steve Albrecht, Gerald W. Wernz, and Timothy L. Williams, *Fraud: Bringing Light to the Dark Side of Business* (Burr Ridge, Ill.: Richard D. Irwin, Inc., 1995).

- **Investment scams:** The sale of fraudulent and often worthless investments, for example, telemarketing and Ponzi scheme frauds.
- **Vendor fraud:** Fraud resulting from overcharging for goods purchased, shipment of inferior goods, or nonshipment of inventory even when payment has been received.
- **Customer fraud:** Fraud committed by a customer by not paying for goods received or deceiving the organization in various ways to get something for nothing.
- **Miscellaneous fraud:** A catch-all category for frauds that do not fit into one of the previous five categories, for example, altering birth records or grade reports.

Although there are many different types and categories of fraud, a fraud examiner should approach each engagement in a systematic manner, as explained in this chapter.

THE FRAUD TRIANGLE

Why do individuals commit fraud? Probably the most common reason is that the perpetrators are greedy and believe that they will not get caught. Various researchers, including criminologists, psychologists, sociologists, auditors, police detectives, educators, and others have studied this issue. They have concluded that three basic factors determine whether an individual might commit fraud. These three factors comprising the fraud triangle include (1) motivation (perceived pressure or incentive), (2) perceived opportunity, and (3) rationalization.[2] All three elements are generally present in the typical case of fraud.

The first element of the fraud triangle is motivation based on perceived pressure or incentive to commit a fraud. An individual's motivation can change due to external forces. An individual who is honest one day might commit fraud the next day due to external pressures. These pressures include financial pressures, vices, and work-related pressures. Typical financial pressures include excessive debt resulting from unexpected high medical bills, uncontrolled spending with credit cards, lifestyle beyond one's means, or outright greed. Vices may include addiction to gambling, drugs, or alcohol. The individual having a vice is sometimes motivated by this pressure to commit a fraudulent act in order to support his or her addiction. Work-related pressures could include not receiving desired job recognition, being overworked and underpaid, or not getting an expected promotion. A formerly honest individual may turn to fraud in order to get even with his or her employer.

The motivation based on perceived pressure or incentive for top management to commit financial statement fraud (management fraud) may include obtaining a bonus or stock option based on the company's financial results, the company's stock price, or meeting regulatory requirements. Similarly, dramatic changes in the organization, such as reengineering or a potential merger, can lead to uncertainty as to the future. This may motivate an individual to become dishonest in order to survive within the organization.

The second element of the fraud triangle is perceived opportunity. All employees have opportunities to commit fraud against their employers, suppliers, or other third parties, such as the government. Perceived opportunity is often driven by the access an individual has to the entity's assets or financial statements, the skill of the individual in exploiting the opportunity to commit fraud, and, in certain cases, the individual's seniority or trust within the organization. Many corporate frauds have occurred due to breaches of trust by employees and managers to whom access privileges were granted. If

> **QUICK FACTS**
> The fraud triangle consists of motivation (pressure or incentive), perceived opportunity, and rationalization.

> **RESEARCH TIPS**
> Examine the fraud probability to plan the fraud investigation.

---

[2] More detailed discussion of the fraud triangle can be found in the following: G. Jack Bologna and Robert J. Lindquist, *Fraud Auditing and Forensic Accounting*, 2nd ed. (New York: John Wiley & Sons, Inc., 1995); W. Steve Albrecht et al., *Fraud Examination* (Cincinnati: South-Western/Cengage, 2009); and Association of Certified Fraud Examiners, *Fraud Examiners Manual*, annual editions.

an individual believes that the opportunity exists to commit a fraud, conceal the fraud in some way from others, and avoid detection and punishment, the probability of the individual committing fraud increases. When an individual's professional aspirations are being met, the individual is generally content. However, when those aspirations are not met, unconventional measures that may include fraud are sometimes pursued.

Conditions (red flags) that may provide the opportunity for fraud include:

- Negligence on the part of top management in enforcing ethical standards or disciplining an individual who commits a fraud.
- Major changes in the entity's operating environment.
- Nonenforcement of mandatory vacation time for employees, preventing others from filling in during absences.
- Lack of supporting documentation for transactions.
- Lack of physical safeguards over assets.

Internal control is an important factor in limiting fraud. The fraud examiner must pay attention to the entity's internal controls and evaluate the weaknesses or red flags that provide the opportunity for fraud.

The third element of the fraud triangle is an individual's rationalization for the actions taken. If an individual can rationalize questionable actions as not being wrong, he or she might justify any improper behavior in his or her mind. Common rationalizations for fraud activity include such statements as:

- "I work long hours and am treated unfairly by my employer. The company owes me more."
- "I will use the funds only for my current financial emergency and will pay them back later."
- "The federal government foolishly wastes my money, so I will not report my extra income this year on my tax return. Besides, no one gets hurt."

What the individual is attempting to do is to rationalize away the dishonesty of any wrongful action.

Individuals use many other rationalizations when committing fraud. However, an important factor, which the fraud examiner will evaluate, in minimizing illicit actions is an individual's personal integrity. An individual's strong personal standards of ethics can offset the temptation to rationalize the fraud activity. The tone set by top management as to proper ethical conduct can have a major impact on actions taken by employees.

Most frauds result when the three elements of the fraud triangle occur in combination: motivation (pressure or incentive), opportunity, and rationalization. If an organization is able to control or eliminate any of the three elements of the fraud triangle, the likelihood for fraud decreases. Knowledge of these three elements provides the fraud examiner with a better understanding of different approaches to take in the investigation.

Fraud comes in many forms. The forensic accountant must tailor the fraud examination to the specific circumstances. Following is an overview of a typical financial statement fraud examination.

OVERVIEW OF A FINANCIAL STATEMENT FRAUD EXAMINATION

Over the years, independent auditors have often not met the expectations of third parties in detecting material fraud when auditing financial statements. Fraud auditing focuses on the detection and prevention of fraud. The fraud auditor should possess the skills of a well-trained auditor combined with those of a criminal investigator.

To further clarify the auditor's responsibility to uncover fraud in a financial statement, SAS No. 99 provides guidance. The auditor has a responsibility to plan and perform the audit in order to obtain reasonable assurance that the financial statements are free of material misstatement, whether caused by error or fraud. Therefore, the auditor/fraud examiner must understand the characteristics and types of fraud, be able to assess fraud risks or red flags, design an appropriate audit, and report the findings on possible fraud to management or the appropriate levels of authority.

Assessing the risk of material misstatement of the financial statements due to the possibility of fraud is a critical part of the first step. The assessment should include attempts to answer the following questions: What types of fraud risk exist? What is the actual and potential exposure to the fraud? Who are the perpetrators? How difficult is it to identify and prevent the fraud? What is the company doing to prevent fraud now? How effective are these measures? This risk assessment aids the auditor in designing the audit program and audit procedures to perform.

In conducting the risk assessment of material misstatement due to fraud, the auditor evaluates fraud risk factors (red flags) that relate to the two basic categories of financial statement fraud: fraudulent financial reporting and misappropriation of assets. A fraud risk factor is a characteristic that provides a motivation or opportunity for fraud or an indication that fraud may have occurred. The risk factors that relate to financial reporting fraud can be placed in the following three groups:

1. **Incentives/pressures:** This group of risk factors relates to the financial stability or profitability of the entity, excessive pressure on management or operating personnel to meet expectations of third parties or financial targets, or a case where the personal situation of management or the board of directors is threatened by the entity's financial performance. Examples of specific red flags include a high degree of competition or market saturation along with declining profit margins, perceived or real adverse effects of reporting poor financial results, or personal guarantees by management or board members for debts of the entity.

2. **Opportunities:** These factors relate to aspects of the industry or the entity's operations that provide the opportunity to engage in fraudulent financial reporting. Examples include significant or highly complex transactions, major operations conducted across international borders, or deficiencies in internal controls.

3. **Attitudes/rationalization:** This category of risk factors reflects the tendency by board members or management to justify or rationalize their motives to commit fraudulent financial reporting. Examples of red flags include ineffective communication or enforcement of ethical standards and excessive interest by management in maintaining or increasing the entity's earnings trend.[3]

Risk factors relating to misstatements arising from the misappropriation of assets are classified into two groups: susceptibility of assets to misappropriation, which relates to the nature of the organization's assets and the probability of theft; and controls, which relate to the lack of measures for preventing or detecting the misappropriation of assets. Examples of red flags for the susceptibility of assets include large amounts of cash on hand; easily convertible assets, such as bearer bonds or diamonds; and lack of ownership identification of fixed assets that are very marketable.

Although fraud is usually concealed, the presence of risk factors (red flags) may alert the fraud auditor to the potential for fraud within the company. If such factors exist and a risk assessment warrants, the auditor should discuss them with management and/or legal

---

[3] AICPA, SAS No. 99, "Consideration of Fraud in a Financial Statement Audit" (October 2002).

counsel. If the conclusion reached is that fraud is likely, a fraud examination would commence. The basic steps of the fraud examination are as follows:

1. Identify the issue/Plan the investigation.
2. Gather the evidence/Complete the investigation phase.
3. Evaluate the evidence.
4. Report findings to management/legal counsel.

Step One: Identify the Issue/Plan the Investigation

> **RESEARCH TIPS**
>
> Identify the fraud issue and create a hypothesis answering when, how, and by whom.

Based upon the circumstances indicating the possibility of fraud, the client and/or the client's legal counsel would usually instruct the fraud examiner to conduct a fraud examination. Management's suspicions as to the possibility of fraud could come from a number of sources. Employees may have observed improprieties committed by fellow employees or observed an employee's lifestyle that is inconsistent with his or her income. Issues may arise from an internal or external audit that has identified missing documents. Not all suspicions result in a finding of fraud, but, by pursuing the evidence and anomalies, the fraud examiner can make a reasoned determination as to its existence. If fraud exists and is not pursued, it will probably continue and more likely increase over time. Based upon the circumstantial evidence, the fraud examiner would create a hypothesis as to when the potential fraud occurred, how it was committed, and by whom.

Step Two: Gather the Evidence/Complete the Investigation Phase

Although different investigation methods exist, the objective of the investigation phase is to gather appropriate evidence in order to determine whether a fraud has occurred or is occurring. Investigations are often contentious and generate a great deal of uneasiness for all parties involved. Each investigation is different, and the suspects and witnesses will often react differently. One mistake in the investigation can jeopardize the entire process.

Also included in the investigation phase is the identification of resources to utilize in the investigation. The fraud examiner needs to know what resources are available: primary, secondary, or third parties. Various types of resources are discussed later in the chapter.

The investigation technique used will often depend on the type of evidence the fraud examiner is attempting to gather. One approach is to classify the evidence into four types with the related investigative techniques to gather the evidence as follows:[4]

> **QUICK FACTS**
>
> The investigative technique used often depends on the type of evidence sought.

Type of Evidence	Investigative Technique
1. Documentary evidence (hardcopy or electronic)	Examination of documents, searches of public records, searches of computer databases, analysis of net worth, or analysis of financial statement
2. Testimonial evidence	Interviewing, interrogations, or polygraph tests
3. Observational evidence (investigator's personal observation)	Physical examination (counts/inspections) or surveillance (close supervision of suspect during examination period)
4. Physical evidence (such as tire marks or fingerprints)	Use of forensic expertise

---

[4] Albrecht et al., op. cit.

Two examples of gathering evidence as to the existence of fraud are presented below:

Case One: Management has experienced lower profit margins than expected. In this investigation, the fraud examiner might review inventory procedures to determine whether employees are stealing inventory. The investigation might identify shrinkage in the actual counts of high-dollar inventory items, and a review of surveillance records may show whether anyone has removed inventory during off hours.

Case Two: A co-worker has reported that an employee appears to be living well above his known means. In such a case, the fraud investigator might review payment records to determine whether sales proceeds were diverted into an employee's personal account. A net worth analysis can also identify inconsistencies, and a review of the suspect's brokerage statements (with legal permission) may show whether the deposit dates correspond to the dates when questionable business transactions occurred.

The investigation phase of the examination requires strong analytical skills. These skills are important in the analysis of the financial information and other data for any trends or anomalies.

In gathering testimonial evidence, interviewing skills are critical for the fraud examiner. Interviewing skills require an ability to extract testimonial evidence from collaborators, co-workers, or others related to the case, as well as the suspect, in hopes of obtaining a confession. Fraud-related interviews are carefully planned question-and-answer sessions designed to solicit information relevant to the case.

Also, information technology skills are required in order to search public records and other electronic databases in the gathering of evidence for the investigation. The use of computer databases and software in evidence gathering for a fraud investigation is discussed later in this chapter.

> **QUICK FACTS**
>
> Fraud investigations identify the issues, gather the evidence, evaluate the evidence, and report the findings.

Step Three: Evaluate the Evidence

After completing a thorough investigation, the fraud examiner will evaluate the evidence in order to determine whether the fraud has occurred or is still occurring. One can draw sound conclusions only if the information was properly collected, organized, and interpreted. Once fraud is discovered, the fraud examiner attempts to determine the extent of the fraud. Was it an isolated incident? Was there a pattern connecting the incidents? When did the fraud begin? By identifying how long and to what extent the fraud occurred, the investigator may be able to provide critical information to help the client recover missing funds from the perpetrator or obtain reimbursement from an insurance company.

> **RESEARCH TIPS**
>
> Ask many questions in a fraud examination to determine the extent of the fraud.

Step Four: Report Findings to Management/Legal Counsel

Upon completing the evaluation of the evidence, the fraud examiner needs to document the results of the investigation and prepare a report on the findings. The report should use the writing concepts discussed in Chapter 2. Any report should use coherent organization, conciseness, clarity, Standard English, responsiveness, and a style appropriate to the reader.

At times, the client's legal counsel may request that the fraud examiner serve as an expert witness in a court case. A fraud examiner might win or lose a court case against a perpetrator depending upon the accuracy and technical rigor of the examiner's investigation and report. However, the fraud examiner's report needs to avoid rendering an opinion as to the guilt or innocence of the suspect. The report should state only the facts of the investigation and the findings. The report should present answers as to when the fraud occurred, how it was committed, and by whom.

Because fraud investigations are considered litigation support services, which are considered consulting services, the CPA/fraud investigator needs to adhere to professional standards during the investigation, as well as in developing the report. Relevant standards and guidance are issued by the AICPA's Management Consulting Services Committee and related subcommittees.

BUSINESS INVESTIGATIONS

A business or due diligence investigation is sometimes performed by professional accountants to help management minimize business risks. At times, a client may need help to verify information about an organization before entering into a joint venture or corporate merger. Or perhaps the client needs a background information check before hiring a new corporate officer or other employee. In other situations, the client may need to know about any related parties associated with the corporation or the reputation of a potential new vendor. In each of these examples, a business or individual background investigation might prove valuable in obtaining desirable information for managing business risks.

A "documents state of mind" is needed in most types of investigative work, Many types of documents, or paper trails, can be used by the investigator to gather facts about the issue under investigation. Such documents are classified as either primary or secondary sources. A typical secondary source would be a newspaper article about a company acquiring a subsidiary or doing business in a certain country.

Primary documents are readily available in many types of investigations. For example, if one is attempting to gather background information on a new corporate executive, typical primary sources would include voter registrations, tax records for property ownership, details of civil and criminal lawsuits, and divorce and bankruptcy records. Corporations have similar types of paper trails. For example, an entity's articles of incorporation are roughly equivalent to an individual's birth certificate.

FIGURE 10-3 | INVESTIGATIVE TECHNIQUE: "WORKING FROM THE OUTSIDE IN"

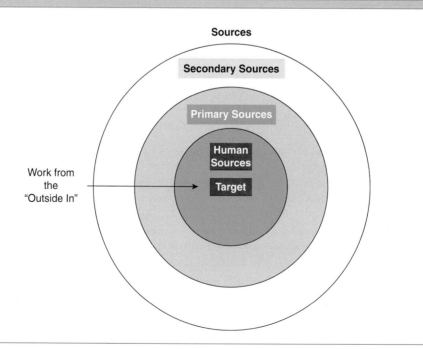

In gathering background information, the investigator typically follows a technique referred to as "working from the outside in." This technique is depicted in the form of concentric circles, with the larger circle representing the secondary sources, as illustrated in Figure 10-3. The middle circle contains the primary sources that often substantiate the secondary information. The inner circle could include personal interviews for facts concerning the target or the issue under investigation. In many investigations, the investigator needs to use creativity in gathering and analyzing the data.

COMPUTER TECHNOLOGY IN FRAUD INVESTIGATIONS

In the Information Age, fraud potential is wider in scope. However, new tools and techniques are available to combat this expansion of fraud. Uncovering signs of fraud among possibly millions of transactions within an organization requires the fraud examiner to use analytical skills and work experience to construct a profile against which to test the data for the possibility of fraud. Three important tools for the fraud examiner are data mining software, public databases, and the Internet.

Data Mining Software

Data mining software is a tool that models a database for the purpose of determining patterns and relationships among the data. This tool is an outgrowth of the development of expert systems. Computer-based data analysis tools can prove invaluable in searching for possible fraud. From the analysis of data, the fraud examiner can develop fraud profiles from the patterns existing within the database. Through identifying and understanding these patterns, the examiner may uncover fraudulent activity. The use of data mining software also provides the opportunity to set up automatic red flags that will reveal discrepancies in data that should be uniform. Some of the common features of data mining software include the following:

- **Sorting:** Arranging data in a particular order such as alphabetically or numerically
- **Occurrence selection:** Querying the database to select the occurrences of items or records in a field
- **Joining files:** Combining selected files from different data files for analysis purposes
- **Duplicate searches:** Searching files for duplication, such as duplicate payments
- **Ratio analysis:** Performing both vertical and horizontal analyses for anomalies

Following is a brief description of some of the more common commercial data mining software products used by fraud examiners.

WizRule This software package is used for many different applications, such as data cleaning (searching for clerical errors) or anomaly detection in a fraud examination. The program is based on the assumption that, in many cases, errors are considered as exceptions to the norm. For example, if Mr. Johnston is the only salesperson for all sales transactions to certain customers, and a sales transaction to one of the customers is associated with salesperson Mrs. Allen, the software could identify the situation as a deviation or a suspected error.

WizRule is based on a mathematical algorithm that is capable of revealing all the rules of a database. The main output of the program analysis is a list of cases found in the data that are unlikely to be legitimate in reference to the discovered rules. Such cases are considered suspected errors.

RESEARCH TIPS

Use software
packages that utilize
various mathematical
algorithms to
examine the data.

Financial Crime Investigator This program offers a systematic approach for investigating, detecting, and preventing contract and procurement fraud. The software, using artificial intelligence, provides instructions on how to query databases to find fraud indicators and match them to the appropriate fraud scheme. It provides a detailed work plan to investigate each scheme, converts probable schemes to the related criminal offenses, outlines an investigative plan for each offense based on the elements of proof, and generates interview formats for debriefing anonymous informants for each contract fraud scheme.

IDEA (Audimation Services, Inc.) This product is a powerful generalized audit software package that allows the user to display, analyze, manipulate, sample, or extract data from files generated by a wide variety of computer systems. The software provides the ability to select records that match one's criteria, check file totals and extensions, and look for gaps in numerical sequences or duplicate documents or records. The investigator can conduct fraud investigations; perform computer security reviews by analyzing systems logs, file lists, and access rights; or review telephone logs for fraudulent or inappropriate use of client facilities.

Monarch This software program allows the investigator to convert electronic editions of reports from programs such as Microsoft Access into text files, spreadsheets, or tables. Monarch can then break this information into individual reports for analysis.

RESEARCH TOOLS

ACL
AICPA reSOURCE
eIFRS
FARS
Internet
i2
LexisNexis
RIA Checkpoint

ACL for Windows ACL Services Ltd., the developer and marketer of ACL for Windows, is considered the market leader in data inquiry, analysis, and reporting software for the auditing profession. ACL's clients include many of the Fortune 100 companies, governmental agencies, and many of the largest international accounting firms. In the software category of fraud detection and prevention, ACL for Windows is the most commonly used software package.

This software product allows the fraud examiner to perform various analytical functions without modifying the original data. The software can sort data on multiple levels as well as locate numerical gaps in the sequencing of data. Graphical display options allow the investigator to create graphs from the Histogram, Stratify, Classify, and Age commands. ACL is very beneficial in fraud detection due to its ability to quickly and thoroughly analyze a large quantity of data in order to highlight those transactions often associated with fraudulent activity.

QUICK FACTS

Software can often
assist in highlighting
transactions often
associated with
fraudulent activities.

As a world leader in data inquiry, analysis, and reporting software, ACL is very effective in such areas as identifying trends and bringing potential problem areas, highlighted errors, or potential fraud to the auditor/fraud examiner's attention by comparing files with end-user criteria and identifying control concerns. In the specific area of fraud detection, ACL can identify suspect transactions by performing such tests as matching names between employee and paid vendor files, identifying vendor price increases greater than an acceptable percent, identifying invoices without a valid purchase order, and identifying invoices with no related receiving report. As the forensic accountant attempts to sort through a massive volume of data in order to detect the possibility of fraud, ACL is a major software product available for the fraud examiner. Figure 10-4 shows the opening screen for ACL software.

RESEARCH TOOLS

ACL
AICPA reSOURCE
eIFRS
FARS
Internet
i2
LexisNexis
RIA Checkpoint

Analyst's Notebook This software package, developed by i2 Inc., is a visual investigative analysis product that assists investigators by uncovering, interpreting, and displaying complex information in easily understood charts. In many investigations,

FIGURE 10-4 | OPENING SCREEN OF ACL SOFTWARE

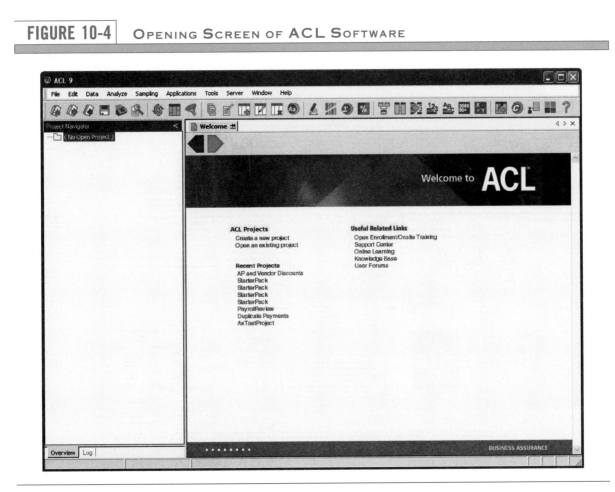

one must carefully analyze large amounts of multiformatted data gathered from various sources. The software provides a range of visualization formats showing connections between related sets of information and, in chart form, revealing significant patterns in the data. The software is excellent for extracting sections from large and complex investigation charts in order to produce smaller, more manageable presentation charts.

A visual presentation is a powerful tool to use in discussing the case with legal counsel and in presenting findings in court. For example, if the fraud examiner has a complex investigation chart of individuals and locations of suspects, and legal counsel is interested in one particular individual, the software can immediately produce a smaller chart showing only the information relating to that one individual. Figure 10-5 provides an example of i2's charting capabilities with respect to a drug cartel investigation.

In a fraud investigation, the Analyst's Notebook can aid the fraud examiner in developing building blocks that support the key issues of how and why. The software can help manage the large volume of information collected; help in understanding the information by providing a link analysis to build up a picture (chart) of the individuals and organizations involved in the fraud; help in the examination of the fraudsters' actions by developing a timeline analysis as to the precise sequence of events in the fraud case; and help in the discovery of the location of the stolen money or assets. Figure 10-6 provides an example of a timeline chart of the famous Bonnie and Clyde investigation.

Typical investigations using the Analyst's Notebook include money laundering activities, securities fraud, credit card fraud, insurance fraud, and organized crime cases.

RESEARCH TIPS

Use Analyst's Notebook to help chart your fraud investigation.

FIGURE 10-5 | i2's CHART OF A DRUG CARTEL INVESTIGATION

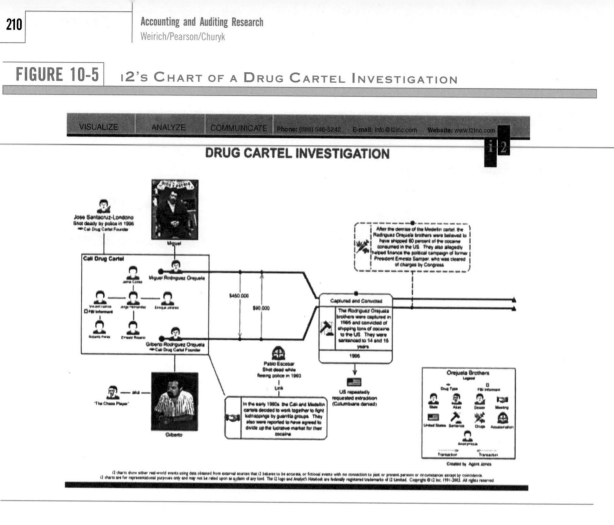

Additional tools available to the fraud investigator from i2 Inc. include iBase and iBridge. iBase is a state-of-the-art database software tool that not only captures, but also controls and analyzes, multisource data in a secure environment. With iBase, one can quickly build a multi-user investigative database that can provide information in a unique visual format. iBridge serves as a connectivity solution that provides the user with a live connection to multiple databases throughout one's organization. It provides connectivity to a variety of relational databases for data retrieval and analysis by the fraud investigator.

Public Databases

Given the enormous volume of public records (including information sold to the public for a fee), in certain cases, the fraud examiner or investigator may not need anything else in gathering evidence. These public databases include, among other information, records of lawsuits, bankruptcies, tax liens, judgments, and property transactions from all over the United States and, in certain cases, from around the world. If the examiner cannot locate the information via computerized databases, he or she can still locate the necessary information by personally visiting courthouses, recorder's offices, or city halls.

The fraud examiner/investigator relies heavily on public records/databases. Because these records are in the public domain, there are usually no restrictions in accessing the information. Business intelligence literature commonly cites that 95 percent of spy work comes from public records/databases. Additional reasons for utilizing public records include the quick access time and the inexpensive search costs.

FIGURE 10-6 | I2'S TIMELINE CHART OF THE "BONNIE AND CLYDE" INVESTIGATION

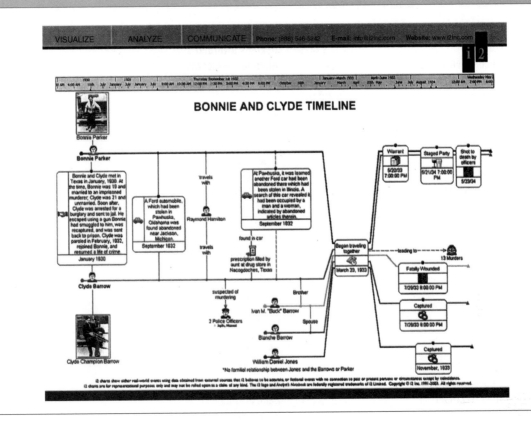

Some of the commonly used public records/databases include courthouse records, company records, online databases, and the Internet. Figure 10-7 presents a summary listing (not all-inclusive) of typical records/files or databases available to the investigator.

Courthouse Records Every county has a courthouse and a place to file real estate records. In both small towns and large cities, lawsuits, judgments, and property filings are found at the courthouse. In addition to county records, the same types of records are filed at federal courts, which also contain bankruptcy filings. These records address the basic questions of a business investigation: Is the subject currently in a lawsuit? Are there unsatisfied judgments? Is there a criminal history? Has the subject filed for bankruptcy?

The existence of these courthouse records tells the investigator something, but buried within the case jackets and docket sheets is even more information. Looking for financial information, the investigator can examine such items as the mortgage on a subject's home. Divorce filings and bankruptcy filings are business investigations in themselves. They contain records on assets and liabilities, employment histories, and pending suits.

Company Records The common starting point in many business investigations is public filings made with the SEC, accessible on the various databases at the SEC Web site. Unfortunately, the great majority of privately held companies need not file with the

> **RESEARCH TIPS**
>
> Use public databases that include courthouse records, company records, online databases, and the Internet

| FIGURE 10-7 | INVESTIGATIVE RESOURCES |

State Records
Driving records
Workers compensation claims
Department of Education records
Licensing Boards (i.e., bar and accountancy boards)
Corporation filings
UCC Records (documents the record of
    a loan or lease with secured assets)
State tax liens
Vehicle ID
Ownership/Property records
Criminal and civil records
Social security number records
Vital statistics (birth, death, marriages)
Bankruptcy records

Locator Records
Phone directories
Zip code directories
Surname directories

Federal Records
Military records
Federal aviation records
SEC filings
UCC filings
Library of Congress
Federal tax liens

Educational Records
Degrees awarded
Attendance records
Teacher certification

Databases
Full Text
LexisNexis
Dow Jones/*Wall Street Journal*
DIALOG
Datatimes

Public Records
PACER
Information America
CDB Infotek

Credit
Experian (formerly TRW)
TransUnion
ChoicePoint (formerly Equifax)

Others
Demographic
Biographical
Internet

RESEARCH TIPS

Examine company
records and other
relevant documents
from online
databases.

SEC. This leaves two primary sources for company information. First, Dun and Bradstreet compiles data on millions of companies. Experienced investigators recognize the shortcomings of these reports, but know that they make great starting points. Second, all businesses file some form of report in either the state or the county where they are located. Proprietorships and partnerships typically file local "assumed name," "d/b/a," or "fictitious name" filings. Corporations, limited partnerships, and limited liability companies (LLCs) file annual reports in their states of registration. These reports will typically identify the officers and registered agent of the company, but most reports will not list ownership data or financial information.

Other sources of company information supplement the various public records and courthouse records. Uniform Commercial Code filings (UCCs) and real estate filings can provide details missing in basic business filings. An investigator may tie an individual to a company because both the individual and the company are co-debtors in a secured agreement. Detailed financial information on private companies often can be gathered from litigation records over contracts, trade secrets, and other issues. Different regulatory bodies may have information on companies, even when they are closely held. State insurance commissions, for instance, have files for the public on companies that sell insurance in their states. Companies awarded government contracts also have to make certain information public. Investigators should try a variety of public records to acquire relevant information on the company under investigation.

Online Databases Many investigators use commercial databases to acquire the majority of their information. As described above, commercial databases give investigators the ability to quickly pull information from all over the world without alerting the subject. The speed and depth of commercial databases make them a must-have for business investigators.

Online databases come in four basic formats. The first type is the full-text database. Full text means that the database stores, for retrieval, the full text of articles. Several databases now have articles from newspapers and magazines from around the world. Databases also carry the full text of transcripts of television and radio broadcasts. LexisNexis, Dow Jones News Retrieval, and Datatimes are examples of full-text databases. Many online databases are now conveniently available on the Web. The online database world provides the majority of information now used by the business investigator.

The second type of database is the public record database. Database companies provide access to many different types of courthouse records as well as company records. Access to federal litigation and bankruptcy records is obtainable through the PACER system. Major vendors of public record databases include Information America, CDB Infotek, and LexisNexis.

A third type of database is the credit and demographic database. The Fair Credit Reporting Act (FCRA) restricts the use of consumer credit information, but credit bureaus offer data not covered by the FRCA. Other databases act as national phone books, providing names and addresses across the country. Credit bureaus include Experian (formerly TRW), Trans Union, and ChoicePoint (formerly Equifax). Suppliers of demographic data such as names and addresses include Metronet and DNIS.

Finally, there are databases that provide additional types of information. Vendors like Dialog and LexisNexis also provide company directories, abstracts, and biographical records such as "Who's Who."

The Internet

Fraud examiners/investigators utilize the Internet beyond accessing commercial databases. Searching the Internet is generally not as precise as searching most commercial databases. Thus, investigators tend to stick with LexisNexis and Dialog. However, Internet online magazines often provide breaking news stories not covered elsewhere. Newsgroups and mailing lists contain raw (but often erroneous) data on companies. Finally, the first source of information on a company these days is often its own corporate Web site. For example, companies place detailed background information on themselves as well as profiles of their key executives on their Web sites.

Internet Web sites utilized by fraud examiners/investigators include KnowX, Switchboard, and others described in the following paragraphs.

KnowX (www.knowx.com) Many of the previously cited public documents are currently accessible via the Internet. KnowX, a LexisNexis company, is an online public record service. This Web site provides the fraud investigator with inexpensive searches to do background checks on a business, locate assets, and investigate for property values. Typical searches available include aircraft ownership records, a business directory, corporate records, date-of-birth records, lawsuits, real estate tax assessor records, stock ownership records, and watercraft ownership records.

QUICK FACTS

Online databases include full-text documents, public records, credit information, and other valuable information.

RESEARCH TOOLS

ACL
AICPA reSOURCE
eIFRS
FARS
Internet
i2
LexisNexis
RIA Checkpoint

RESEARCH TIPS

Use notable Web sites to assist in finding helpful research information.

Zoominfo.com (www.zoominfo.com) This Web site collates information from various Web sites through its software bots, also known as intelligent agents, which capture and match information to a particular person or company. You can search by company, person or industry. However, this information is generated from other Web sites and needs to be verified.

Other Web sites Other specific Internet sites related to fraud include:

- Association of Certified Fraud Examiners (www.acfe.com). This Web site provides information on fraud and the Certified Fraud Examiners Program.
- Online Fraud Information Center (www.fraud.org).
- Fraud Information Center (www.echotech.com/fmenu.htm).

FRAUD INVESTIGATION REGULATIONS

QUICK FACTS

Conducting a professional fraud investigation requires following the law.

Many different types of information are available to fraud investigations. One must gather the information legally in order to provide the evidence in a court of law. Some federal acts that govern access to information are the Freedom of Information Act (FOIA), the Fair Credit Reporting Act (FCRA), and privacy laws that restrict the type of information that organizations may provide.

The FOIA increased the availability of many government records. Typical information available under the FOIA includes tax rolls, voter registration, assumed names, real property records, and divorce/probate information. Information not available under the FOIA includes such items as banking records, telephone records, and stock ownership.

The FCRA regulates what information consumer reporting agencies can provide to third parties. Under the FCRA, an individual cannot obtain information about a person's character, general reputation, personal characteristics, or mode of living without notifying that person in advance. Thus, a fraud examiner/investigator should learn more about the legality of evidence gathered.

SUMMARY

As discussed in this chapter, fraud is a major risk to society. As fraud increases, businesses are turning to fraud examiners/investigators to help fight it. Therefore, professional accountants are offering additional services to clients in the area of forensic accounting or litigation support services related to the audit. Fraud examination steps include identifying the issues and planning the investigation, gathering the evidence in an investigation phase, evaluating the evidence, and reporting findings to entity management or legal counsel. Software and database tools are used to help the professional gather and organize the evidence for such engagements. Each fraud investigation is unique and requires strong critical thinking skills as it proceeds.

DISCUSSION QUESTIONS

1. Describe four different examples of fraud engagements.
2. Define forensic accounting.
3. Define fraud and identify four examples of fraud.
4. What are the three components of the fraud triangle? Of what concern are they to the fraud examiner?

5. What is a risk factor or red flag?

6. Differentiate between management fraud and employee fraud.

7. What are some risk factors associated with management fraud and employee fraud?

8. Identify the basic steps of a fraud examination.

9. Provide two examples of a business/due diligence investigation.

10. Describe three computerized tools used by the fraud examiner/investigator.

11. Explain the difference between data mining software and public databases.

EXERCISES

1. Access the KnowX Web site (www.knowx.com) and enter a free search. Discuss what you searched for and what you found. Provide two examples of how the fraud examiner/investigator can utilize this Web site.

2. Access Zoominfo.com and search for a business. What were your results?

3. Access the Fraud Information Center (www.fraud.org) and locate and describe three types of fraud reported by the Fraud Information Center.

4. Acquire information about the Bernie Madoff investment management scandal, as revealed in 2009. Integrate the theory presented in this chapter with the facts of the case to explain the scandal. Why were government investigators so slow to uncover this record-breaking $50 billion fraud?

5. Access a recently issued SEC Accounting and Auditing Enforcement Release related to a fraud action (www. sec.gov/divisions/enforce/friactions.shtml), and determine incentive(s)/pressure to commit the fraud, accounting issue(s), and the motive for the fraud.

6. Access the Association of Certified Fraud Examiners Web site (www.acfe.com) and complete the following:

   a. List three qualifications for becoming a CFE.

   b. List three items located in the ACFE's resource library.

7. Locate four Web sites on fraud and briefly describe the contents of the sites.

INDEX